EEO

1993

DISCRIMINATION IN EMPLOYMENT

• • • • • • • • • • • •

Published by

California Chamber of Commerce

Editor
Ronald Hoh

Published by
California Chamber of Commerce
P.O. Box 1736
Sacramento, CA 95812-1736

ISBN 1-878630-39-3

The information compiled in this guide is being provided by the California Chamber of Commerce as a service to the business community. Although every effort has been made to ensure the accuracy and completeness of this information, the California Chamber of Commerce and the contributors and reviewers of this publication cannot be responsible for any errors and omissions, nor any agency's interpretations, applications and changes of regulations described herein.

This publication is designed to provide accurate and authoritative information in a highly summarized manner with regard to the subject matter covered. It is sold with the understanding that the publisher and others associated with this publication are not engaged in rendering legal, technical or other professional service. If legal and other expert assistance is required, the services of competent professionals should be sought.

This publication is available from:

California Chamber of Commerce
P.O. Box 1736
Sacramento, CA 95812-1736
(916) 444-6670

Here's What's New for 1993

General

Over the last two years, and particularly for 1993, the editor has attempted to move the content of the *EEO Discrimination in Employment Digest* toward a more comprehensive, easier-to-read, narrative form, containing references and footnotes for each chapter. I believe this new format not only makes it easier for the reader to understand the complex interactions and requirements of the EEO laws, but also offers a more complete explanation of those laws and recommendations for employer policy decisions in these areas.

Chapter 1: Equal Employment Opportunity — An Introduction

Completely rewritten chapter emphasizing the importance of good equal employment business decisions, and describing some of the most important elements of equal employment law (Pages 1-5).

Chapter 2: Laws Governing Employment Discrimination.

- New section summarizing the requirements for non-discrimination by federal contractors and subcontractors under Executive Order 11246 (Page 10).
- Clarifications of employer requirements for retirement programs under the Age Discrimination in Employment Act (Pages 10-11).
- Summary of protections against discrimination against agricultural workers for exercise of their right to unionize or engage in other protected activities under the Agricultural Labor Relations Act (Page 12).
- Clarification of I-9 identification requirements under the Immigration Reform and Control Act (Page 13).
- Summary of discrimination provisions of the Americans with Disabilities Act (Page 14).
- Summary of the discrimination provisions of federal and state pregnancy discrimination laws (Page 14).
- Summary of discrimination provisions of the Equal Pay Act (Page 14).
- Description of California laws prohibiting discrimination on various public policy grounds (Pages 14-15).
- Footnotes and references (Page 17).

Chapter 3: Guidelines for Avoiding Employment Discrimination Claims.

- Summary of new state law requiring employers to post a notice and distribute pamphlets concerning significant components of prohibitions against sexual harassment (Page 20).
- Explanation of requirement for reasonable accommodation to employee's religion or disability (Page 21).
- Discrimination exceptions to prohibitions against age discrimination (Page 25).
- Clarification on requirements for an employer's early retirement programs (Page 25).
- New section on prohibitions against race discrimination (Page 26).
- Summary of new state law prohibiting discrimination on the basis that a person has AIDS or has been diagnosed as HIV-positive (Page 26).
- Summary of new state law prohibiting discrimination on the basis of sexual orientation (Pages 26-27).

- New section on prohibitions against sex discrimination (Page 27).
- New section on marital status discrimination, focusing upon an employer's "no employment of spouses" policy (Page 27).
- Clarifications of prohibitions against discrimination on the basis of religious creed (Pages 27-28).
- Clarifications of prohibitions against national origin discrimination, focusing upon an employer's "English only" rule (Page 28).
- Clarifications on guidelines to employers in avoiding discrimination (Pages 29-32).
- Footnotes and references (Page 32).

Chapter 4: Hiring and Recruitment

- New introduction stressing the importance of questions asked by companies in job applications, job interviews and reference checks (Page 33).
- Clarifications of application form and interview do's and don'ts (Pages 34-37).
- Clarifications of timing and legalities of pre-employment physicals (Page 38).
- Clarifications of requirements for retaining payroll records (Page 39).
- Updates on chart outlining acceptable and unacceptable pre-employment inquiries (Pages 40-41).

Chapter 5: Statistics Required of Employers

- Clarifications of EEOC-required retention of data for percentages of minorities and non-minorities (Page 50).
- New section on required EEO reporting forms (Pages 50-51).
- New section on required state contractor reporting forms (Page 51).

Chapter 6: Affirmative Action

Completely redone and condensed chapter on affirmative action (Pages 53-61). Topics covered include:

- What affirmative action is and is not.
- Who is required to have affirmative action programs.
- Voluntary affirmative action programs.
- Developing affirmative action goals and timetables.
- Eliminating existing equal employment problems.
- Development of an acceptable affirmative action program.
- Footnotes and references.

Chapter 7: Sexual Harassment

- Description of new state law prohibiting discrimination on the basis of sexual orientation (Page 64).
- Clarification of proper basis for a claim of "hostile environment" sexual harassment (Page 65).
- New section on constructive discharge and sexual harassment (Page 65).
- Summary of new state law requiring employers to both post a new Department of Fair Employment and Housing poster and distribute a pamphlet to employees outlining prohibitions against sexual harassment (Pages 65-66).
- Footnotes and references (Page 70).

Chapter 8: Pregnancy Discrimination

- Clarifications of federal and state pregnancy leave requirements (Page 75).
- Clarification of the definition of "disabled" for purposes of pregnancy leaves of absences (Pages 75-76).
- Clarifications on timing of pregnancy leave (Page 76).
- Summary of new state law requiring employers to provide pregnant employees upon request with temporary transfer rights to a less strenuous or hazardous position (Page 76).
- Clarification of method of calculation pregnancy leaves for employers covered by state, but not federal, law (Page 76).
- Footnotes and references (Page 86).

Chapter 9: The Family Rights Act

Newly rewritten, more comprehensive chapter further explaining this new law and incorporating new Fair Employment and Housing regulations for implementing the law (Pages 87-92). Topics covered include:

- Purposes and reasons for leave.
- Benefits eligibility and payment.
- Procedure for requests.
- Interaction with maternity leave.
- Limitations on use.
- Undue hardship.
- Protections against discrimination.
- Notice posting requirements.
- Suggested notice.
- Footnotes and references.

Chapter 10: The Americans with Disabilities Act and State Regulation of Disability Discrimination

- Summary of new law expanding state definition of disability to include mental disability, and clarifying definitions of "public accommodation" and "full and equal access" (Pages 93-94).
- New section outlining the interaction of the ADA and workers' compensation laws (Page 101).
- New subsection on job areas where disability discrimination can occur (Page 101).
- New section on ADA remedies and enforcement (Page 102).
- New section on ADA qualification standards (Page 104).
- Information on newly issued ADA poster (Page 104).
- New subsection on public accommodation responsibilities of landlord and business tenant (Page 106).
- Updates on sources for information and assistance (Page 110).
- Footnotes and references (Page 112).

Chapter 11: AIDS in the Workplace: An Employer's Response

- Summary of new law making AIDS and HIV-positive status protected disabilities under state law (Page 115).
- New section on AIDS and the state prohibition against discrimination on the basis of medical condition (Page 115).

- New section concerning state protection against discrimination against persons exposed to the AIDS virus (Pages 116-117).
- Updates and clarifications to commonly asked questions and answers in this area (Pages 118-121).
- Footnotes and references (Page 121).

Chapter 12: The Civil Rights Act of 1991

New chapter detailing the requirements of the Civil Rights Act of 1991, which again expands employee rights that had been narrowed by the U.S. Supreme Court in seven decisions from 1989 through 1991 (Pages 123-127). Topics addressed include:

- Introduction.
- Compensatory and punitive damages in cases of intentional discrimination.
- Adverse impact cases — burden of proof.
- "Mixed motive" cases.
- Prohibition against discrimination in contracts.
- Reimbursement of expert witness fees.
- Extension of time for seniority system challenges.
- Application of discrimination laws outside the United States.
- Employment test adjustments.
- "Glass-ceiling" commission.
- Encouraging of alternative dispute resolution procedures.
- Footnotes and references.

Chapter 13: Resolving Discrimination Complaints Through Arbitration

New chapter outlining arbitration as an alternative to litigation approved by the U.S. Supreme Court for resolution of discrimination claims in certain circumstances (Pages 129-137). Topics covered include:

- Introduction and background.
- Recent change in legal framework.
- California Arbitration Act.
- Enforcement of agreements to arbitrate in employment contracts.
- Advantages of arbitration over litigation.
- Securing the arbitration agreement.
- Sources of arbitrators and arbitration proceedings.
- Considerations in determining the utility of an arbitration policy.
- Considerations in drafting arbitration agreements.
- Other forms of alternative dispute resolution.
- Footnotes and references.

Chapter 14: Recent EEO Court Decisions

Newly reorganized and updated review of recent case decisions, categorized for the first time by the type of discrimination addressed in the case involved (Pages 139-154). Areas of discrimination laws cases addressed include:

- Sexual harassment.
- Sex discrimination.
- Pregnancy discrimination.

- Age discrimination.
- Race and national origin discrimination.
- Religious discrimination.
- Disabilities discrimination.
- Sexual orientation discrimination.
- AIDS discrimination.
- Immigration discrimination.
- Veteran's status discrimination.
- Workers' compensation discrimination.
- Arbitration and discrimination laws.

Chapter 15: Exhibits and Publications

- Addition: sample of state fair employment poster. Page 158.
- New suggested family leave poster. Page 160.

Have a Question?

Call the California Chamber of Commerce, (916) 444-6670. The California Chamber is here to help your business succeed and operate efficiently.

Is there any charge for answering my question?

No. The **HELPLINE** is one of several free services for companies that are members of the California Chamber.

What if my company is not currently a member of the California Chamber?

Call us anyway. Tell us you just bought a book and you have a question. We appreciate your business, so we'll be happy to answer your question so you can see why thousands of businesses — large and small — all across California invest in membership with the California Chamber.

When you join the California Chamber, you will receive the toll-free 800 telephone number and a brochure introducing you to the **HELPLINE** staff.

HELPLINE assistance provides an explanation and clarification of laws and regulations confronting business (not legal advice for specific situations).

Thank you for this opportunity to be of service.

California Chamber of Commerce
P.O. Box 1736
Sacramento, CA 95812-1736
(916) 444-6670

Table of Contents

Introduction

Equal Employment Opportunity — hasn't such always been practiced at your place of business? So, what's to worry?

Plenty! Your employment practices are subject to governmental scrutiny from the standpoint of potential, as well as actual, discrimination. If you have 15 or more employees (five or more in California) working during 20 or more weeks in the calendar year, federal agencies in California will not apply the state's "five employee" rule, and accede jurisdiction to the State enforcement agencies. If a complaint is received, California may audit, investigate and monitor your records and procedures to determine whether you discriminate against any of the eleven (11) protected classes set forth below. The federal goverment also has the right to investigate, audit and monitor your records and procedures to determine whether you discriminate against any of the 11 protected classes (race, color, religion, sex, national origin or ancestry, physical or mental handicap unrelated to ability, unfavorable military discharge other than dishonorable, those over 40 years old or older, Vietnam era veterans and sexual harassment in employment). If found to be in violation, you may be subject to penalties, including back pay, front pay, attorney's fees, costs, compensatory damages, interest, permanent injunctions or bad press.

Do you have to hire anyone who breathes? No! Can't you hire someone capable of doing the job? Can't you terminate someone who isn't performing at an acceptable level any longer? Of course! But, in so doing you must not discriminate.

"Affirmative action" requires not only avoiding discrimination but also doing more than you might have in the past to utilize persons in the protected classes. If you participate in government contracts (prime or subcontracting) or bid on such, you may be required to have a written affirmative action plan.

Well, you can imagine how complicated the rules and regulations are as state and federal agencies seek to enforce the concept of equal employment and its ramifications. The California Chamber offers this ready reference to help employers qualify for the title of "equal opportunity employer, M/F/H."

Chapter 1
Equal Employment Opportunity — An Introduction

Employment Relationship

The relationship between employers and employees in the workplace is shaped by an ever-changing body of laws and regulations that affect nearly every aspect of that relationship. For example, this book's companion survival guide, the *California Labor Law Digest,* focuses in lay terms on keeping employers in legal compliance regarding all aspects of the employment relationship except those covered in this book. This *Equal Employment Opportunity (EEO) Discrimination in Employment* survival guide focuses on the complexities of compliance in a major generic area of employment law — those laws categorically described as discrimination laws. It provides special emphasis on decisions involving recruitment, hiring, termination, promotion, training, evaluation, managing and supervising on the job.

The foundation for understanding the requirements of the law in the area of employment discrimination is found in Title VII of the Civil Rights Act of 1964, which established an unprecedented body of milestone guidelines concerning equal treatment of all employees and job applicants. Most importantly, this law created the Equal Opportunity Employment Commission (EEOC), the primary agency responsible for enforcing that federal law and those which followed.

Since then, most states and many municipalities have passed similar laws to broaden or clarify the scope of discrimination laws. For instance, California has the Fair Employment and Housing Act, enforced by the Department of Fair Employment and Housing and the Fair Employment and Housing Commission. A limited number of other discrimination laws are enforced in California by the Office of the State Labor Commissioner. In addition, some larger cities have their own human rights ordinances enforced by local human rights commissions.

Effect of Equal Employment Opportunity on Business Decisions

There is a common belief among employers that EEO laws severely limit an employer's ability to operate its business and deal with its employees. The fact is that those laws are generally composed of common sense guidelines to professional conduct, and if followed properly, should do very little to limit effective operations of a company. Properly adhered to, those laws still permit employers to hire, promote and retain the best candidates and/or employees for various jobs.

Put more directly, no law prohibits an employer from rejecting, demoting or discharging employees who are unwilling or unable to do a job, so long as those decisions are based on legitimate business factors which are undiscriminatory in nature. What the laws prohibit are employment decisions based upon discriminatory and/or otherwise illegal factors.

1

Certain terms are used to express certain degrees and standards for legal, non-discriminatory employment decisions. For example, terms such as "job-related" and "valid" are used to describe factors that generally are considered to predict success on the job and thus are relevant, non-discriminatory factors. In contrast, factors that are rooted in prejudice, stereotypes and related inappropriate elements are discriminatory, and thus illegal.

Other terms in discrimination law have particular legal implications. Examples of these terms include "bona fide occupational qualifications" (BFOQ) and "business necessity." These factors may have an impact upon the propriety of an employment-related decision in the discrimination area, and are explained in the contexts of the various applicable laws throughout this Digest.

Fortunately, however, not every employment decision is subject to scrutiny regarding such factors. Instead, EEO law focuses on specific discriminatory or otherwise illegal factors that are judged to be the most likely areas of abuse in the employer/employee relationship. So long as those factors are not a consideration in the employment decision, employers are generally free to make those decisions as they see fit.

Protected Classes

The propriety of any employment decision in the equal employment area is best comprehended by an understanding of what the EEO laws call "protected classes." Simply put, it is illegal to make employment decisions based upon a person's membership in any of the protected classes. Originally, the federal law established only a small number of protected classes. However, over the years the law has been amended to add additional classes or broaden existing classes. In addition, state and local laws frequently add other protected classes to the list maintained under federal law.

Currently, the protected classes under federal law are: race, color, religion, sex (including sexual harassment and pregnancy), national origin, ancestry, age (40 and over), and mental or physical disability. All these protected classes are recognized by the enforcement agencies in California, as well as by the EEOC. California law enforced by the Fair Employment and Housing Commission adds these protected classes: veterans status, religious creed, marital status, ancestry and medical condition. In addition, the Office of the State Labor Commissioner enforces discrimination laws regarding the protected classes of sexual orientation and political activity.

Affirmative Action

Another term frequently misunderstood in EEO law is "affirmative action." The reason for the confusion about this term is that affirmative action is both a philosophical matter and a legal concept. The philosophy of affirmative action refers to the concept of an employer making employment opportunities available to a broader base of recruiting sources and employees than might otherwise exist in the normal course of business.

The general jurisdiction of affirmative action requirements, in contrast to the general belief, is narrow in scope. Affirmative action generally is required only of employers who do business either with the federal or state government, or by subcontractors of those employers. Under such federal and state laws, employers doing business with government agencies must develop written plans to identify underutilization of women and minorities, and establish goals for creating proper balances in comparison with the percentages of those classes within the general population. There is no legal requirement for an affirmative action plan for employers who do not, or will not, do business with either federal or state government.

See Chapter 6 of this handbook for further information concerning the requirements for affirmative action programs.

Enforcement of Equal Employment Opportunity Laws

Defining Illegal Discrimination

Both the EEOC and the DFEH are authorized to investigate fully all charges of discrimination filed with those agencies. If an employer is charged with discrimination, those agencies will normally will take evidence from the charging party initially to determine whether that evidence makes a showing of "prima facie" (on its face) illegal discrimination. The charging party has the burden of proof in such cases. If that prima facie burden is initially met, the investigating agency normally will make a request for information to the employer to determine if any type of illegal discrimination actually has occurred. Such requests must generally be complied with the employer. Upon review of all the evidence, the agency will then make a determination of whether a complaint charging the employer with illegal discrimination should be issued, or whether the charge should be dismissed.

There are two types of illegal discrimination. The first is "disparate treatment," which occurs when an employee is treated differently from another employee because of an illegal criterion such as race. A successful claim of disparate treatment also requires the charging party to have been adversely affected as a result of the different treatment. For example, if a black supervisor is demoted because he/she falsified an employee's time card but a white supervisor is only given a written warning for the same offense, the black supervisor will have a basis for filing a charge. Disparate treatment charges are the most common type of illegal discrimination charge, and usually involve only the individual filing the charge.

The second type of illegal discrimination is "adverse impact." Both federal and state discrimination laws prohibit not only overt discrimination, but also employment practices that appear neutral on their face but are discriminatory in operation. Normally, "adverse impact" cases are those where an employment practice has the effect of establishing a barrier to the advancement of a particular group of employees, irrespective of the employer's motive in establishing the employment practice. Examples of practices that have shown adverse impact upon blacks and hispanics are denial of employment opportunity based on a lack of a high school diploma or solely on the presence of an arrest record.

Establishing the *Prima Facie* Case

The laws prohibiting discrimination in employment do not prohibit all employment decisions an applicant may consider "unfair." Discrimination because of a non-prohibited factor is not a violation of law. For example, Title VII prohibits an employer from discriminating against an individual with respect to enumerated employment conditions and decisions because of the individual's race, color, religion, sex or national origin. Thus, if the employer would have reached the same employment decision without regard to those factors, there is likely to be no violation of Title VII.

In discrimination cases, the charging party (normally the employee) has the burden of proof in establishing a *prima facie* case. In the absence of such a *prima facie* showing, the enforcement agency will dismiss the case prior to full investigation. If in the eyes of the enforcement agency, however, the facts appear to indicate the occurence of discrimination on the basis of the protected class status of the employee or applicant, that agency will pursue the case and require the employer to respond. Most discrimination cases arise out of the termination process and involve a former employee alleging disparate treatment. A typical case may involve a hispanic employee who was fired for excessive tardiness claiming that he was punished more severely than a white male who also had several instances of tardiness.

The Employer's Defense

If an applicant or employee establishes a *prima facie* case of discrimination under the disparate treatment theory, an employer may rebut that evidence by showing that the applicant or employee was not treated any differently from other employees, or that the same decision would have been made irrespective of the protected class status of the employee. This often may be accomplished by the employer providing facts which establish the standard of performance or behavior, verifying the employee's significant deviation from that standard, and showing consistent application of the appropriate punishment. For example, if a woman alleges that she was discharged for tardiness and a man who engaged in similar activity was not fired, the employer may provide a copy of the company's policy on tardiness, documentation of the woman's behavior and disciplinary history, and a copy of the man's disciplinary history, in order to show that she was not treated in any disparate manner.

If the facts of the case do indicate disparate treatment or adverse impact, the employer must then show "business necessity" for the employment decision or practice. As a practical matter, however, the ability to prove business necessity is extremely difficult.

Equal Employment Opportunity and "Quotas"

One of the more controversial issues in the area of equal employment opportunity is "quotas." Many employers and management representatives argue that equal employment law requires employers to hire, promote and retain "by the numbers" to avoid the high cost of defending an adverse impact charge. They contend that such a system amounts to quotas of employees in protected classes. Both EEOC and DFEH claim that the law does not require quotas, and actually consider quotas to be illegal because race, sex and national origin cannot be used blatantly as a basis for employment decisions.

The employer must engage in the delicate balance of avoiding the use of quotas, and yet engaging in some reliable statistical analysis to ensure that employment decisions do not result in adverse impact. The employer must ensure that the method for determining an employee's performance quality is not inherently flawed, or utilize some alternate selection for employment decisions which is not subject to criticism, such as seniority.

Management Practices and Success Guidelines

The key to establishing appropriate management practices is to have a strong commitment to EEO concepts, coupled with a focus on the success of the organization. One important step in this direction is to provide EEO compliance training for managers. Employers must develop a perspective that factors in the necessity for EEO compliance. For example, a high degree of intelligence and leadership skills may be necessary for some jobs, but not for all. Moreover, enthusiasm may be a positive quality for assembly line workers, but perseverence may be much more useful to the employer's overall goals. Likewise, while high school diplomas might arguably create a more capable workforce, some high school graduates are illiterate, while such areas as the computer skills of many high school freshman often are greater than those of their parents.

An employer that requires all employees to have a high school diploma, be enthusiastic and have proven leadership skills may be turning its back on the people most suitable for success for the particular job involved. Furthermore, race, sex, national origin, age, marital status, etc., do not indicate the presence of desirable or undesirable traits or characteristics in employees. Those classifications simply cannot be disregarded in making employment-related decisions.

In addition to training managers concerning equal employment opportunity, employers must become sensitive to what is "reasonable." Determinations of what is reasonable must take into account that employees possess different perspectives and may question what an employer considers reasonable or appropriate. For example, what is considered "reasonable" may differ depending upon a person's sex, race or ethnic background. Both employers and their representatives must realize that what they say and do may both be taken out of context and viewed in a different context. Before making any employment decision, employers must ask themselves if others would likely reach the same conclusion given the same set of relevant facts.

The employment-related decision not only must be able to stand on its own as being reasonable; it must also be considered in light of other decisions. Indeed, the reasonableness of all responses becomes questionable if an employer responds differently to similar situations. Although employers are not bound in perpetuity by the action that they take in one situation, any change in policy should have sound reasoning and should be communicated to employees in advance, if possible. In the absence of strong business necessity, an employer should resist any temptation to respond differently to a similar incident occurring in the future. If an employer's initial response later proved harmful to the employer and was believed to therefore be inappropriate, the impact of that decision should be noted so that a different response to future incidents can be justified easily, and employers should notify their employees of the change.

Gathering Only Relevant Facts

EEO law recognizes that an employer must ask questions to determine if applicants or employees are willing and able to perform a job. The law is not intended as a barrier to prohibit the gathering and retention of relevant information. However, many employers gather information that is simply unnecessary for employment decisions, and retain documentation of this information along with other information used in making employment decisions. Although this practice is not specifically illegal, it can and often is used against an employer as evidence of discrimination, since it tends to give an appearance of such discrimination.

Not only should employers restrict the questions on an application to gather only the necessary information, but completed application forms should be reviewed periodically to ensure that applicants do not routinely provide requested but irrelevant information. For example, if age is not important to the performance of the job, why ask someone the year they graduated from high school? Additionally, any notes on employment applications and related materials should contain statements of facts such as "held three jobs in two years" rather than statements of opinion such as "shaky work history." An extremely helpful chart listing both discriminatory and non-discriminatory employment inquiries is contained in Chapter 5 of this handbook.

Guidelines for Success

EEO regulations should be viewed as guidelines for successfully recruiting and developing employees to make the most of their human resources, rather than as government interference. Here are four guidelines commonly followed by EEO-conscious employers:

1.   All employment decisions should be based on relevant factors.
2.   Be reasonable and consistent.
3.   Avoid gathering information which has no effect on an employee's ability to perform the job.
4.   If it's good, document it. If it's bad, don't do it.

The following chapters are designed to provide employers with the step-by-step information needed to achieve these goals.

Chapter 2
Laws Governing Employment Discrimination

California Fair Employment and Housing Act

An employer is subject to the California Fair Employment and Housing Act (FEHA) if it: 1) employs, or has employed, five or more employees within California during 20 or more calendar weeks within the calendar year preceding an alleged violation of the act; 2) is a public employer, regardless of the number of employees; 3) for harassment cases only, regularly employs one or more persons. Religious non-profit employers are generally excluded from coverage under the FEHA.

To be processed as timely filed, a charge must be filed within one year of the alleged violation. This deadline may be extended by 90 days if the individual learns of the alleged violation after the expiration of one year from the date of the occurence.

The FEHA prohibits employment discrimination on the basis of race, color, national origin, sex, physical and mental disability, age (40 and above) and religious creed. While FEHA covers any employer employing five or more employees, employers employing only one employee are prohibited from harassment on the basis of any classification protected by the FEHA.

An employer commits an unlawful employment practice under the FEHA if it, among other things:

1. Inquires on a written job application (except in limited circumstances) whether a job applicant has ever been arrested.
2. Refuses to hire, segregates or acts adversely with respect to recruitment, hiring, promotion, renewal of employment, selection for training or apprenticeship, discharge, discipline, tenure or terms, conditions or privileges of employment on the basis of race, color, religion, national origin, ancestry, age (40 and over), sex, marital status, physical or mental disability or medical condition.
3. Engages in, or permits its employees or agents to engage in, harassment of any protected class.
4. Retaliates against an employee or applicant for opposing sexual harassment or other unlawful discrimination, or for filing a complaint, testifying, assisting or participating in an investigation, proceeding or hearing under the FEHA.
5. Bases any adverse employment decision in whole or in part on the complainant's protected class status.
6. Refuses to honor an otherwise eligible employee's request for pregnancy disability leave or for leave for certain designated family care responsibilities in accordance with the California Family Rights Act of 1991.

An employee who believes that he/she has been discriminated against in violation of the FEHA must file a charge with the California Department of Fair Employment and Housing (DFEH) to trigger the enforcement mechanism of the act. The DFEH investigates the charge. The initial burden of proof is on the charging party, and the employer is innocent until proven guilty. If DFEH determines there is no substantial evidence, the charge will be dismissed and the charging party notified that he/she may seek review of the dismissal order before the California superior court. If DFEH determines there is substantial evidence to support the charge, DFEH will attempt to remedy the matter by means of conference and conciliation. If conciliation is unsuccessful, the DFEH will issue a complaint and set a hearing before an administrative law judge (ALJ). The decision of the ALJ is reviewed by the Fair Employment and Housing Commission and can be adopted or modified by the FEHC. The final order of the Commission is enforceable by and appealable to the California superior court.

DFEH may grant a right-to-sue letter and terminate its investigation upon request of the complaining party. Complainants automatically receive an authorization to file suit if an investigation has not been completed 150 days after filing. In the latter circumstance, DFEH will continue the investigation unless the complainant actually files suit.

In accordance with the California Supreme Court's 1991 decision in the case of *Rojo v. Kliger*, DFEH no longer provides the exclusive remedy for employee challenges to alleged employment discrimination. The court determined that, since the California Constitution protects persons from sex, race, color, religious and national origin discrimination, employees claiming such discrimination could bypass the DFEH administrative processes and go directly to court to pursue common law claims that are related to employment discrimination but were not covered by the Fair Employment and Housing Act, such as claims for intentional infliction of emotional distress.

Effective January 1, 1993, the law gives the FEHC authority, upon the finding of an unlawful employment practice, to award actual damages, including damages for emotional injuries, administrative fines and other affirmative or prospective relief to prevent the recurrence of unlawful practices. The combined amount of an award for emotional damages and other administrative fines may not exceed $50,000 per aggrieved person per respondent.[2] The new law also gives the FEHC the power to award victims of hate crimes up to $150,000 in actual damages[3] and to assess fines of up to $25,000 against perpetrators of hate violence.[4]

An employer found to have engaged in an employment practice unlawful under the FEHA can be required to:

1. Hire an applicant for employment who was unlawfully denied a job.
2. Reinstate an employee who was unlawfully discharged or promote an employee unlawfully denied a promotion.
3. Pay back wages and other benefits lost by an employee or applicant as a result of the employer's unlawful employment practice.
4. Pay actual damages for injuries or losses suffered by the complainant.
5. If the matter goes to court, pay compensatory damages (for pain, suffering, humiliation and embarrassment) and punitive damages (to punish the employer for particularly egregious conduct).
6. In the case of an employer that is a party to a public contract, cancel the contract, refrain from participating in any public contract for up to three years, and pay a penalty equal to the profit derived by the employer as a direct result of the unlawful employment practice.

7. Post notices of an employer's obligation to cease discriminatory practices.
8. Pay attorney's fees.

Title VII of the Civil Rights Act of 1964[5]

An employer is subject to the discrimination provisions of Title VII if it is engaged in an "industry affecting commerce;" and employs, or has employed, 15 or more employees for each working day in 20 or more calendar weeks in the current or preceding calendar year.

To be processed by the EEOC as timely filed, a charge must be filed within 180 days. If a charge is first filed with the DFEH, then a charge can be filed with the EEOC within 300 days of the alleged violation or within 30 days from receiving notice that the state has terminated its proceedings, whichever is earlier.

An employer commits an unlawful employment practice under Title VII if it, among other things:

1. Uses an individual's race, color, religion, sex or national origin as a basis for:
   — failing or refusing to hire an applicant for employment;
   — discharging or otherwise disciplining an employee;
   — determining an employee's compensation, including fringe benefits or other terms, conditions or privileges of employment; or
   — limiting, segregating or classifying an employee or an applicant for employment in a way that would tend to deprive him/her of an employment opportunity or otherwise adversely affect his/her status as an employee.

2. Discriminates against an employee or applicant for employment because he/she has opposed an employment practice unlawful under Title VII, or because he/she has filed a charge, testified, assisted or participated in any manner in an investigation, proceeding or hearing under Title VII.

An employee who believes that he/she has been discriminated against on the basis of race, color, religion, sex and/or national origin must file a charge with the Equal Employment Opportunity Commission (EEOC) to trigger the enforcement mechanism of Title VII. The EEOC investigates the charge and attempts to convince the parties to reach a mutually satisfactory conciliation agreement. If conciliation is not forthcoming, the EEOC will, in rare cases, file a suit in federal district court on the behalf of the employee or, more often, issue a "right-to-sue" letter to the employee, advising him/her that he/she may file a suit in federal district court.

An employer found to have engaged in an employment practice unlawful under Title VII can be required to, among other things:

1. Hire an applicant for employment who was unlawfully denied a job;
2. Reinstate an employee who was unlawfully discharged;
3. Pay back wages and other benefits lost by an employee or applicant as a result of the employer's unlawful employment practice;
4. Pay the costs and attorney's fees of the prevailing employee or applicant; and
5. Pay compensatory damages including damages for emotional injuries.

Executive Order 11246: Non-Discrimination Under Federal Contracts

Executive Order No. 11246 requires every federal contractor and subcontractor to agree not to discriminate against any employee or applicant because of race, color, religion, sex or national origin, and to take affirmative action to ensure that all applicants and employees are employed without regard to those factors. Contractors and subcontractors having 50 or more employees and a contract or subcontract of $50,000 or more, and banks receiving deposits of any type of federal funds, must develop written affirmative action plans. These plans must contain such elements as an analysis of the contractor's workforce by race and sex, an analysis of the labor force by race and sex, a determination of whether the contractor is underutilizing minorities or women in any job categories, and the establishment of goals and timetables to correct any such underutilization.

The obligations of federal contractors and subcontractors under E.O. No. 11246 are enforced by the Office of Federal Contract Compliance Programs (OFCCP). Allegations of violations of E.O. 11246 may result in an OFCCP audit of the employer's employment practices by OFCCP, and substantial evidence of support of the employee's charge may result in formal adjudication before the OFCCP, the EEOC or the Department of Justice. A finding that a contractor or subcontractor has violated the requirements of E.O. No. 11246 can result in an OFCCP order that, among other things, may result in cancellation, termination or suspension of the contractor's or subcontractor's government contract(s), and/or debarment from holding government contracts in the future.

For further information concerning the elements of affirmative action programs required under Executive Order 11246, please see Chapter 6 of this handbook.

Age Discrimination in Employment Act of 1967[6]

A private sector employer is subject to the Age Discrimination in Employment Act (ADEA) if it is engaged in an "industry affecting commerce," and employs, or has employed, 20 or more employees for each working day in each of 20 or more calendar weeks in the current or preceding year. Public sector employers are covered regardless of the number of employees.

The protections of the ADEA generally are available to employees and applicants for employment who are at least 40 years of age. There is no upper age limit.

Age is not a factor when differentiations are based on the terms of a bona fide seniority system or any bona fide employee benefit plan, such as a retirement, pension or insurance plan. Employee benefit plans may not, however, excuse the failure to hire any individual, and no such seniority system or employee benefit plan may require or permit the involuntary retirement of an individual upon attainment of any specific age. The exception of a bona fide seniority system does not authorize an employer to require or permit mandatory retirement of any employee. The mandatory retirement prohibition applies to all new and existing seniority systems and employer benefit plans. Therefore, any system or plan provision requiring involuntary retirement is unlawful.

An exception to the prohibition of mandatory retirement at any age, effective January 1, 1987, covers states and localities with mandatory retirement ages for firefighters and law enforcement officers, and institutions of higher education with a mandatory retirement of age 70 for tenured faculty (could be age 65 until January 1, 1987). In addition, the ADEA requires that persons who are in an executive capacity for at least two years before retirement and who will receive a retirement benefit of at least $44,000 annually still may be retired mandatorily at age 65.[7] The state of California requires only a $27,000 annual retirement benefit.

An employer commits an unlawful employment practice under the ADEA if it:

1. Places an employment notice or advertisement indicating a preference, limitation or specification based on age;

2. Uses an individual's age as a basis for:

    — failing or refusing to hire an applicant for employment;
    — discharging or otherwise disciplining an employee;
    — determining an employee's compensation or other terms, conditions or privileges of employment;
    — limiting, segregating or classifying an employee or applicant for employment in a way that would tend to deprive him/her of an employment opportunity or otherwise adversely affect his/her status as an employee; or
    — reducing the wage rate of an employee in order to comply with other requirements under the ADEA; or

3. Discriminates against an employee or applicant for employment because he/she has opposed an employment practice unlawful under the ADEA, or because he/she has filed a charge, testified, assisted or participated in any manner in an investigation, proceeding or litigation under the ADEA.

The ADEA contains five specific exemptions to its prohibition against age discrimination. It is not unlawful for an employer to take any action where:

1. Age is a bona fide occupational qualification reasonably necessary to the operation of its business;
2. The action is based on reasonable factors other than age;
3. The action is in observance of a bona fide seniority system;
4. The action is in observance of a bona fide employee benefit plan; and
5. The employer has good cause to discipline or discharge the employee.[8]

An employer found to have engaged in an employment practice unlawful under the ADEA can be required to:

1. Hire an applicant for employment who was unlawfully denied a job;
2. Reinstate an employee who was unlawfully discharged;
3. Pay back wages and other benefits lost by an employee or applicant as a result of the employer's unlawful employment practice (maximum liability: two-year period preceding the date on which the employee files his/her charge, unless the employer's conduct is found to be willful, in which case liability may extend back through the three-year period preceding the date on which the employee files the charge);
4. Pay liquidated damages equal to the amount of back wages awarded (if the employer's conduct is found to be willful);
5. Pay "front pay" until the employee reaches age 70; and
6. Pay the costs and reasonable attorney's fees of the prevailing employee or applicant.

A prevailing plaintiff may be entitled to double damages in cases of willful violations of the ADEA.[9] Willful conduct is evidenced if an employer knows or shows reckless disregard for whether its conduct is prohibited by the ADEA.[10]

National Labor Relations Act[11]

The National Labor Relations Act (NLRA) is designed to protect employees' rights to organize and form unions, or to engage in other mutual aid and protection. It enforces that right by prohibiting certain actions of both employers and unions as "unfair labor practices." An employer commits an unfair labor practice under the NLRA if it:

1. Interferes with, restrains or coerces employees in the exercise of their right "to engage in. . . concerted activities for the purpose of. . . mutual aid or protection. . . ";
2. Dominates or interferes with the formation or administration of any labor organization;
3. Discriminates against any employee in regard to hire, tenure or other term or condition of employment to encourage or discourage membership in a labor organization;
4. Discharges or otherwise discriminates against an employee because he/she has filed charges or given testimony pursuant to the provisions of the NLRA; or
5. Refuses to bargain collectively with a representative lawfully chosen by its employees.

An individual or labor organization may file an unfair labor practice charge with a regional office of the National Labor Relations Board (NLRB). The region will investigate the charge and usually attempt to settle the underlying dispute. If a settlement cannot be reached, the region generally will either issue a formal complaint against the employer or dismiss the charge. Its action will, of course, depend on its view of the merits of the charge.

If a complaint issues and the matter is not settled, an evidentiary hearing will be convened before an administrative law judge of the Board. The judge's opinion can be appealed to the NLRB in Washington, D.C., and thereafter, to the federal appellate courts.

An employer found to have engaged in an unfair labor practice under the NLRA can be required to:

1. Cease and desist from any such further conduct;
2. Reinstate an employee who has been unlawfully discharged; and
3. Pay back wages and restore benefits lost by an employee as a consequence of the employer's unfair labor practice.

Similiar procedures and protections for agricultural employees in California exist under the California Agricultural Labor Relations Act.[12]

For further information, please see Chapter 4 of the *California Labor Law Digest*, the companion handbook to this publication.

Immigration Reform and Control Act of 1986[13]

The Immigration Reform and Control Act makes it an unlawful employment practice to: 1) knowingly hire an alien who is not authorized to work in the United States; 2) hire anyone without verifying the individual's legal employment status; or 3) continue the employment of an alien properly hired in accordance with the new verification procedures once the employer learns that the alien is or has become unauthorized to work. In other words, even if an employer employs no illegal aliens, that employer still can violate the law if he/she has failed to verify the legality of the status of all employees.

Ban on Employment Discrimination

The law makes it an "unfair immigration-related employment practice" to discriminate against any person because of the national origin or, in the case of a citizen or "intending" citizen, because of the person's citizenship status. This provision of the statute was included to prevent employers who are fearful of unwittingly hiring illegal aliens from discriminating against all "foreign-looking" or "foreign-sounding" individuals. For employers with more than 15 employees, national origin discrimination has long been covered under Title VII of the Civil Rights Act of 1964. The national origin discrimination provision of this statute covers employers with more than three and less than 15 employees.

The ban on discrimination against citizens and "intending citizens" was intended to act as an extra deterrent to employers who prefer to hire illegal aliens (or authorized aliens) because they are willing to work for substandard wages.

Verification and Recordkeeping Requirements

To avoid liability and penalties under the law, an employer must verify that every new hire is either a U.S. citizen or is authorized to be employed in the United States. Those documents which must be inspected to verify the prospective employee's identity and authorization to work are any one of the following:

1. U.S. passport;
2. Certificate of citizenship;
3. Certificate of naturalization;
4. Unexpired foreign passport if it contains an endorsement by the Attorney General of the United States; or
5. A "green card" with photo (starting August 1, 1989, the revised alien card is mostly pink).

If the prospective employee has none of the above five documents, he/she may still be hired if he/she can prove his/her identity with a photo driver license or other state-issued identification with a photo *and* a Social Security card or a birth certificate, either of which establishes his/her employment authorization. An employer satisfies the legal requirement if the document provided by the prospective employee "reasonably appears in its face to be genuine." The verification forms must be kept and made available for government inspection beginning on the date of hire for a minimum of three years or, if employment has been for more than two years, one year after the employee terminates.

There is a special form, the I-9 form, on which the employer must attest to every new employee's legal status under penalty of perjury. The I-9 lists the most frequently used documents that will suffice for verification of the new hire's identification and/or work authorization. On this same form, each new employee similarly must attest to his/her to legal status. Covered employers who don't receive the form must contact their nearest Immigration and Naturalization Service office. The I-9 verification form must be completed for *all* new hires.

For additional information, see Chapter 18 of the *California Labor Law Digest*, the companion to this publication.

Americans with Disabilities Act[14]

The Americans with Disabilities Act (ADA), which took effect in 1992 for employers of 25 or more employees, requires that employers may not discriminate against any qualified individual with a disability. The ADA covers hiring procedures, job training, promotions, terminations, employee wages and all terms and conditions of employment. Its employment provisions become effective in 1994 for employers with 15 or more employees.

The ADA also provides that no person may be discriminated against or prevented from equal enjoyment of goods, services, facilities and accommodations of any place that accommodates the public, because he/she is disabled. This includes hotels, restaurants, theaters, retail sales service establishments and any other place that may have the potential for being places of employment or public access, and requires these places to be physically accessible to persons with disabilities.

For further information on both the employment and public accomodation provisions of the ADA, please see Chapter 10 of this handbook.

Pregnancy Discrimination Act of 1978 and California Pregnancy Discrimination Laws[15]

The Pregnancy Discrimination Act of 1978, an amendment to Title VII, provides that a pregnant employee is to be treated the same as any other employee, and that when a female employee becomes unable to work due to pregnancy, childbirth or related medical conditions, her disability is to be treated the same as any other disability. State law provides that an employer grant up to four months of pregnancy leave once it is determined that an employee is unable to continue working due to pregnancy. Employees are entitled to return to the same job they left due to pregnancy, so long as the return occurs within the four months or any longer period allowed under an employer's policy concerning return from disability leave. It is unlawful for an employer to discriminate against an employee in any way due to that employee's pregnancy.

For further information concerning maternity leave and reinstatement requirements, please see Chapter 9 of this handbook.

Equal Pay Act[16]

The Equal Pay Act is part of the federal Fair Labor Standards Act, and provides for the payment of equal pay for "equal work" by both sexes working in the same establishment. The Act prohibits discrimination on the basis of sex in wages paid for "equal work" on jobs requiring equal skill, effort and responsibility when those jobs are performed under similar working conditions. It allows unequal pay, however, where the disparity is due to a seniority or merit system, a system that measures earnings by quantity or quality of production, or a differential based on any factor other than sex.

California Labor and Government Codes[17]

The California Labor Code and Government Code prohibit discrimination in employment on a variety of public policy grounds. Employers are prohibited from retaliating against an employee for:

1. Filing for or receiving workers' compensation benefits;[18]
2. Filing a claim with the Labor Commissioner;[19]
3. Filing an Occupational Safety and Health Administration (OSHA) complaint;[20]
4. Disclosing information to a government or law enforcement agency;[21]
5. Serving on a jury;[22]
6. Disclosing the employee's illiteracy.[23]

Employers also are prevented from imposing any policy that prevents employees from disclosing the amount of their wages or salary to other persons, and from discharging, disciplining or otherwise discriminating against employees who do disclose the amount of their wages.[24] In addition, California law prevents employees from unlawfully being denied the benefits of, or unlawfully being subjected to discrimination under any program or activity funded by or receiving funds from the state, on the basis of any ethnic group identification, religion, age, sex, color or physical or mental disability.[25] Finally, employers may not reject or terminate from employment, nor deny coverage under an insurance policy to, individuals whose blood tests reflect thay they have been exposed to the AIDS virus. Such a blood test may not be used in any instance to determine insurability or suitability for employment.[26]

Employer Defenses, Employment Discrimination

Under either the Fair Employment and Housing Act or Title VII, employment discrimination can be lawful where the employer can show both a proper, relevant affirmative defense and that less discriminatory alternatives are not available. Except where otherwise specifically noted, one or more of the following affirmative defenses may be appropriate in a given situation to justify the employment practice in question. The following defenses generally are referred to in the text of California regulations as "permissible defenses."

Bona fide occupational qualification (BFOQ). Discrimination based on religion, sex or national origin is not illegal where it can be proven that "religion, sex, or national origin is a *bona fide occupational qualification* (BFOQ) reasonably necessary to the normal operation of the business enterprise."[27] To establish a BFOQ defense, an employer must prove: 1) a relationship between the classification and job performance; 2) the necessity of the classification for successful performance; and 3) that the job performance affected is the essence of the employer's business operation. Usually asserted with respect to sex, BFOQ is construed very narrowly by the courts.

Where an employer or other covered entity has a practice that excludes an entire group of individuals on a basis enumerated in the act, e.g., all women or all individuals with lower back defects, the employer or other covered entity must prove the practice is justified because all or substantially all of the excluded individuals are unable to safely and efficiently perform the job in question, or because the essence of the business operation would otherwise be undermined.

Business necessity. Where an employer or other covered entity has a practice that appears neutral but has an adverse impact, i.e., is discriminatory in effect, the employer or other covered entity must prove there exists an overriding legitimate business purpose such that the practice is necessary to the safe and efficient operation of the business, and that the challenged practice effectively fulfills the business purpose it is supposed to serve. This practice still may not be permissible where it is shown there exists an alternative practice that would accomplish the business purpose equally well with a less discriminatory impact.

The Supreme Court has stated:

"The applicable test is not merely whether there exists a business purpose for adhering to a challenged practice. The test is whether there exists an overriding legitimate business purpose such that the practice is necessary to the safe and efficient operation of the business. Thus, the business purpose must be sufficiently compelling to override any racial impact; . . . there must be available no acceptable alternative policies or practices which

would better accomplish the business purpose advanced, or accomplish it equally well with a lesser differential race impact." [28]

Job-relatedness. Any selection device or pre-employment, promotional, etc., criterion or qualification must be a valid predictor of the applicant's success at performing the job in question.[29] Example: typing and spelling tests are related to the job of secretary. Requiring a driver license or high school diploma for a labor job would be difficult to justify.

Security regulations. Notwithstanding a showing of discrimination, an employment practice that conforms to applicable security regulations established by the United States or the state of California is lawful.

Non-discrimination plans or affirmative action plans. Notwithstanding a showing of discrimination, such an employment practice is lawful which conforms to:

1. a bona fide voluntary affirmative action plan;[30]

2. a non-discrimination plan pursuant to Labor Code Section 1431[31]

3. an order of a state or federal court or administrative agency of proper jurisdiction.

Otherwise required by law. Notwithstanding a showing of discrimination, an employment practice is lawful where required by state or federal law or where pursuant to an order of a state or federal court of proper jurisdiction.

Once the employer presents a legitimate non-discriminatory reason for its decision, the employee must prove that the reason the employer has given is a pretext for unlawful discrimination.[32]

Remedies to Employees

All the standard remedies available under Title VII of the federal regulations are available under California state regulations. They include injunctive relief, backpay, affirmative relief including promotion and reinstatement, orders directing employers to change or abolish employment practices, and reasonable attorney's fees. Under the Age Discrimination in Employment Act and the Equal Pay Act, an individual can recover unpaid wages and liquidated damages in an equal amount, plus reasonable attorney's fees. Punitive and compensatory damages may be awarded when violations are particularly deliberate, egregious or inexcusable.

All relief generally available in non-contractual actions, including compensatory damages, may be obtained by the employee from the employer. An employee may seek punitive damages where the employer has been found guilty of oppression, fraud or malice. Such damages can be awarded by the courts, but the Fair Employment and Housing Commission may only impose administrative fines.

Retaliation Not Permitted

Employers may not retaliate against persons because of their activities in furtherance of the enforcement of employment discrimination laws. The retaliation prohibition is quite broad, and includes retaliation against a person who objected to a practice that is legal but which the person "reasonably believed" to be illegal. However, if the employee's action was extremely disruptive and inappropriate, he/she may be disciplined. This protection is not limited to applicants and employees, but reaches all individuals, including former employees.[33]

An employee who thinks he/she has been discriminated against has the right to bring up the matter with the supervisor, other persons in management or a governmental agency. Any retaliation for making a complaint is strictly illegal, whether the retaliation is obvious (such as discharging the complaining person) or subtle (such as denying a merit increase for "uncooperativeness"). A complaint should not be viewed as a sign of disloyalty. It should be taken seriously and investigated objectively. Although some complaints of discrimination are insincere and harassing, the great majority are sincere complaints of perceived mistreatment.

References

1. Government Code 12900, et seq.
2. Government Code §12970(a)(3)
3. Government Code §12970(a)(4)
4. Government Code §12970(e)
5. 42 U.S.C. §2000(e), et seq.
6. 29 U.S.C. §621, et seq.
7. 29 U.S.C. §631(c)(l)
8. 29 U.S.C. §623(f)
9. 29 U.S.C. §626(o)
10. *TransWorld Airlines, Inc. v. Thurston* 469 U.S. 111 (1985).
11. 29 U.S.C. §151, et seq.
12. Labor Code §1160, et seq.
13. 8 U.S.C. §1324(a) and (b).
14. 29 U.S.C. §101, et seq.
15. 42 U.S.C. §2000(e)(k), et seq.
16. Government Code §12945, et seq.
17. 29 U.S.C. §201-219.
18. Labor Code §132(a).
19. Labor Code §98.6.
20. Labor Code §6310.
21. Labor Code §1102.5.
22. Labor Code §230.
23. Labor Code §1044.
24. Labor Code §232.
25. Government Code §11135.
26. Health and Safety Code §199.21.
27. Title VII, §703(e)(1).
28. *Griggs v. Duke Power Company* 401 U.S. 424 (1971).
29. *Griggs v. Duke Power Company* 401 U.S. 424 (1971).
30. *United Steelworkers v. Weber* 443 U.S. 193 (1979); *Johnson v. Santa Clara County Transportation Agency* 480 U.S. 616 (1987).
31. Government Code §12990
32. *Board of Trustees v. Sweeney* 439 U.S. 24 (1978).
33. *Sherman v. Burke Contracting Co.* 891 F. 2d 1527 (11th Cir., 1990).

Chapter 3
Guidelines for Avoiding Employment Discrimination Claims

Background

The word "discrimination" often has been overused and stretched beyond its real meaning to cover anything an employee may subjectively feel is "unfair." But the real meaning of the word is much more limited. A supervisor needs to have a basic working knowledge of what it really means. The following outline is a practical guide to what discrimination is, and how to avoid claims of discrimination.

Protected Classes

The first thing to understand about "discrimination" is that legally it covers only actions taken against people because of their being in certain protected categories. It means treating those people in some way differently than other people not in the same category. In California, the basic protected categories are:

1. Race/color.
2. National origin/ancestry.
3. Sex.
4. Religious creed.
5. Age (for persons 40 and older).
6. Mental or physical disability including AIDS or HIV positive status.
7. Veteran status.
8. Medical condition.
9. Marital status.
10. Sexual orientation.

What Discrimination Is

Discrimination can occur in different ways. It usually is not willful. For example, a supervisor does not simply decide not to promote a person because he is black, or because she is female, etc. But certain acts can constitute unlawful discrimination because of their effect, even if they are not purposeful. Here are the ways unlawful discrimination can occur:

1. *Unequal (disparate) treatment.*
   If similarly situated or equally qualified persons receive unequal treatment and at least one of those persons is a member of a protected class, unlawful discrimination may have occurred. For example, if a black employee and a white employee get into a fight, both are equally at fault, and the black employee is discharged while the white employee is only reprimanded, unlawful discrimination has likely occurred. Or if an Hispanic employee is discharged for theft when a black employee, months previously, was only reprimanded for the same kind of theft, unlawful discrimination has likely occurred.

19

2. *Unequal (disparate) impact.*

A practice or procedure may appear neutral on its face, but its application may have a more negative impact on members of a protected classification. In such a case, unlawful discrimination may have occurred. For example, a rule that all employees must have their own car to get to work may have a greater impact on minorities than whites. If it does, it is unlawful unless it is proved to be necessary to the normal operation of the business. Although a rule that is necessary (such as an attendance rule) is lawful even if it has a greater impact on minorities than non-minorities, the burden is always on the employer to show the necessity for the rule.

Stereotyping

Because there are differences in appearance and physical characteristics between whites and blacks, males and females, young and old, etc., it is easy to make stereotype assumptions about people because of those qualities. But such stereotyping is likely to be unlawful discrimination. For example, not giving a job to a healthy 55-year-old because it involves lifting would likely be unlawful age discrimination based on stereotyping. Refusing to promote a qualified and willing female because the new job required out-of-town travel would also likely be unlawful sex discrimination based on stereotyping. This kind of discrimination is particularly noticeable in decisions made because of assumed limitations based on age and sex. The discrimination laws require that all employment-related decisions be based on individual merit rather than stereotypes or class assumptions.

Sexual Harassment

California employers of one or more employees are required to take all reasonable steps necessary to prevent harassment from occurring in the workplace. Although this requirement applies to harassment on the basis of any of the protected categories set forth above, one of its most common forms is sexual harassment. Sexual harassment generally falls into two types: the "quid pro quo" type, which conditions job continuance, benefits, promotions, etc. on receipt of sexual favors; and the "hostile environment" type, where the unwelcomed sexual comments, touching and/or visual displays of a supervisor or co-worker create an environment poisoned by the harassment. It also is unlawful for a supervisor to fail to act to cure any atmosphere of sexual harassment of which he/she is aware. While this does not mean all "shop talk" involving vulgarities is necessarily illegal, it does mean that any such words from a supervisor or co-worker **could** be illegal if reasonably viewed as having unwelcome sexual connotation by the person either to whom they are directed or who regularly is exposed to such vulgarities. To be safe, a supervisor simply should never engage in sexual banter with persons under his or her charge, and should discourage such actions among employees. Additionally, the requirement that an employer take all reasonable steps necessary to prevent the occurrence of harassment should include an anti-harassment policy.

Effective January 1, 1993, employers are required to post an amended Department of Fair Employment and Housing poster including information relating to the illegality of sexual harassment,[1] and to distribute to employees an information sheet outlining the significant components of sexual harassment prohibitions.[2] See Chapter 7 of this digest for further information about sexual harassment and guidelines for establishing policies prohibiting sexual harassment.

Failure to Accommodate Religion or Disability

Unlike the other protected classes, the categories of "religion" and "disability" have the added legal protection that the employer and the supervisor must attempt to "reasonably accommodate" employees in these categories.[3] For example, a person must be given time off for religious observance if it can be done without seriously hurting the employer's regular business activities; a disabled person must be provided physical accommodations to his/her disability if that can be done at reasonable cost; and the job environment and schedule must be tailored to make it possible for persons with disabilities to work where reasonably practical. For example, a person who suffers from night blindness must be allowed to work an altered schedule to avoid night driving if it can be done without unreasonable hardship to the employer or fellow workers. Examples of these accommodations include varying the days off to accommodate an employee's religious beliefs, providing readers or braille materials to qualified blind applicants or employees, and making existing facilities accessible to and usable by disabled individuals.

Even with a reasonable accommodation requirement, employers are permitted to enforce work rules that ensure the efficient operation of the business, so long as they demonstrate a flexibility in rule enforcement where those rules conflict with accommodation of their employee's religious beliefs.

Reasonable accommodation to an employee's religious requirements might include adjusting any required uniform to meet the religious needs of the employee, so long as such an accommodation does not produce an undue hardship upon the employer's operations.[4]

Avoiding Discrimination Claims in Various Employment-Related Areas

Unlawful discrimination can occur almost any time a manager makes a decision. In avoiding charges of unlawful discrimination, it is important that the employer not only avoid actual discrimination, but also any appearance of such discrimination. Below are common manager decisions with suggestions for avoiding discriminatory actions.

Promotions and Demotions. Be sure that qualified protected class employees are promoted where underutilization exists. Also be sure qualified protected class employees are given equal opportunity to compete for promotional advancement in all areas, not merely jobs at the entry level. Assure that any demotion decisions are neither based upon nor appear to be based upon the employee's protected class status.

Training. Include all protected class employees in any training that might help them to qualify for better positions. Explore both outside and on-the-job training opportunities.

Performance Evaluation and Counseling. Any performance evaluation should relate only to the actions of the employee on the job or conduct off the job that has an impact upon the employee's job performance. Evaluations should be performed objectively based upon standard job-related factors, and should not result in disparate impact upon protected classes.

Layoff and Recall. Layoff decisions should be related either to clear job-related performance standards, to seniority, or to a combination of those factors. Because seniority seldom involves any subjective determination, it often is the easiest layoff system to defend in the face of discrimination charges. Any method used in layoff decisions may be questionable if it has a disparate impact upon protected classes.

The same rationale applies to recall decisions. Any statistics showing proportionately more protected class members being laid off, or more non-minorities being recalled, calls into question the possible discriminatory basis for those decisions.

Terminations. It is vital to document the reasons for any terminations of employees, including work standards expected, notification to the employee of the potential results of his/her failure to meet those standards, counseling sessions, disciplinary actions, warnings, etc. This is particularly helpful in the face of a charge of discrimination in the termination decision. Such records should be kept for at least two years after the termination. (See Chapter 11 of the *California Labor Law Digest*, the companion publication to this handbook, for extensive further information in this area.)

Equal Pay. Assure that any jobs with "substantially similar" content, skill effort, responsibility and working conditions are compensated in the same pay range. There is no requirement that work be identical in order to be considered equal.

Employee Benefits. Employee benefit plans must be administered in a manner that does not adversely affect protected class employees, and must assure that pregnancy is treated the same as any other disability. The only exceptions are employers of 5-14 employees covered by the Fair Employment and Housing Act, but not federal law. Those employers may exclude childbirth and pregnancy coverage from any medical insurance.

The amount of employer payment or cost incurred for employee benefits for older workers may be no less than that incurred for younger workers, in accordance with the Older Workers Benefit Protection Act.[5] In addition, employees who work past any "normal" retirement age are eligible for whatever benefits or contributions are incurred under employer-sponsored qualified retirement plans for employees who have not yet reached that "normal" retirement age.[6]

Harassment in the Workplace

The employer must provide a workplace that is free of discrimination against protected classes. This includes the requirement that a workplace is free of harassment, whether it is intentional or unintentional. Employees and applicants for employment must be free of harassment on the basis of race, religious creed, color, national origin, ancestry, physical or mental handicap, medical condition, marital status, sexual orientation, sex or age. Sexual harassment in the workplace is illegal no matter what its form; even innocently intended remarks or uninvited touching may be seen as harassment. The employer may become liable if he/she knows or even should have known of conduct considered harassment and failed to take immediate and appropriate corrective action. This applies not only to employers, but also to labor organizations, employment agencies, apprenticeship programs or any of their agents or supervisors. Employers should have a program in place to prevent discrimination and harassment in the workplace, and should take all reasonable steps to prevent harassment and discrimination from occurring. Exempted are religious organizations or corporations not organized for private profit.

Sexual harassment includes, among other things, verbal, physical or visual harassment. It also includes conditioning a promotion or benefits on sexual favors. Although other provisions of the Fair Employment and Housing Act apply only to employers with five or more employees, the harassment provisions apply to all employers who regularly employ one or more persons.

Where the employee establishes that the violation was willful, the employer becomes liable for damages. Regardless of whether the employee proves intent, the employer will be liable for court costs and reasonable attorney's fees if a violation is proven. If an individual supervisor failed to take action to warn the harassing party and failed to report the incident, the supervisor may be individually liable.

The Equal Employment Opportunity Commission has published the following guidelines on harassment because of sex.

Unwelcome sexual advances, requests for sexual favors, and other verbal or physical conduct of a sexual nature constitute sexual harassment when:

Submission to such conduct is made a condition of employment; or

Submission to or rejection of such conduct is used as the basis for employment decisions; or

Such conduct has the purpose or effect of unreasonably interfering with an individual's work performance or creating an intimidating, hostile or offensive working environment.

"Unwelcome" conduct. The commission considers as "unwelcome" conduct that the victim did not solicit or incite and which the victim regarded as undesirable or offensive. The commission will look at whether the victim's conduct was consistent with the assertion that the sexual conduct was unwelcome.

Evaluating evidence of harassment. Although not a necessary element of a claim, whether the charging party made a contemporaneous complaint or protest will be looked at carefully by the commission when evaluating evidence of sexual harassment.

"Hostile" environment. In California, a "reasonable woman" standard will be used in determining whether a hostile environment existed. No violation is likely to be found "if the challenged conduct would not substantially affect the work environment of a reasonable woman."

Employer liability. The employer will always be held responsible for acts of "quid pro quo" sexual harassment. In hostile environment cases, the commission will examine carefully whether the employer has in place an appropriate and effective complaint procedure designed to encourage victims to come forward, and if so, whether the victim used it.

Remedies. If it finds that the "harassment has been eliminated, all victims made whole and preventive measures instituted," the commission normally will administratively close the charge on the basis the employer took prompt remedial action.

An employer is held strictly liable for harassment of an applicant or employee through the employee's supervisors or agents. The employer also can be held liable for harassment if one employee harasses another employee and if the employer fails to have a policy about the harassment and fails to take corrective action. Therefore, the employer, supervisor or agent should take immediate corrective action at the highest level. This should include speaking to the involved employees (complainant, accused and witnesses) and/or taking immediate disciplinary action. It would be wise to establish an ongoing program to eliminate harassment in the workplace.

In addition to publishing a policy outlining the company's non-discrimination policy, employers should specify the person to whom complaints of harassment or any other form of discrimination may be directed.

Because the threshold of offense varies between and among individuals, and because avoiding harassment is so important in the workplace, an employer should focus on this issue with supervisors and management. The following are dos and don'ts for your consideration:

Do write and distribute a clear statement of the company's position on harassment of employees and visitors to the workplace.

Do train employees and supervisors about what harassment is, and that harassment will not be tolerated.

Do train supervisors how to investigate harassment complaints.

Do take any complaints seriously, even if your initial judgment is that the complaint is trivial or unwarranted.

Do investigate complaints, take corrective action and keep the complainant informed at all steps of the investigation and any corrective action.

Don't use your management position to request personal favors of any kind.

Don't wait for a complaint if you personally observe something that is likely to be offensive.

When an incident occurs involving harassment — sexual, racial or otherwise — the employer should:

1. Document the event.
2. Treat it confidentially.
3. Treat it seriously.
4. Have management address the situation as far up the chain of command as necessary.

See Chapter 7 of this digest for further information on sexual harassment prohibitions and suggested company policies to combat sexual harassment.

Workers' Compensation Discrimination

It is illegal to discharge, threaten or discriminate in any way against an employee because he/she has received an award from, has filed or even intends to file a claim with the Workers' Compensation Appeals Board. If the employer demotes or transfers an employee because he/she has filed, intends to file or has received a workers' compensation award, such action constitutes unlawful discrimination against the employee. If found to be in violation of the law, the employer is subject to heavy financial penalties of up to $10,000. Further, the employer may be required to reinstate the employee and reimburse him/her for lost wages and benefits. Given the difficulty of answering the charge of discrimination, it is considered unwise to take any adverse action against an employee who is on workers' compensation, unless the employer has substantial written evidence of a job-related reason for discharging, demoting or transferring an individual.

Age

Employers cannot refuse to hire applicants simply because they are more than 40 years of age, or express a preference for individuals under 40 years of age.[7] In addition, employers are prohibited from discriminating on the basis of age between two individuals, both of whom are in the protected age group. The employer may require an applicant over 40 years of age to undergo a physical or medical examination to determine whether the applicant meets job-related physical or medical standards. An employer can require an employee over 40 years of age to undergo a physical or medical examination at reasonable times and intervals during employment to determine if the employee meets medical or physical standards for the position held. If such medical or physical examinations are required, they must be at the expense of the employer and required equally and uniformly of all applicants or employees regardless of age, as the case may be, applying for or holding that same position.

Just as Title VII and the Fair Employment and Housing Act prohibit an employer from creating or maintaining a hostile work environment on the basis of race, sex, religion or national origin, the Age Discrimination in Employment Act (ADEA) prohibits such an environment based upon age.[8]

It is not unlawful for an employer to either limit eligibility for promotion to employees in an existing workforce, to give selection preference for promotion to an incumbent employee, or to promote a candidate under age 40 in preference over a candidate over age 40 based on the younger candidate's superior experience or other work-related qualification. The ADEA permits an employer to "observe the terms of a bona fide seniority system" in hiring or promoting a younger employee with more years of seniority over an older employee with less seniority.[9]

In order to show a violation of the ADEA in layoffs, the plaintiff must show that the employer intended to discriminate in laying off the older employee rather than the younger employee.[10] The fact that an older employee is laid off and eventually replaced by a younger employee is not sufficient alone to establish that the employer's action violated the ADEA.[11] Additionally, layoff schemes based on qualifications and performance, rather than age, are permitted.[12] The ADEA neither guarantees continued employment for those over 40, nor gives older employees the right to bump a younger employee simply because the older employee is also qualified to perform that job.[13]

Retirement

Employers with 20 or more employees (five or more employees in California) cannot have a mandatory retirement age. The original age 70 ceiling has been eliminated under the federal Age Discrimination in Employment Act (ADEA). Separations from employment must now be for reasons other than simply reaching a certain age.

As a result of this prohibition, an employer cannot give employees an ultimatum that they either accept retirement under a special early retirement plan or be subject to adverse treatment such as demotion, reduction in pay, or diminished chance of career advancement.[14] However, early retirement programs that are purely voluntary, and are offered to reduce costs, are lawful.[15] An employer's offer of an early retirement option to an employee slated for termination due to non-discriminatory work deficiences has been found by at least one court not to violate the ADEA.[14]

An employer with a private pension or retirement program must take the following steps to retire an employee:

1. The employer must advise the employee nearing a retirement date that if the employee intends to work beyond the normal retirement date, he/she must file a written notice of this intention.
2. The employer's notice must be in writing no later than 90 days before the normal retirement date (NRD).
3. If the employee wishes to continue to work beyond the NRD, he/she must advise the employer in writing, not more than 45 days after receiving the employer's notification.
4. An employee choosing to work beyond the NRD has an obligation to notify his/her employer of an intended retirement date at least 60 days before the anticipated date of retirement.

The employer may send a normal retirement date letter to the employee two years after the date the employee decided to continue beyond normal retirement. After the second NRD, the employer may send the employee subsequent NRDs not more frequently than one a year.

All private sector employees who desire and demonstrate the ability to continue to work may continue their employment beyond the normal retirement date. Law enforcement, firefighting employees and other public sector employees are governed by state regulations.

Race Discrimination

Section 1981 of the Reconstruction Era Civil Rights Act[15] guarantees to all persons, regardless of race, the right to make and enforce contracts, and provides that those who deprive others of their civil rights may be sued and held personally liable for the harm caused by such deprivation. The 1991 Civil Rights Act reverses the Supreme Court's narrow interpretation of Section 1981 coverage, by expressly providing that the statute applies to all aspects of contractual relationships, including the making, performance, notification and termination of contracts and the enjoyment of all benefits, privileges, terms and conditions of the contractual relationship.[18]

Title VII prohibits discrimination in all aspects of employment relationships. For example, a company's failure to criticize and counsel a black employee about job performance in an effort to avoid charges of race discrimination ultimately backfired into proof of discriminatory conduct when the employee was ultimately terminated.[19] In addition, Title VII protections have been applied to a plaintiff's interracial association, where an employer created a hostile work environment by discriminating against a white women on the basis of her husband's Hispanic race.[20]

AIDS or HIV-Positive Status

Effective January 1, 1993, state law has joined federal law in declaring that AIDS or HIV-positive status is a protected disability.[21] In addition to including AIDS as a disability, California law specifically prohibits employers from rejecting or terminating from employment, or denying coverage under an insurance policy to, or discriminating in any way against, individuals exposed to the AIDS virus. Also prohibited is the use of blood tests in any instance to determine insurability or suitability for employment.[22]

Sexual Orientation Discrimination

Effective January 1, 1993, California law prohibits discrimination or different treatment in any aspect of employment or opportunity for employment on the basis of actual or perceived sexual orientation.[23] This prohibition places in law an existing practice of the Labor Commissioner and the courts in recognizing homosexual rights advocacy, including those in the field of employment, as "political activity." Employers are prohibited from making, adopting or enforcing any policy that tends to control or direct employees' political activities or affiliations, and from attempting to coerce or influence employees to adopt or refrain from adopting or following any particular line of political activity, by threatening loss of employment.[24]

In contrast to the large majority of other discrimination laws, the prohibition against discrimination on the basis of sexual orientation is enforced by the California Labor Commissioner's office under a procedure less time-consuming and costly than those utilized for cases arising before the Fair Employment and Housing Commission or the Equal Employment Opportunity Commission.

Sex Discrimination

Both California and federal law prohibit any distinction because of gender in the workplace. However, personal privacy considerations may justify a gender requirement in very limited circumstances, including when: 1) the job requires an employee to observe other individuals in a state of nudity or to conduct body searches; 2) it would be offensive to prevailing social standards to have an individual of the opposite sex present; or 3) it is detrimental to the mental or physical welfare of individuals being observed or searched to have an individual of the opposite sex present.[25]

Marital Status

In contrast to federal law, state law prohibits discrimination on the basis of marital status. The Fair Employment and Housing Act defines marital status as an individual's state of marriage, non-marriage, divorce or dissolution, separation, widowhood, annulment or other marital status.[20] Employers may not condition fringe benefits or other employment decisions upon whether the employee or prospective employee is considered a "principal wage earner" or "head of household."

Employers generally may not impose a "no employment of spouses" rule. However, an employer may refuse either to place one spouse under the direct supervision of the other, or to place both spouses in the same department, division or facility, if it can show a reasonable business basis concerning supervision, safety, security or morale,[26] or if the work involves potential conflicts of interests or other hazards that are greater for married couples than for other persons.[27] In addition, Fair Employment and Housing Commission regulations make exceptions for fringe benefits, such as health insurance plans, permitting employers to cover only one spouse or the other to avoid unnecessary double coverage of both spouses.

Religious Creed

Employers may not deny employment benefits to any employee because of his/her religious creed, or lack of one. Religious creed is broadly defined to include any traditionally recognized religion as well as beliefs, observances or practices that are sincerely held by an employee and are similarly important in his/her life.[28]

The definition of religion necessarily includes the absence of religion. Discrimination against an individual because he/she is atheistic or agnostic is thus also prohibited, as is requiring an employee to participate in a particular religious observance or practice.[29]

However, religious organizations are permitted to discriminate only on the basis of religion (not on other protected class status) and only with regard to jobs for which "the practice of and belief in the religion of the organization is a legitimate, job-related requirement" so long as the work involved is connected with the carrying on by such organizations of its religious activities.[30]

Employers are required to make reasonable accommodations for employees when there is a conflict between the employee's religious belief or observance and any employment requirement, so long as the accommodation does not cause an undue hardship to the employer. If an employee brings charges against the employer for failure to make reasonable accommodation, then the employer must demonstrate that he/she has explored all available and reasonable alternative means of accommodating the employee's religious belief or observance. The employer may be relieved of religious discrimination charges if he/she can demonstrate the employee cannot be reasonably accommodated without undue hardship on the employer. Factors considered in determining undue hardship include the size and nature of the business, the type and cost of the accommodation required, and notice of the requested accommodation.

National Origin

"National origin" has been broadly interpreted to mean the country from which the applicant or employee, or his/her ancestors, came.[31] An employer may not, for example, deny a person an employment opportunity because of that person's foreign accent or inability to communicate well in English, unless the employer meets the burden of showing that ability to communicate effectively in English is necessary to the job and thus a bona fide occupational qualification.[32]

English Only Rules
An employer's blanket "English only" rule is normally held to violate prohibitions against national origin discrimination, unless the employer can show that it is justified by business necessity.[33] An employer generally cannot enforce English only requirements in private conversations or during an employee's work breaks or lunch hours.[34]

Immigration Reform and Control Act of 1986

Employers cannot discriminate against job applicants on the basis of national origin or citizenship status. However, the employer is permitted to select a U.S. citizen over an alien if the U.S. citizen is equally qualified. The burden of proof for the choice is on the employer if a discrimination case is filed.

Federal law establishes civil and criminal penalties for knowingly hiring, referring, recruiting or retaining in employment "unauthorized aliens" when they are identified.

It is important for the employer to treat all applicants equally, requiring the same identification from all of them. Every new hire must be a U.S. citizen or authorized to work in the United States. If an applicant cannot produce a valid driver license or a Social Security number, one of the following identifications is acceptable:

1. A valid U.S. passport.
2. INS form N-560 or N-561 (a certificate of U.S. citizenship).
3. INS form N-550 or N-570 (certificate of naturalization).
4. An unexpired foreign passport which:
    — contains an unexpired stamp that reads "processed for I-551. Temporary evidence of lawful admission of permanent residence. Valid until _____ Employment Authorized"; or
    — has attached thereto a form I-94 bearing the same name as the passport and containing an employment authorization stamp.

5. INS form I-151 (Alien Registration Receipt Card) or INS form I-511 (Resident Alien Form), provided it contains a photograph of the bearer (the "green card").
6. INS form I-688 (Temporary Resident Card).
7. INS form I-688A (Employment Authorization Card).

The employer should photocopy any such documents and keep those copies on file. The employer must be ready to state under oath that he/she examined the copied documents. Each new hire must attest on the verification form that he/she qualifies for employment. Be sure the new hire knows to what he/she is attesting.

Retain all of the above gathered records for at least three years from date of hire and at least one year from date of termination, whichever is longer.

For additional information, see Chapter 18 of this book's companion publication, the *California Labor Law Digest.*

Dress Standards

An employer may require reasonable dress standards. However, such standards may not discriminate between men and women, or on any other basis enumerated in either the federal or state anti-discrimination laws (i.e., women must be permitted to dress in slacks the same as men) if the standard either financially or otherwise burdens the employee's ability to work. An employer must reasonably accommodate an employee's religious creed that affects dress standards, physical appearance and grooming.[35] It may be considered undue hardship for an employer to totally abandon an otherwise reasonable uniform, clothing or grooming requirement if it relates directly to bona fide and identifiable business reasons, or if it is mandated by government occupational safety regulations.[36] Careful consideration of the specific job-relatedness of particular dress requirements can prevent much of the risk in such policies.

Height and Weight Standards

An employer cannot establish height or weight standards which, in effect, discriminate against a particular class of people. If the employer can show that a weight or height restriction relates directly to the job and is an essential function of the job, then selection according to justifiable height and weight standards is not discriminatory (examples: firefighting, police protection, piloting, certain jobs concerning public safety.)

Highway Carriers

No highway carrier may have a contractual or business relationship with another carrier that relates to providing transportation services, based upon race, religious creed, color, national origin, ancestry, physical or mental disability, medical condition, marital status, sex or age. Such a violation of law would permit the injured person to institute an action against the carrier for damages or an injunction or both.

Guidelines to Avoid Discrimination

Some acts and omissions by supervisors look a lot like unlawful discrimination, even though in the end it can be proven that they were not. Anything that has the appearance of unfairness may be initially viewed as discrimination if it happens to minorities or females. Any decision that is based on subjective "feelings" about people rather than objective facts can look like discrimination, as can any negative decision about employees without a full, fair investigation.

The best way to prevent the appearance of discrimination is to always follow these basic rules in making decisions about employees:

1. *Apply all rules and standards equally to everyone.* Treating all employees equally seldom results in claims of unlawful discrimination.

2. *Give consistent signals and candid appraisals.* The most difficult employment discrimination case to defend is a discharge for unsatisfactory performance shortly after a "merit" increase intended to motivate substandard performance. Mixed signals breed discrimination charges.

3. *Don't delay decisions.* Problems not acted upon immediately often create a sense that a bad situation has been accepted or condoned. Delay in the decision may greatly enhance the appearance of arbitrariness or unfairness. Moreover, delay in addressing a bad situation often creates worse problems and may result in more severe action than originally called for.

4. *Assume everyone wants to advance within the organization.* Supervisors may assume certain employees have no interest in advancement or better salaries because of attitudes they appear to display. That is a bad assumption. All employees should be considered for advancement. Choices should be made on the basis of the best qualifications, but don't overlook anyone because he/she "appears" not to be interested in promotion.

5. *Give clear instructions and warnings.* Don't ever think that employees "should have known" what was expected. Tell everyone clearly what is expected. To hold employees to certain rules of conduct, the rules must be made clear.

6. *Always hear an employee's side of the story before taking action against him/her.* This is an application of the fundamental idea of "due process." A supervisor can take action against an employee, but should not do so until all the facts are in, and a full investigation has been conducted.

7. *Avoid making decisions on the basis of subjective "feelings" about people — rely on objective facts.* A person's performance in a current job is usually a good predictor of success in an upgraded job, especially if some upgraded tasks have been assigned to see how the person responds to the additional responsibilities. Subjective "feelings" as to promotability are neither as dependable or as explainable if a charge of discrimination results from such a decision.

8. *Explain decisions to affected employees.* Many cases of discrimination are filed because adverse action was taken against a minority employee and no one explained to the employee why it happened. For example, while a very detailed explanation is not always in order, an employee who knows he/she is being considered for a promotion but is not selected should be given some explanation for the decision.

9. *Make sure communication channels are open.* Frequent conversations and meetings at regular intervals are essential. A "one-way mirror" in which supervisors only talk and employees only listen is bad. Communication has to flow up as well as down.

10. *Keep complete and accurate records and documentation of all incidents.* This includes testimony of witnesses, employer response, charges filed by the complainant, etc. Date and attest all documents accurately.

Sensitive Personnel Points

Every managerial decision, act or omission is theoretically a point at which discrimination could occur or be claimed. But some situations are more likely than others to lead to an accusation of discrimination. It is particularly important for supervisors and managers to apply these guidelines in the following situations and decision points:

Hiring. Is each candidate being evaluated objectively, avoiding any stereotype assumptions? Is each candidate given the same chance to show he/she is best for the job? Decisions should be guided objectively by the requirements of the job and the qualifications of the applicant.

Evaluation and performance reviews. Are the same standards used to evaluate everyone? Is their actual performance being objectively considered, avoiding any pre-conceived notions about their abilities? Are you being fully candid with them, directly addressing problems rather than hoping they will go away?

Promotion considerations and decisions. Are all possible candidates being considered? Are assumptions that certain people simply are not promotable being avoided? Are you requesting second opinions where possible? Are you saying something positive to each unsuccessful candidate after the decision is made?

Discipline and discharge decisions. Are the rules clear and well-disseminated to all employees? Are you sure you have all the facts? Was the accused employee interviewed about the incident before a decision was finalized, and were any plausible explanation he/she has made checked out? Have all facts been gathered? Did you apply the same penalty for this infraction in the past? Did you confront the issue directly with the employee, and avoid the inclination to be vague about unpleasant matters? Did you document everything in writing in objective language? (See Chapter 11 of the *California Labor Law Digest* for further information on employee termination.)

Assignment and change in work content. Are job assignments and reassignments fair as to content and complexity? Are all employees adequately trained for jobs they are expected to do? Do you seek out the preferences of employees before finalizing changes, and determine how employees react to changes?

Scheduling work and people. Are expectations reasonable about the time needed to complete a task? Given differences in abilities, are the best employees performing each job? Are you aware of employees' views about who is best at what? Have you ever done each job yourself? How do you know what it takes and how a particular job should be done?

Working conditions. Are conditions reasonably set so work can be done without unnecessary interruptions, inconveniences, etc.? Is there a mechanism for complaints about equipment safety, etc.? Do you accommodate mental or physical disabilities where reasonably possible? Do you have an open mind to employees' suggestions for improvement — and not a defensive attitude? Do you watch for physical and mental "fatigue factors," and reduce them when you can?

Fielding complaints/grievances. Is there an established and known procedure for employees to use to make complaints known? Do you have regular meetings with staff to discuss problems and ideas? Do you have individual conversations often enough to have a "pulse" of things? Do you try to solve legitimate complaints, and do you explain the reason when complaints can't be solved in the way an employee wants?

Conflict resolution. Do you accept your responsibility as mediator of disputes and keeper of the department morale and productivity? Do you know your staff well enough to avoid putting clashing personalities together when not necessary? Do you deal with employees in a manner that does not bruise their dignity? Do you attempt to discern the basis for abrupt, negative mood changes? Do you try to understand different goals and motivations of each of your employees?

A supervisor who can objectively answer "yes" to all of these questions has an excellent chance of avoiding any appearance of unlawful discrimination. Most discrimination charges arise when an employee feels he/she has been treated unfairly or insensitively. Fair dealing, candid communications, objective evaluation of persons and situations, and an ongoing regard for the personal dignity of each employee are the basics for avoiding any appearance of discrimination.

References

1. Government Code §12950(a)
2. Government Code §12950(b)
3. 42 U.S.C. §2000e(j)
4. *Bhatia v. Chevron U.S.A., Inc.* 734 F. 2d 1382 (9th Cir., 1984).
5. ????
6. ????
7. Government Code §12941
8. *Blake v. J.C. Penney Co.* 894 F. 2d 274 (8th Cir., 1990).
9. *Dalton v. Mercer County Board of Education* 887 F. 2d 490 (4th Cir., 1989).
10. *Matthews v. Allis-Chalmers* 769 F. 2d 1215 (7th Cir., 1985); *Holley v. Sanyo Mfg., Inc.* 771 F. 2d 1161 (8th Cir., 1985).
11. *Chappell v. GTE Products Corp.* 803 F. 2d 261 (6th Cir., 1986).
12. *Arnell v. Pan American World Airways, Inc.* 611 F. Supp. 908 (S.D.N.Y. 1985).
13. *Accord Ridenour v. Lawson Co.* 791 F. 2d 52 (6th Cir. 1986).
14. *Ackerman v. Diamond Shamrock Corp.* 670 F. 2d 66 (6th Cir., 1982); *Kneisley v. Hercules, Inc.* 577 F. Supp. 726 (D. Del., 1983).
15. *Coburn v. Pan American World Airways, Inc.* 711 F. 2d 339 (D.C. Cir., 1983). cert. denied 464 U.S. 994 (1983).
16. *Sutton v. Atlantic Richfield Co.* 646 F. 2d 407 (9th Cir., 1981).
17. 42 U.S.C. §1981.
18. 42 U.S.C. §1981 (b).
19. *Vaughn v. Edel* 918 F. 2d 517 (5th Cir., 1990).
20. *Chacon v. Ochs* 780 F. Supp. 680 (C.D. Cal. 1991).
21. Chapter 912, Acts of the 1992 General Assembly.
22. Health and Safety Code §199.21
23. Labor Code §1102.1
24. Labor Code §1101 and §1102
25. 2 California Code of Regulations §7290.8(b)
26. Government Code §12940(a)
27. Government Code §12940(a)(3)
28. 2 California Code of Regulations §7292.5
29. Government Code §12926(i)
30. *Church of Jesus Christ of Latter-Day Saints v. Amos* 483 U.S. 327 (1987).
31. 42 U.S.C. §2000(e)(l); *McClure v. Salvation Army* 460 F. 2d 553 (5th Cir., 1972).
32. *EEOC v. Townley Engineering and Manufacturing Co.* 859 F. 2d 610 (9th Cir. 1988).
33. *Espinoza v. Farah Manufacturing Co.* 414 U.S. 86 (1973)
34. *Fragante v. City of Honolulu* 888 F. 2d 591 (9th Cir., 1989)
35. *Richardson v. Quik Trip Corp.* 591 F Supp. 1151 (S.D. Iowa, 1984); *Karriem v. Oliver T. Carr Company* 38 FEPC 882 (D.D.C., 1985)
36. 29 CFR Section 1606.7
37. *Gutierrez v. Municipal Court* 838 F.2d 1031 (9th Cir., 1988)
38. *Bhatia v. Chevron U.S.A., Inc.* 734 F. 2d 1382 (9th Cir., 1984).

Chapter 4
Hiring and Recruitment

Because of the variety of prohibitions in both federal and state equal employment opportunity laws, company managers involved in the hiring process must take special care in the questions they ask of applicants both in the job application, in the job interview itself, and in reference checks made to an applicant's or employee's former employer.

The following sections address areas that an employer should consider in attempting to avoid discrimination complaints in the areas of recruitment, interviewing and hiring.

Advertising

Avoid headings under Male or Female in want ads, employment agencies, radio, etc. Only list a job opening under MALE or FEMALE if there is a *bona fide occupational qualification* (BFOQ) for it being listed as such, e.g., clothing model. Otherwise, list openings under MALE AND FEMALE section. If dual listing (MALE - FEMALE) run in both columns. Add "Equal Opportunity M/F/H" on all ads. If pictures or drawings of employees are used in your ads, include minorities and women and other protected classes in these pictures.

In designing want ads, do not suggest that the job opening is designed for men or women unless there is a BFOQ why it should be so. Do not request that applicants send their picture. Avoid sex stereotype words such as "salesman;" instead use "salesperson." Avoid such phrases as "young and aggressive salesperson," or "recent graduate" to prevent contentions of age discrimination.

Notify all recruitment sources of your policy as an equal opportunity employer. An appropriate example of such notices is set forth below.

> *To Whom It May Concern:*
> *On behalf of _____, I want to call to your attention our policy of Equal Employment Opportunity, specifically as it relates to the hiring process.*
>
> *In accordance with this policy, we are committed to ensuring that:*
>
> 1. *Selection criteria bear a direct relation to job performance and do not screen out individuals on the basis of their race, color, sex, religion, national origin, age or other protected classification;*
>
> 2. *All applicants have an equal opportunity to compete for employment;*
>
> 3. *Employment practices do not eliminate qualified applicants of any race, color, sex, religion, national origin or age group at a significantly higher rate than other qualified applicants;*

4. *Qualified disabled individuals and Vietnam-era veterans are protected against discrimination in hiring and promotion;*

In addition, we make an active effort to generate an applicant pool that reflects the availability of qualified women and minorities in the applicable labor market. In support of this important objective, we ask your cooperation in helping us identify qualified minority and female applicants to fill openings as vacancies occur.

Please share this letter with those in your organization who are involved in making applicant referrals. Thank you.

Sincerely,

_____
(Company Representative)

Application Form Dos and Don'ts

(See pages 42 - 48 for an example of an acceptable employment application.)

Do not ask questions about an applicant's religion, race, color, age, national origin or ancestry, sex, marital status, family plans, disability, physical or mental condition, or type or date of military discharge, unless such information can be shown to have a valid relationship to the job in question. The term "marital status" includes whether the applicant is married, divorced, separated, widowed, has dependents or is in the process of having a marriage annulled or dissolved.

Do not ask questions about the applicant's height and weight or other physical qualifications, unless it is demonstrated that such questions are job-related.

Do not ask applicants to attach a picture. Pictures are irrelevant to an applicant's ability to perform the job, and may expose an employer to charges of discrimination on the basis of race, sex or national origin.

You can ask, "Have you been convicted of a felony?" You cannot ask, "Have you ever been arrested?"

General questions about physical or mental disabilities are not allowed. It is discriminatory to deny employment because of a physical or mental defect where the essential functions of the position do not require such a distinction, or where a reasonable accommodation to the disability can be made without undue hardship to the employer. However, an employer may ask whether the applicant is able to perform the functions of a job, and make an employment offer contingent upon the applicant passing a job-related physical examination, so long as all new applicants must also undergo such a physical examination.

Questions concerning information that it is legal to obtain, but on the basis of which a company must not discriminate, should be footnoted, e.g., age, sex. The footnote should read something like: "This company does not discriminate on the basis of. . . ."

You may not ask for the applicant's birthplace or birthday. You may ask if the applicant can furnish proof of age and citizenship if hired.

Under the federal immigration law, an employer must verify that the applicant is legally authorized to work in the United States. However, do not ask about an applicant's immigration status before making a job offer. Simply give applicant notice on the application form that an I-9 (U.S. immigration form) must be completed within three days of hiring.

You may inquire about the applicant's work experience and generally about his/her references, so long as those questions do not elicit information concerning the applicant's protected class status.

You may request information about an applicant's academic achievement and schools attended, but avoid inquiries concerning specific grades or years of attendance/graduation.

You may request information about languages spoken, relatives already employed and whether the applicant maintains membership in a professional organization.

You are prohibited from asking:

1. Have you ever been treated for any of the following diseases or conditions?
2. Are you now receiving or have you ever received workers' compensation?
3. Do you have any particular disabilities?

You may condition an offer of employment on the results of a medical examination before the employee assumes of the duties of the job in order to determine fitness for the job if:

1. All prospective applicants for similar positions are given the same examination as an employment offer condition.
2. The results of such an examination would result in disqualification and the applicant is given the opportunity to submit independent medical opinions before a final determination is made.

You cannot ask about an applicant's:

1. Draft classification.
2. Dates and conditions of discharge.
3. Military experience other than the U.S. Armed Forces.
4. Assignment to the National Guard or a reserve unit.

You may ask an applicant if he/she is a U.S. veteran, including any relevant skills acquired while in the military. You may use veteran status as a factor in hiring and also may give special consideration to Vietnam-era veterans. Avoid questions about military service in other countries and circumstances under which applicant was discharged from military service.

However, you can request information about applicant's military experience, such as:

1. Have you received any notice to report for duty?
2. Were you separated from service for any reason other than an honorable discharge?
3. What was your military experience in the armed forces?

During interviews, you must make reasonable accommodation to the needs of disabled individuals by such actions as providing interpreters for the hearing impaired or scheduling the interview in a room accessible to individuals in wheelchairs.

You should avoid making any notations at all on application forms. Additional information from interviews, reference checks, etc., may be attached, but coding, numbers and cryptic shorthand notes on the application itself could be misinterpreted and should be avoided.

Interviewing Dos and Don'ts

Do make sure interview checklists comply to the same restrictions as the application form.

Do be ready to back up any prerequisites for hiring, or determinations of the "essential functions" of a job, with statistical data proving their validity or documenting bona fide occupational qualifications.

Do keep objective notes as to why a employee is hired, or why not. To say "not impressed" or "bad attitude" is not enough.

Do keep records of resumes, applications and interviews for at least two years, whether or not the applicant was hired.

Do ask questions that are job-related or necessary for determining an applicant's qualifications for employment.

Do question the applicants in a consistent and uniform manner, regardless of race, sex, national origin, age, disability or other protected class status.

Do evaluate applicants on job-related criteria, in accord with the actual requirements for successful performance of the job.

Do not ask questions concerning age, number of children, color of eyes or hair, height or weight, garnishment record, marital status or maiden name, since such questions are not viewed as job-related.

Do not ask any questions of a female applicant that would not be asked of a male candidate, i.e., inquiries pertaining to child care, marital status, birth control methods or hindrances to travel or working weekends.

Do not ask questions of one race that would not be asked of another, i.e., questioning one's ability to work in a location with members of another racial group.

Do not establish a negative tone to the interview in an effort to discourage any applicant from seeking the position.

Do not give undue emphasis to the hazardous or tedious aspects of a job, especially if such occurs on an infrequent basis.

Do not inform an applicant that the position is "reserved" or must be filled by a female or minority group applicant due to equal opportunity or affirmative action obligations or regulations.

Do not impose additional "desirable" qualifications, in excess of actual requirements of the job opening.

Do not ask questions in the oral interviews that cannot be asked on the application form.

Do not devise additional testing requirements as part of a pre-employment screening procedure, unless such testing is job-related and properly validated.

Do not ask about an applicant's type of military discharge or general military service. You may ask about job-related experience in the Armed Forces of the United States.

Do not ask if the applicant has ever been arrested. You may ask if the person has ever been convicted of a felony.

Do not ask questions on the general physical or mental condition of an applicant. You may ask if the applicant is able to perform the functions of the job. If applicant voluntarily discloses a disability, you may ask whether he/she can perform the job notwithstanding the disability or with reasonable accommodation, and what kind of accommodation would be required.

Selection Guidelines

Objective criteria such as the following are acceptable:

1. Typing or shorthand skills criteria for different clerical or secretarial jobs.
2. Specific physical qualifications (able to climb ladders, etc.)
3. Past specific job-related experience
4. Hair style or length, complexion, clothing, unshined shoes or gum chewing.

Job descriptions, if they exist, must be accurate in relation to actual job function and duties. Education or experience requirements must be relevant to the performance of the duties of the job.

Avoid setting minimum educational requirements, e.g., high school diploma or college degree, unless you can prove they are essential to job performance. The same pertains to minimum experience requirements. Also avoid "over-qualification" as a reason for failure to hire. It is generally inadvisable to base hiring decisions on such subjective criteria.

If an applicant is not hired, the reasons should be clearly documented (it can vary from a simple notation "hired someone better-qualified" to a detailed explanation of why this applicant was rejected).

Testing

If the use of tests results in an adverse or disparate effect on protected classes, the employer must validate the relationship between those tests and actual job requirements. The same standard of evidence of validity applies to interviews, application blanks and performance evaluations. The employer should be prepared to defend their use.

The Department of Fair Employment and Housing (DFEH) has indicated that it will closely scrutinize the job-relatedness of tests for job applicants or job promotions given to disabled applicants or employees that are not given to another applicant or employee or which are not job-related. If the employer can demonstrate that hiring and providing special accommodations for a disabled person is an undue hardship, the DFEH will take this factor into consideration if required to review the case. An undue hardship includes, among other things, the costs of accommodation and the costs of fringe benefits. It is likely that similar scrutiny will be utilized by the Equal Employment Opportunity Commission in cases arising under the Americans with Disabilities Act.

An employer is not subject to any legal liability resulting from refusal to employ or to discharge an employee who, because of medical condition or disability and after reasonable accommodation, is unable to perform his/her duties, or cannot perform such duties in a manner that would not endanger the employee's health and safety or the health and safety of others. In addition, the law does not require an employer to make any accommodation for a disabled employee that would produce undue hardship on the employer. The burden of proof in showing such matters is generally on the employer, and the employer must therefore be prepared to defend its interpretations in these areas. See Chapter 10 of this digest for further related information.

Pre-Employment Physicals
Introduction
After a job offer has been made and before the applicant begins his/her employment duties, medical and psychiatric examinations can be used to screen applicants for employment who would be unable to perform a particular job safely and efficiently, so long as: 1) all prospective applicants are given the same examination after an offer of employment; and 2) the information obtained regarding the applicant's medical condition or history is collected and maintained on separate forms and in separate medical files. Occasionally, physical and psychiatric examinations have been misused in employment screening to reject qualified disabled applicants. Consequently, disability discrimination law regulates the role of physical and psychiatric examinations in employment screening to use only after a job offer is made. Any exclusion from employment on the basis of such physicals must be shown to be job-related and consistent with business necessity, and that no reasonable accommodation is possible.

Use of lower back x-rays in employment screening
Physical examinations should not be used to disqualify applicants whose conditions merely pose a risk of future injury. Current medical opinion questions the value of lower back x-rays in predicting propensity for future injury. Employers should be careful not to disqualify applicants on the basis of lower back x-rays unless injury or disorder of the back exists and the evidence is convincing that the applicant would be unable to perform a specific job safely. Physical examinations should not be used to screen applicants for a job category unless each position in that category requires a physical examination. Physical examinations can be conducted to determine what kind of an accommodation would be appropriate.

Suggestions for selecting a doctor
In selecting a physician or psychiatrist to screen applicants, consider the physician's specialty and qualifications for making occupational placement decisions. Once selected, a physician should have a clear understanding of the demands of the job(s) for which applicants are being screened. Request that the physician's recommendations be as specific as possible. Be wary of vague language in the job specifications, such as "no heavy lifting."

Personnel Records
Records retention
All job applications, personnel records after discharge, union membership or employment referral records and files must be maintained for a minimum of two years. Payroll records must be kept for three years. See Chapter 8 of this handbook's companion *California Labor Law Digest* for further information.

Arrest records

California law prohibits employer inquiries about arrests that did not result in convictions. It further outlaws use of information about such arrests in hiring, promotion or termination decisions. In addition, employers may not inquire about or use information concerning "detentions," defined as an arrest in which no charge was filed with a court. The only exceptions to these general prohibitions are where the arrestee applies for work as a law enforcement officer or other position having access to criminal records data.

Where an employer violates this law he/she becomes liable to the injured employee for full actual damages or $200, whichever is greater. However, where the employee establishes that the violation was willful, the employer becomes liable for either treble damages or a liquidated penalty of $500, whichever is greater. Regardless of whether the employee proves intent, the employer will be liable for court costs and reasonable attorney's fees if a violation can be proven.

Medical records for disabled employees

The medical records of disabled employees should be kept in a place separate from the main file for employees. It is a good idea, however, to advise managers and/or supervisory persons of the work or duty restrictions placed on a disabled employee so that the accommodations required by his/her disability can be made in the workplace. The employer also should provide first aid and personnel safety training where necessary.

> *Note:* *Although the employer's job application form cannot request information from the applicant about his/her sex, race or national origin, an employer is required to maintain a record of the sex, race and national origin in a separate record, apart from the main personnel files for employees and job applicants. The purpose of the file is to demonstrate to the Department of Fair Employment and Housing (DFEH), if necessary, that the employer's recruiting program is reaching minority groups and that the employer is making an honest effort to develop a workforce that reflects the community's ethnic profile.*

Guide for Pre-Employment Inquiries
(either on application form or during interview)

Category			It is discriminatory to inquire about:	Examples of acceptable inquiries:
☐	1.	Name	a. The fact of a change of name or the original name of an applicant whose name has been legally changed. b. Maiden name.	a. Information relative to change of name, use of an assumed name or nickname necessary to enable a check on applicant's work records.
☐	2.	Birthplace and Residence	a. Birthplace of applicant. b. Birthplace of applicant's parents. c. Requirement that the applicant submit birth certificate, naturalization or baptismal record (see citizenship item).	a. Applicant's place of residence. b. Length of applicant's residence in city where the employer is located.
☐	3.	Creed and Religion	a. Applicant's religious affiliation. b. Church, parish or religious holidays observed by applicant, and whether religious beliefs prevent applicant from working on those days.	a. None; however, an employer may state the regular work days, hours and shifts to be worked, as well as religious days on which operations are closed.
☐	4.	Race or Color	a. Applicant's race. b. Color of applicant's skin, eyes, hair, etc.	
☐	5.	Photographs and Fingerprints	a. Photographs with application. b. Photographs after interview, but before hiring. c. Fingerprinting of applicant or employee.	a. Statement that photograph may be required after employment

☐	6.	Age	a. Date of birth or age of an applicant except when such information is needed for or to:
			  (1) maintain apprenticeship requirements based upon a reasonable minimum age.
			  (2) satisfy the provisions of either state or federal minimum age statutes.
			  (3) avoid interference with the operation of the terms and conditions and administration of any bona fide retirement pension employee benefit program.
			  (4) verify that applicant is above the minimum legal age but without asking for a birth certificate.
			b. Age specifications or limitations in newspaper advertisements which might bar workers under or over a certain age.
			c. Dates of attendance or completion of elementary or high school.
				a. Statement that applicant's hire is subject to verification that he/she meets legal age requirements.
				a. If hired, can you furnish proof of age?
				b. Are you over 18 years of age?
				c. If under 18, can you after employment submit a work permit?

☐	7.	Education	a. Specific years of attendance or graduation. b. Who paid for educational expenses while in school c. Whether applicant still owes on loans taken out while in school.	a. Academic, vocational or professional education and the public and private schools attended.
☐	8.	Citizenship	a. Any inquiry into whether applicant is or intends to become a citizen of the United States. b. Any requirement that applicants produce naturalization or alien registration prior to employment. c. Requirement of production of naturalization or alien registration prior to employment.	a. Are you a citizen of the United States or have a visa which permits you to work here? You must furnish proof of such if hired.
☐	9.	National Origin and Ancestry	a. Applicant's lineage, ancestry, national origin, descent, parentage or nationality. b. Language commonly used by applicant. c. How applicant acquired the ability to read, write or speak a foreign language.	a. What language the applicant speaks, writes, reads or understands (may be asked only if language other than English is relevent to the job being applied for).

Category	It is discriminatory to inquire about:	Examples of acceptable inquiries:
☐ 10. Language	a. Applicant's mother tongue. b. Language commonly used by applicant at applicant's home. c. How the applicant acquired ability to read, write or speak a foreign language.	a. Languages applicant speaks and/or writes fluently.
☐ 11. Relatives	a. Name and/or address of any relative of applicant.	a. Names of relatives already employed by the company or by a competitor.
☐ 12. Military Experience	a. Applicant's military experience in other than U.S. Armed Forces. b. National Guard or Reserve Units of applicant. c. Draft classification or other eligibility for military service. d. Dates and conditions of discharge.	a. Military experience of applicant in the U.S. Armed Forces, including any relevant skills acquired. b. Whether separation from military service was for any reason other than an honorable discharge. c. Whether applicant has received any notice to report for duty in the Armed Forces.
☐ 13. Organization(s)	a. Clubs, societies, lodges or organizations to which the applicant belongs, which might indicate race, religion, etc. b. Names of any service organizations of which applicant is a member.	a. Applicant's membership in any union or professional or trade organization, unless they indicate applicant's race, religion, color, national origin, ancestry, sex or age.
☐ 14. References	a. The name of the applicant's pastor or religious leader. b. Any questions of applicant's former employers or acquaintances that elicit information concerning applicant's race, sex, color, religion, national origin, physical handicap, marital status, age, sex or medical condition.	a. Names of persons willing to provide professional and/or character references for applicant. b. Names of persons who suggested applicant apply for a position with the employer. c. Request of applicant for written consent to a former employer's giving of a narrative job reference.
☐ 15. Sex and Marital Status	a. Sex of applicant. b. Marital status of applicant. c. Dependents of applicant. d. Whether applicant has made provisions for child care. e. Whether applicant is pregnant, or uses birth control. f. With whom applicant resides. g. Whether applicant lives with his/her parents. h. Applicant's maiden name. i. Name of spouse or children. j. Child support obligations.	a. The name and address of applicant's parent or guardian (for minors only, if applicable to the job). b. Name and position of any relatives already employed by the company.
☐ 16. Arrest Record	a. The number and kinds of arrests of an applicant. b. Convictions for possession or sale of a controlled substance that are more than two years old.	a. Number and kinds of convictions for felonies (must be accompanied by a statement that a conviction will not necessarily disqualify an applicant for employment).
☐ 17. Height or Weight	a. Any inquiry into height or weight of applicant, except where it is a bona fide occupational requirement.	
☐ 18. Disability or Physical or Mental Condition	a. Inquiry into applicant's general medical condition, state of health or illness, physical or mental disabilities. b. Questions regarding receipt of workers' compensation.	a. Whether applicant is able to perform the functions of this job (if applicant voluntarily discloses a disability, can inquire whether applicant can perform the job not withstanding the disability or with reasonable accommodation, and what kind of accommodation would be required). b. Statement that employment offer may be made contingent to applicant passing a job-related physical exam.

41

Employment Application

Please Print   Date _____

Name _____
            Last   First   Middle

Telephone No. (_____) _____ Social Security No. _____-_____-_____

Present Address _____
                No.   Street   City   State   Zip

Permanent Address if different from present address

_____
   No.   Street   City   State   Zip

Employment Desired

Are you applying for:

Regular full-time work? .... Yes___ No___

Regular part-time work? .... Yes___ No___

Temporary work, e.g., summer or holiday work? .... Yes___ No___

What days and hours are you available for work? _____

If applying for temporary work, during what period of time will you be available?

From _____

Are you available for work on weekends? .... Yes___ No___

Would you be available to work overtime, if necessary? .... Yes___ No___

If hired, on what date can you start work? _____

Salary desired: _____

Personal Information

Have you ever applied to or worked for (your company name) before?............................ Yes___ No___

If yes, when? _____

Do you have any friends or relatives working for (your company name)? .... Yes___ No___

If yes, state name(s) and relationship _____

_____

Why are you applying for work at (your company name)? _____

_____

If hired, would you have a reliable means of transportation to and from work? .... Yes___ No___

Are you at least 18 years old? .... Yes___ No___
(If under 18, hire is subject to verification that you are of minimum legal age.)

If hired, can you present evidence of your U.S. citizenship or proof of your legal right
to live and work in this country? .... Yes___ No___

Do you have any limitation on your ability to perform the duties of the job for which
you are applying? .... Yes___ No___

If yes, describe the conditions and the nature of your work limitations _____

_____

_____

_____

(Note: Hire may be subject to passing a job-related physical examination after employment offer is made.)

Have you ever been convicted of a felony? .... Yes___ No___

If yes, state nature of the crime(s), when and where convicted and disposition of the case _____

_____

_____

(Note: No applicant will be denied employment solely on the grounds of conviction of a criminal offense.
The nature of the offense, the date of the offense, the surrounding circumstances and the relevance of the
offense to the position(s) applied for may, however, be considered.)

Education, Training and Experience

School	Name and Address	No. of years Completed	Did you Graduate?	Degree or Diploma
High School			Yes ___ No ___	
College/ University			Yes ___ No ___	
Vocational/ Business			Yes ___ No ___	
Health Care			Yes ___ No ___	

Many of our customers (clients) do not speak English. Do you speak, write or understand any foreign languages? .... Yes___ No___

If yes, which language(s)?_____

Do you have any other experience, training, qualifications or skills which you feel make you especially suited for work at (your company name)? If so, please explain

_____
_____
_____

Answer the Following Questions if you are Applying for a Professional Position

Are you licensed/certified for the job applied for? .... Yes___ No___

Name of license/certification _____

Issuing state_____

License/certification number _____

Has your license/certification ever been revoked or suspended? .... Yes___ No___

If yes, state reason(s), date of revocation or suspension and date of reinstatement _____

_____
_____
_____
_____

Employment History

List below all present and past employment starting with your most recent employer (last 10 years is sufficient).

Name of Employer _____

Address _____
        No.   Street   City   State   Zip

Type of Business _____

Telephone No. (_____) _____ Your Supervisor's Name _____

Your Position and Duties _____

_____

_____

Date of Employment: From _____ To _____

Weekly Pay: Starting _____ Ending _____

Reason for Leaving: _____

_____

_____

_____

Name of Employer _____

Address _____
        No.   Street   City   State   Zip

Type of Business _____

Telephone No. (_____) _____ Your Supervisor's Name _____

Your Position and Duties _____

_____

_____

Date of Employment: From _____ To _____

Weekly Pay: Starting _____ Ending _____

Reason for Leaving: _____

_____

_____

_____

Name of Employer _____

Address _____
        No.   Street   City   State   Zip

Type of Business _____

Telephone No. (_____) _____ Your Supervisor's Name _____

Your Position and Duties _____

_____

_____

Date of Employment: From _____ To _____

Weekly Pay: Starting _____ Ending _____

Reason for Leaving: _____

_____

_____

_____

Name of Employer _____

Address _____
        No.   Street   City   State   Zip

Type of Business _____

Telephone No. (_____) _____ Your Supervisor's Name _____

Your Position and Duties _____

_____

_____

Date of Employment: From _____ To _____

Weekly Pay: Starting _____ Ending _____

Reason for Leaving: _____

_____

_____

_____

Military Service

Have you obtained any special skills or abilities as the result of service in the military? .. Yes___ No___

If so, describe: _____

_____

_____

_____

_____

_____

References

List below three persons who have knowledge of your work performance within the last three years.

Name _____

Address _____
        No.   Street   City   State   Zip

Occupation _____

Telephone No. (_____) _____ Number of Years Acquainted _____

Name _____

Address _____
        No.   Street   City   State   Zip

Occupation _____

Telephone No. (_____) _____ Number of Years Acquainted _____

Name _____

Address _____
        No.   Street   City   State   Zip

Occupation _____

Telephone No. (_____) _____ Number of Years Acquainted _____

Please Read and Sign Below

I hereby certify that I have not knowingly withheld any information that might adversely affect my chances for employment and that the answers given by me are true and correct to the best of my knowledge. I further certify that I, the undersigned applicant, have personally completed this application. I understand that any omission or misstatement of material fact on this application or on any document used to secure employment shall be grounds for rejection of this application or for immediate discharge if I am employed, regardless of the time elapsed before discovery.

I hereby authorize (your company name) to thoroughly investigate my references, work record, education and other matters related to my suitability for employment and, further, authorize my former employers to disclose to the company any and all letters, reports and other information related to my work records, without giving me prior notice of such disclosure. In addition, I hereby release the company, my former employers and all other persons, corporations, partnerships and asso-ciations from any and all claims, demands or liabilities arising out of or in any way related to such investigation or disclosure.

I understand that nothing contained in the application or conveyed during any interview which may be granted is intended to create an employment contract between me and the company. In addition, I understand and agree that if I am employed, my employment is for no definite or determinable period and may be terminated at any time, with or without prior notice, at the option of either myself or the company, and that no promises or representations contrary to the foregoing are binding on the company unless made in writing and signed by me and the company's designated representative.

Date_____ Applicant's Signature _____

Chapter 5
Statistics Required of Employers

Records Retention

Federal and state laws vary regarding what records the employer must retain and for how long. Some general guidelines set forth below should be of help:

Fair Employment and Equal Opportunity: General personnel records (including application forms, promotion and discharge, tests, physical exams, etc.) — two years; payroll records (name, address, sex, race, age, occupation, pay rates and earnings) — three years.

OSHA: All federal, e.g., Form 200, — five years. Medical records for Cal/OSHA must be retained 30 years after discharge or retirement.

ERISA (Pension Reform Act): All records pertinent to covered plans — six years.

Immigration and Naturalization Service: Verification Form I-9, three years, or one year after termination, whichever is later.

Age Discrimination in Employment Act: Payroll records (name, address, age, sex, occupation, pay rate and earnings) — three years; job applications, personnel records — one year

Americans with Disabilities Act: All pertinent records — one year.

The laws themselves are the final word. Records pertaining to a pending case should be kept until the case is closed. Anything used to determine the status of an employee with the employer which was intentionally omitted from the employee's records cannot be used by the employer to defend a lawsuit relating to employment.

In addition, records pertaining to the following should be maintained on a monthly basis and kept for minimum of two years for Equal Employment Opportunity Commission and Fair Employment and Housing Commission purposes:

1. Job applications (including reason for rejection);
2. Hires;
3. Promotions and demotions;
4. Transfers;
5. Layoffs and recalls;
6. Training;
7. Disciplinary action;
8. Terminations (including reasons);
9. Employment referral records;
10. Union membership.

Any willful violation of these requirements is a misdemeanor punishable by a maximum $500 fine or up to six months' imprisonment under state law.

Equal Employment Opportunity Commission regulations require that employer-retained data for commission statistical purposes should include only name, sex, race and EEO-1 category. Race is defined as black, white, Asian or Hispanic. An employer must be able to show percentages of minorities and non-minorities and men and women in each of these classifications:

1. Officials and managers;
2. Professionals;
3. Technicians;
4. Sales;
5. Office and clerical;
6. Crafts-skilled;
7. Operatives-semi-skilled;
8. Laborers-unskilled;
9. Service workers.

Explanations will be required if under-representation of minorities or women exists in any of the above. Acceptable explanations might include:

1. Statistics showing a limited number of minorities or women both in the area from which the employer recruits, and in the workforce.
2. Statistics showing the limited number of available minorities or women possessing the required skills for specific jobs.
3. Lack of available transportation to and from the work facility.
4. Limited training capability both inside and outside the workplace

Required EEO Reporting Forms

All employers with 100 or more employees and all federal government contractors and subcontractors who have both a contract of $50,000 or more and 50 or more employees, are required to file the federal EEO-1 form. The filing deadline for 1993 is September 30. An employer may use any payroll period in the third quarter of the calendar year to report the required employment data, although other periods that have been specifically approved by the Equal Employment Opportunity Commission (EEOC) may be substituted. Completed EEO-1 forms, or requests for additional forms, must be sent to the following address:

Joint Reporting Committee
P.O. Box 779
Norfolk, VA 23501
(804) 461-1213

Questions concerning EEO-1 filings should be directed to the above number, or to the EEO-1 coordinator in Washington D.C. at (202) 663-4968.

Computer printouts may be substituted for the survey forms, but those printouts **must** contain all address label codes, follow the format of the prior year's printed report, and respond to all questions contained on the EEO-1 form. The consolidated report **must** be submitted on an actual EEO-1 form, and the EEO-1 computer format designed by the EEOC must be utilized for computerized reports. That format is available from the following address:

EEO-1 Coordinator
EEOC Survey Division, Room 9602
1801 L Street N.W.
Washington D.C. 20507

Single establishment employers may meet the requirements of the EEO-1 report by timely submitting one completed form. A completed form for a multi-establishment company must include:

1. A consolidated report that tallies all employees throughout the entire company (including those counted on lists).
2. A headquarter's report covering the corporate office only of the parent company.
3. A report for each establishment with 50 or more employees.
4. A list of each establishment with fewer than 50 employees, giving establishment name, address, number of employees and major activity.

Although the EEO-1 form is normally sent annually to covered employers, failure to receive the form does not excuse the employer from the obligation to timely file the EEO-1 report. The burden to complete the form rests with the employer.

Required State Contractor Reporting Forms

A contractor receiving state service or supplying contracts in excess of $25,000 must file a California Employment Identification Report Form (DFEH-OCP-002). This form may be obtained as follows:

Department of Fair Employment and Housing
Office of Compliance Programs
2014 T Street, Suite 210
Sacramento, CA 95814
(916) 739-4631

VETS - 100 Form

Employers with federal contracts of $10,000 or more must file an annual form reporting:

1. The number of special disabled and Vietnam-era veterans they employ, by job category and hiring location.
2. The total number of all new employees hired during the previous 12 months.
3. The number of special disabled and Vietnam-era veterans hired during the previous 12 months. Special disabled veterans generally are those with a 30 percent or higher disability rating from the Veterans Administration.

The reporting date is March 31 each year, and is to be completed using data for a twelve-month period ending no later than March 1. For information or forms if you have not filed previously contact:

U.S. Department of Labor
Office of Veterans Employment and Training
P.O. Box 4228
Woodbridge, VA 22191
(800) 535-2446.

Chapter 6
Affirmative Action

What Affirmative Action Is

Affirmative action is a systematic effort to implement equal employment opportunity policies by identifying discrimination based upon protected class status. In addition, it is an effort to eliminate the past effects of discrimination on protected classes. Affirmative action plans are deliberate organizational strategies for interrupting discriminatory processes and creating self-sustaining, non-discriminatory processes.

Affirmative action requires the employer to do more than ensure employment neutrality with regard to race, color, religion, sex, disability, veteran's status or national origin. As the phrase implies, affirmative action requires the company to make additional efforts to recruit, hire and promote qualified members of groups formerly excluded, even if that exclusion cannot be traced to specific discriminatory actions on the part of the company. The premise behind the affirmative action concept is that unless positive steps are taken to overcome the effects of unintentional discrimination, the status quo will be perpetuated as a result of an otherwise benign and neutral employment practice.

In essence, affirmative action is an outreach activity to recruit, hire and train minorities (or females) who historically have been under-represented in the workforce. It involves identifying areas of workforce under-representation, locating qualified minority or female candidates through expansion of recruiting sources, and providing those under-represented minorities with the training necessary to succeed in those positions.

Affirmative action means making necessary efforts to assure that minorities understand the performance and conduct standards required. It means that all supervisors should have increased awareness of the impact of past exclusion that may be borne by minorities, including females. It means that supervisors should be sensitive to feelings of "discomfort" some minorities may feel in a predominantly white environment. It also means accommodating the problems of the disabled where reasonably possible.

An "affirmative action plan" is a formal, written employer program with the long-range goal of employing minorities and females at every level of the workforce in about the same proportions as those persons are available in the general workforce. Affirmative action programs have short-range, annual goals in areas of underutilization. That is, numerical goals are set for hiring and promoting minorities and females in areas of the workforce where they appear to be under-represented. These annual goals are not "quotas" which must be met. Rather, they are reasonable goals an employer believes can be met without discriminating against non-minorities and males. The purpose of such a plan is to increase integration, not discriminate in reverse.

Both the state and federal government require that any employer contracting or subcontracting on a government job must have a written affirmative action plan. An affirmative action plan has only one legitimate purpose — to help accelerate the participation of protected classes into the workforce. Another category of affirmative action agreements includes those that are voluntary. Voluntary agreements do not involve admission of past discrimination, but do involve a company's commitment to assist in incorporating protected classes into the workforce. A third category, imposed affirmative action plans, are individually designed by the Office of Federal Contract Compliance Programs (OFCCP) to meet the needs of particular areas, i.e., Chicago Plan, Philadelphia Plan, etc., so no two are precisely alike.

In general, an affirmative action plan must identify specifically where underutilization exists with respect to minorities and females. The employer is then required to establish reasonable and reachable goals, along with the methods for achieving these objectives, within a given time.

Employers also are required to ensure that barriers to employment and advancement of qualified mentally or physically disabled individuals, including veterans, are removed and that such individuals are, in fact, employed and promoted. Most accommodations require more imagination than expense. Examples may include setting a desk on blocks to accommodate a wheelchair user, or an amplifier on the telephone for a hearing-impaired employee.

What Affirmative Action Is Not

Real affirmative action is not equivalent to reverse discrimination against non-minorities nor males. It is not a "quota" system for hiring minorities in preference to better-qualified non-minorities. Affirmative action programs are designed to give minorities and females the opportunity to progress on an equal basis with non-minorities and males.

An affirmative action program is not intended as a basis for lowering performance or conduct standards in order to accomodate the previously disadvantaged. It is a program of finding and preparing previously disadvantaged minority group members to compete on an equal footing with others. A supervisor does a real disservice to a minority person and to the company if he/she expects and requires less because of the person's minority status.

At the same time, an affirmative action program is not a mechanism for hiring minorities in lower-skill jobs and failing to provide them with equal opportunity for advancement. Promotion of qualified minorites is as important as providing them the initial opportunity for employment. In fact, prohibited discrimination often occurs when employers concentrate on hiring minorities at entry-level positions and then show a pattern of promoting a higher percentage of whites, leaving "pockets" of minorities in low-skill jobs with limited advancement opportunities.

Who is Required to Have Affirmative Action Programs?

Affirmative action programs are not required of all California employers. With limited exceptions, such programs are required only of employers who enter into contracts with the federal or state government or subcontractors of federal or state contractors, and of certain public sector employers such as community colleges and school districts. Additionally, affirmative action obligations may be imposed as part of a court-approved consent agreement, or when a court order of such obligations has been adopted as a remedy following the finding of employment discrimination in a class action lawsuit.

Federal contractors and subcontractors

Federal contractors and subcontractors are prohibited from discriminating against any employee or applicant for employment based on race, color, religion, sex or national origin. Employers are also required to take affirmative efforts in employment and promotions, so that minorities and women will be employed at all levels of the workforce.[1]

All contractors and subcontractors having 50 or more employees and a contract or subcontract of $50,000 or more must develop a written affirmative action plan under the federal guidelines. The plan is also required of federal contractors or subcontractors who:

1. Have contracts totaling $50,000 or more in any 12-month period;
2. Serve as a depository of government funds in any amount; or
3. Function as a financial institution that is the issuing and paying agent for U.S. savings bonds and savings notes in any amount.

The affirmative action plan must include, among other things, an analysis of the contractor's workforce and the labor force by race and sex; a determination of whether the contractor is underutilizing minorities or women in any job groups; and the establishment of goals and timetables for correcting any underutilization.[2]

The obligations of federal contractors and subcontractors under Executive Order 11246 are enforced by the Office of Federal Contract Compliance Programs (OFCCP). Alleged violations of an employer's equal employment opportunity or affirmative action obligations are investigated, conciliated, and in some cases adjudicated by formal adminstrative procedures before the OFCCP. If the OFCCP finds that a federal contractor or subcontractor has violated its affirmative action obligations, it may seek relief for the particular individual or individuals affected, including backpay and reinstatement. Significantly more important, the OFCCP can order, among other things, that the contractor or subcontractor be barred from any future federal contracts until it is determined to be in compliance with the Executive Order.[3]

State contractors and subcontractors

Any employer who is a contractor with the state of California for public works, goods or services in any amount must prepare a non-discrimination program, including an affirmative action plan. Included in the program must be an analysis of the contractor's workforce by job, race and sex, as well as an outline of the contractor's equal employment efforts. The state non-discrimination program differs from the federal affirmative action plan in that no hiring goals or timetable need be included.

The Department of Fair Employment and Housing (DFEH) has issued regulations detailing the requirements of state-mandated non-discrimination programs and affirmative action plans.[5] The Office of Compliance Programs (OCP), a branch of DFEH, is responsible for reviewing and monitoring state contractors' discrimination programs. The OCP is empowered to establish and maintain a list of debarred contractors which it updates monthly and places in the *California Notice Registry* published each month. No contractor, during the performance of any contract with the state, may enter into any subcontract with any employer listed on the OCP list of debarred contractors. To do so may constitute a material breach of the contract.

Under state regulations, an employer with a state contract must do the following under its non-discrimination and affirmative action programs:

1. Develop or affirm the contractor's equal employment opportunity policy that applies to all personnel actions;
2. Formally disseminate the contractor's policy internally and externally, and inform all employees and applicants of that policy;

3. Establish personnel policies to implement the contractor's program;
4. Annually identify all existing practices that have resulted in disproportionaly inhibiting the employment, promotion or retention of those protected by the plan;
5. Develop and execute action-oriented programs designed to correct problems preventing equal employment opportunities for all applicants and employees; and
6. Design and implement an internal audit and reporting system to measure the effectiveness of the entire program.

A contractor receiving state service or supply contracts in excess of $25,000 must file a California Employment Identification Report (Form DFEH-OCP-002). This form may be obtained through:

Department of Fair Employment and Housing
Office of Compliance Programs
2014 T Street, Suite 210
Sacramento, CA 95814
(916) 739-4631

Voluntary Affirmative Action Plans

In the past 20 years, many employers have developed affirmative action plans to increase the hiring of women and minorities in their workforce, even though they were not required to do so under any federal, state or local law. The validity of such voluntary affirmative action plans has been upheld by the U.S. Supreme Court under certain criteria for plans addressing past racial balance[5] and sexual discrimination.[6] In both of those cases, the Court concluded that the plan was lawful because it:

1. Was meant to correct imbalances against protected classes and traditionally segregated job categories;
2. Did not result in the discharge or exclusion of white employees who were not members of a protected class;
3. Did not create an absolute bar to the advancement of non-protected class employees; and
4. Was temporary and was designed to eliminate a manifest imbalance against protected classes.

Developing Affirmative Action Goals and Timetables

In developing affirmative action goals and timetables, an employer must address a number of important factors. The first of these is a written equal employment opportunity statement. Such a statement should indicate that the company is fully committed to equal employment opportunity both in principle and as a matter of company policy. An example of such a policy is contained in Chapter 12 of this book.

The written policy should be signed by the company's chief executive, distributed to all units and posted prominently. Such a statement should set forth the company's equal employment opportunity and affirmative action goals, and identify the person responsible for implementation of the equal employment opportunity policy.

As soon as it is developed, the EEO policy statement should be included in any employee handbook and in union agreements, if applicable. The policy should also be distributed to all recruitment sources. Moreover, the statement "an equal employment opportunity employer (M/F/H)" should be included on the following communications items:

1. Advertisements for employees — internal and external.
2. Company or facility newspaper.
3. Purchase order forms.
4. Employment application forms.

Second, the company should assure conspicious posting of the following state and federal posters on all company bulletin boards and in the employment office:

Federal Posters

1. Employers with 15 or more employers are required to display the revised poster "Equal Employment Opportunity is the Law" (OFCCP 1420). That poster must be posted by all contractors and subcontractors who enter into any agreement with the federal government in excess of $2,500 for the principal purpose of furnishing services. A copy of that poster may be found in Chapter 15 of this book.

2. A poster entitled "Your Rights Under the FLSA" (WH 1088) is required of all employers covered by the Fair Labor Standards Act.

3. The poster "Notice to Employees Working on Federal or Federally Financed Construction Projects" (WH 1321) must be posted at the job site if the company is engaged in work covered by the Davis-Bacon Act (the prevailing wage statute for such projects) or one of the federal laws applicable to federal or federally assisted construction.

4. The poster "Notice to Employees Working on Government Contracts" (WH 1313) must be posted by contractors and subcontractors with contracts in excess of $10,000 under the Walsh Healy Public Contract Act dealing with prevailing wages, or for contracts in excess of $2,500 under the Service Contract Act.

All of these posters may be obtained by writing to:

U.S. Department of Labor
Wage and Hour Division
211 Main Street, Room 341
San Francisco, CA 94105

State Posters

California employers are required to post the state Department of Fair Employment and Housing "Discrimination in Employment is Prohibited by Law" poster. A copy of this poster may be found in Chapter 15 of this book. This poster can be obtained from:

Department of Fair Employment and Housing
2014 T Street, Suite 211
Sacramento, CA 95814
(916) 739-4616

The third element in developing affirmative action goals and timetables is the identification of problem areas. Problem areas in affirmative action programs may include such elements as:

1. Any phase of hiring or on-the-job activities that shows protected classes as not receiving equal treatment with non-protected persons;
2. Underutilization of protected classes in any job, group or category in any department, with "underutilization" defined as having fewer minorities or women in a particular job classification than would reasonably be expected by their availability; and
3. Making little or no use of an employee's talents and/or education; i.e. a women with a bachelor's degree utilized in a clerical position.

In determining whether underutilization exists in any job title, the following factors should be considered:

1. The number and sources of minorities and women in the area from which the employer can reasonably be expected to recruit;
2. The number of minorities and women in the area workforce;
3. Unemployment rates of minorities and women;
4. Ability to train or hire minorities and women;
5. The number of minorities and women not currently in the workforce;
6. Whether the employer has trainable (qualifiable) minority and female employees within the organization; and
7. The availability of minorities or women with requisite skills.

If underutilization is determined, the employer must set goals to correct such under-utilization. Such goals must not be rigid or inflexible, and must aim to increase the number or percentage of minorities and women by some reasonably attainable amount. Timetables to obtain these goals should be set for 12 months (short range) and three to five years (long range), with an ultimate goal. Goals themselves should be based on projected openings resulting from expansion and turnover. Contingency goals must be set to cover unanticipated openings should any occur.

Elimination of Existing Equal Employment Problems

Efforts or plans to eliminate existing equal employment problems through affirmative action goals should include such factors as a monthly analysis of employee training; advancement and turnover; sensitivity training of managers, supervisors and employees; and dissemination of the exising EEO policy to all personnel. Moreover, one person in the company should be specifically appointed to receive and investigate EEO problems and complaints. In addition to that function, company staff responsible for carrying out EEO policy should review all procedures on a continuing basis to assure that the affirmative action plan is being carried out. Such an audit should include:

1. Periodic monitoring of personnel activities for evidence of possible adverse impact;
2. Periodic review of the recruiting and hiring processes;
3. Scheduled monitoring of goal achievement on existing on-the-job programs (especially training, promotions, counseling, discipline or discharge procedures);
4. Dissemination of EEO policy by management throughout the organization, through facility newspapers, bulletins, etc.; and
5. Training managers and supervisors on EEO policy and company affirmative action goals.

In addition to the above, an employer might also consider the following affirmative action steps designed to make its affirmative action program more effective:

1. Enlist participation in or support of the program by local or national community action programs such as National Alliance of Business, the Urban League, United Way agencies or other community projects. An example of such outreach programs would be scholarships offered in conjunction with local or national community action programs.
2. Require notification to all labor unions and subcontractors of their responsibilities under EEO requirements and secure their acknowledgement and certification of compliance with those requirements.
3. Assure minority/female participation in company-sponsored social and recreation activities.

Developing an Acceptable Affirmative Action Program

The following outline contains the factors to be considered and emphasized in developing an acceptable affirmative action program (AAP). It is not intended as an absolute procedure or order in developing such a program. Your company's affirmative action program might be more or less detailed and might well emphasize different points.

The basic goals of any affirmative action program include identifying and eliminating discriminatory practices, taking remedial action to address past discrimination, setting goals and timetables and monitoring results.

Internal Communications

1. State where the company policy on non-discrimination is posted and where copies may be obtained
2. State how often and by whom the EEO policy is reviewed, and with whom, in order to ensure proper implementation.
3. Explain the role of corporate staff in keeping the company informed about proper steps, actions, legal requirements, etc.
4. Explain the method of appointing an AAP coordinator and his/her duties.
5. Plan periodic encouragement for employees to discuss any EEO question or problems with the AAP coordinator.
6. Assure the non-discrimination policy is reviewed with all new hires.
7. Assure that any union representing company employees is periodically advised of the AAP and changes in it.
8. Negotiate changes in the company-union contract, if applicable, to bring it into compliance with the law and the policy.
9. Forward a copy of the company's AAP to the corporate offices, if applicable.

External Communications

1. Set forth all steps to be taken to advise recruitment sources of the company's non-discrimination policy on hiring, recruitment and promotion.
2. Notify all suppliers of the company's policy that suppliers also meet the affirmative action requirements.
3. Set forth the steps to notify local recruitment sources of the company's policy, and the fact that the company will be asking them for referrals as the needs arise.

4. Outline rules to be followed about any pictures in position vacancy advertisements.
5. List employees currently serving on community boards or agencies directly related to human relations and equal opportunity, and encourage others to become involved in such activities.

Responsibility for Implementation

1. Appoint an affirmative action coordinator who reports to the top executive at the facility and detail the coordinator's duties.
2. Define the steps necessary for designated plant or unit managers and/or supervisors to implement the AAP.
3. Require coordination of the filling of employment vacancies through the AAP coordinator to assure that hiring procedures conform with the AAP.

Analysis of Current Employment Situation and Problem Areas

1. Analyze present workforce by job title, race and sex.
2. List current area employment statistics, based on Department of Fair Employment and Housing (DFEH) data.
3. Review population mix based on latest census and local DFEH figures for city and county.
4. List institutions in the area available for providing training employees in requisite skills.

Corrective Action

1. Set corrective short-term goals for next 12 months.
2. Set ultimate or long-range goals.
3. Develop plans for correcting underutilization, such as broadening recruiting sources, looking for present employees who can be promoted, and providing additional employee training.
4. List all positive steps already taken in implementing the program, such as the contacting of protected class sources, recent promotions of protected class members, employee participation in civic organizations directed toward better human relations, and other activities to improve community relations.

Internal Audit and Reporting

1. Review total employment procedure.
2. Require quarterly reports to corporate headquarters, if applicable.
3. Require no less than annual reviews by the AAP coordinator to keep the program adapted to current situations, requirements, steps, actions, etc.

Recommended Listing of Exhibits Used to Support AAPs

1. Copy of company non-discrimination policy.
2. Copy of the AAP itself.
3. Samples of letters to recruitment sources.
4. Letters of AAP obligation to vendors and subcontractors and certification of their responses.

5. List of agencies and individuals concerned with protected class employment in the company's recruitment area.
6. Current EEO situation of the company and goals.
7. Samples of recruitment ads.
8. List of schools in the area providing training necessary for advancement within all areas of the company.
9. Copies of regular corporate reports concerning protected class hiring.
10. Organizational charts.
11. Job progression charts.
12. Employment application form.
13. Purchase order, including certification that contractor follows AAP guidelines.
14. Samples of company-sponsored recreational activities.
15. Employee benefits booklets.

References

1. Executive Order 11246 (September 24, 1965)
2. 41C.F.R. Parts 60-1, 60-2
3. 41C.F.R. Parts 60-1, 60-2
4. 2CCR §8101, et seq.
5. *United Steelworkers of America v. Weber* 443 U.S. 193 (1979)
6. *Johnson v. Transportation Agency of Santa Clara County* 480 U.S. 116 (1987)

Chapter 7
Sexual Harassment

Introduction

As more and more women have entered the workforce in the last 20 years, there has been a heightened awareness of the problem of sexual harassment. The recent spate of successful employee litigation in this area, combined with an extension of an employer's liability for acts of its supervisors and often its rank-and-file employees, has created an area of serious concern to employers. This is particularly so given the heightened awareness to the issue inherent in the Supreme Court confirmation hearings of Judge Clarence Thomas.

What is Sexual Harassment?

The Equal Employment Opportunity Commission (EEOC), which enforces federal prohibitions against sexual harassment, defines sexual harassment as "unwelcome sexual advances, requests for sexual favors, and other verbal or physical conduct of a sexual nature."[1] Such requests, advances or sexual conduct constitute sexual harassment when:

1. It is an employment condition — submission to such conduct is made a term or condition of employment;

2. It is an employment consequence — submission to or rejection of such conduct is used as a basis for employment decisions affecting individuals;

3. It is an offensive job interference — such conduct has a purpose or effect of unreasonably interfering with an employee's work performance or creating an intimidating, hostile or offensive work environment.[2]

The California Fair Employment and Housing Commission, which enforces state law on the subject, further defines sexual harassment to include verbal harassment, such as epithets, derogatory comments or slurs; physical harassment such as assault or physical interference with movement or work; and visual harassment, such as derogatory cartoons, drawings or posters.[3]

Over the years, the courts have separated sexual harassment into two main categories:

1. "Quid pro quo" sexual harassment. This occurs when a supervisor or manager conditions an employment benefit or continuing employment on the employee's acquiescence in the form of sexual behavior.

2. "Hostile" or "offensive" work environment sexual harassment. No employment benefits need be lost or gained, and this type of harassment may be engaged in, not only by management or supervisors, but also by co-workers or persons who are not even employed by the employer. Offensive work environment sexual harassment occurs where sexual jokes, suggestive remarks, cartoons, physical interference with movement such as blocking or following, and sexually derogatory comments create an offensive working environment.

Sexual harassment applies to both sexes, can occur in either direction and may include sexually explicit statements or creation of a hostile environment by women toward men. In addition, although discrimination on the basis of sexual preference is not unlawful under federal law, harassment of a homosexual or lesbian on the basis of his/her sex is also unlawful sexual harassment.[4] Effective January 1, 1993, discrimination on the basis of perceived sexual orientation is unlawful under state law.[5]

Employer Liability

In California, an employer is strictly liable for the sexual harassing conduct of managers and supervisors in both the "quid pro quo" and "hostile environment" situations, on the common law theory that holds an employer liable for injuries committed by employees during the course of their employment. The employer is liable for harassment of an employee by co-workers, and possibly even of non-employees, if the employer knew, or should have known, of such conduct and failed to take immediate and appropriate action. Sexual harassment also may occur where employment benefits are granted because of one employee's submission to a supervisor's request for sexual favors, but where other employees equally or better qualified to receive the benefits are denied them.[6] If the employer did not know of the conduct, the FEHC will consider that the employer had notice unless the employer can establish that it took reasonable steps to prevent the harassment from occurring. Such reasonable steps may include having a sexual harassment policy in place, as well as providing sexual harassment training to supervisors and managers.[7]

Federal Sexual Harassment Policy Guidelines

In late 1988, the Equal Employment Opportunity Commission (EEOC) issued comprehensive policy guidelines on sexual harassment.[8] Some of the highlights of those guidelines are as follows:

1. *Unwelcome sexual conduct*
    The guidelines indicate that to be unlawful, sexual conduct in the workplace must be unwelcome in the sense that the employee did not solicit or incite it, and that the employee regarded the conduct as undesirable or offensive. It also focuses on a careful examination of the victim's behavior toward the alleged harasser. In evaluating the evidence as to "welcomeness," the EEOC looks at the totality of the circumstances and analyzes each situation on a case-by-case basis.

2. *"Hostile" work environment*
    A single sexual advance may create a "quid pro quo" case of sexual harassment if the advance is linked to the granting or denial of employment benefits. To create an offensive work environment case, however, the sexual conduct must be sufficiently severe and/or pervasive so as to alter the conditions of the victim's employment and create an offensive working environment. In evaluating a hostile work environment claim, the EEOC examines the following factors: whether the conduct was verbal or physical, or both; how frequently it was repeated; whether the conduct was hostile or patently offensive; whether the alleged harasser was a co-worker or supervisor; whether others joined in perpetuating the harassment; and whether the harassment was directed at more than one person.

Standards For Evaluating Sexual Harassment — the "Reasonable Woman" Standard

In deciding whether harassment is sufficiently severe or pervasive to create a hostile work environment, the Equal Employment Opportunity Commission has traditionally evaluated the harasser's conduct from the objective viewpoint of a "reasonable person." If the challenged conduct would not substantially affect the work environment of a reasonable person, then no violation existed. However, in a 1991 case, the 9th U.S. Circuit Court of Appeals (which covers California) held that when determining whether a sexually harassing hostile work environment exists, a court should determine whether a "reasonable woman," rather than a "reasonable person," would consider the conduct sufficiently severe or pervasive to create a hostile or abusive working environment. In rejecting the "reasonable person" standard, the court held that applying this theoretically "sex-blind" standard to female employees "tends to be male-biased and systematically ignores the experiences of women."[9]

The court also noted that the concept of what a "reasonable woman" would consider sufficiently severe or pervasive to create a hostile work environment may change over time, and that the standard of what is acceptable behavior should mirror those changes. However, although the federal statutory prohibition against sexual harassment does require a totally de-sexualized workplace, even the well-intentioned compliments of a co-worker could form the basis of a sexual harassment claim if a "reasonable woman" would consider such compliments as altering her conditions of employment.[10]

Even where only limited offensive sexual conduct in the workplace is directed toward a complaining employee, the employee may still pursue a hostile environment claim. Both federal[11] and California[12] courts have considered as relevant evidence of a hostile work environment proof that pervasive sexual harassment was directed at other female employees.

Sexually Oriented Posters and Obscenities

Both sexually oriented posters in the workplace and a supervisor's vulgar comments could create a hostile work environment sufficient to constitute sexual harassment. In a recent case, a female shipyard worker sued her employer, claiming that a number of posters and calendars depicting nude or scantily dressed women were consistently allowed to be posted in the shipyard. The court held that such sexually oriented pictures created a hostile work environment, and that such "cheesecake" posters unlawfully stereotyped women as sex objects.[13]

In another case, the state Fair Employment and Housing Commission determined that a supervisor who constantly used obscenities such as "son-of-a-bitch" and "goddamn," and accompanied these expressions by sexual jokes about oral copulation and attempts to peak under women's skirts, created a hostile work environment and engaged in sexual harassment. The commission found not only the employer liable for the harassment, but also the supervisor personally liable as an agent of the employer.[14]

Constructive Discharge

A "constructive discharge" exists where an employer imposes intolerable working conditions which foreseeably would compel a reasonable employee to quit, whether or not the employer specifically intended to force the employee's resignation.[15] To succeed in a constructive discharge claim, the employee may be required to leave his/her job within a "reasonable amount of time" after the last act of discrimination or harassment.[16] However, if the alleged victim without good reason bypasses an existing internal complaint procedure that the victim knew to be effective, particularly if the company took sufficient remedial action after investigating the victim's complaint, neither the Equal Employment Opportunity Commission nor the courts would likely find the existence of a constructive discharge.[17]

Posting and Employee Notification Requirements

Effective January 1, 1993, employers are required to post an amended state Department of Fair Employment and Housing (DFEH) poster, including information about the illegality of sexual harassment, in a prominent and accessible location in the workplace.[18]

In addition, employers are required to obtain from DFEH an information sheet on sexual harassment, and to thereafter assure distribution of this information to all employees. Any such distributed information sheet shall include, at a minimum, components of the following:

1. The illegality of sexual harassment;
2. The definition of sexual harassment under applicable state and federal law;
3. A description of sexual harassment, utilizing examples;
4. The internal complaint process of the employer available to the employee;
5. The legal remedies and complaint process available through DFEH;
6. Directions on how to contact DFEH; and
7. The DFEH regulatory protections against retaliation for opposing sexual harassment, filing a complaint with, or participating in an investigation, proceeding or hearing conducted by DFEH. These regulations are found in Title 2, of the California Code of Regulations, §7287.8.[19]

Preventing Sexual Harassment Claims:
Developing and Implementating a Sexual Harassment Policy

In light of the increase in sexual harassment claims and wrongful termination lawsuits alleging sexual harassment, and in view of the potential liability to which managers and supervisors are subject, and particularly in view of the employee notification requirements set forth above, it is important that all employers implement sexual harassment policies, particularly since an effective sexual harassment policy may prevent employer liability for an offensive work environment claim. It is imperative that such policies contain, among other things, effective internal complaint procedures. Recent cases have held employers liable for sexual harassment because their investigation of sexual harassment complaints were inadequate and their policies prohibiting sexual harassment were insufficient.[20] The fact that an employer has an anti-discrimination policy and an internal complaint procedure will not insulate it from liability for sexual harassment, especially if the employer's policy does not specifically prohibit sexual harassment and its internal procedures require initial resort to a supervisor who might actually be the harasser or who might condone harassment.

Preventive Steps

1. *Have an effective sexual harassment policy*
    A sexual harassment policy should clearly describe the kinds of conduct that constitute harassment, and include an enforceable statement that such conduct is prohibited by the company's rules as well as state and federal law. The policy should include a statement about an employee's right to complain about harassment without fear of retaliation, and contain a procedure providing that the employee does not have to complain directly to the harasser. The policy should explain the employer's procedure for promptly and objectively investigating all sexual harassment complaints, and should include a statement that appropriate and immediate measures will be taken to discipline offenders. A policy also may state that if the harassment has caused harm to the employee, the harm will be redressed. An example of a non-harassment policy is contained at the end of this chapter.

2. *Conduct appropriate investigations*

   In an investigation, the employer should fully inform the complainant of his/her rights under any company sexual harassment policy, as well as under any other relevant policy, such as one relating to internal grievances. The employer should fully and effectively conduct an investigation that includes interviewing the complaining employee, the alleged harasser, any witnesses to the conduct, and any other person who may be mentioned during the course of the investigation as possibly having relevant information. The resulting determination should be communicated to the complaining employee and the alleged harasser, and if sexual harassment is found, a prompt and effective remedy should be provided to the complaining employee and disciplinary action taken against the harasser. The employer should ensure that no further harassment occurs, as well as no retaliation against the complaining employee or any other employee who participated in the investigation.

Guidelines for Developing a Sexual Harassment Policy

A sexual harassment policy should explain what constitutes sexual harassment, include procedures for internal resolution of sexual harassment complaints, and promise to remedy the situation if the investigation warrants. The policy should be prepared and distributed to all employees by memorandum. In addition, both employees and supervisors should be educated about their liability and that of the employer for sexual harassment, including the possibility of compensatory and punitive damages. An employer's policy should include a sexual harassment complaint procedure. An example of such a procedure is contained at the end of this chapter.

Questions and Answers on Harassment in the Workplace

Employer liability

Q. *An employer having only three employees has one employee who utters racial slurs about another employee. Is the employer liable for a harassment suit?*

A. Yes, if he/she makes no attempt to stop it. An employer having one or more employees is liable under California law if he/she fails to make substantive efforts to eliminate acts of harassment among employees. The harassment charge is the only charge under state fair employment law that covers all employers. All other Fair Employment and Housing Commission regulations apply to employers having five or more employees.

Q. *What is the employer's liability if he/she fails to deal with a harassment problem in the workplace?*

A. The employer can be held liable if the employer or his/her supervisors or agents knew or should have known about the harassment. Treat such charges seriously and investigate them thoroughly. Most importantly, the employer should document these efforts completely.

Q. *What is likely to happen if a supervisor does not take the employee's complaint seriously?*

A. He/she places the company in jeopardy of being found in intentional violation of the law by an EEO enforcement agency. In such instances, the enforcement agency could take the position that the company was placed on notice and intentionally failed to act. Supervisors should take any comments or statements seriously, no matter how casual, and report the incident.

Q. *What can an employer do about harassment in the workplace?*
A. You should tell your employees that harassment is any form of remark that slurs a person racially, sexually or in any other of the categories protected by law. Tell your employees that it is against company policy and against the law to harass another person in the workplace. The employer should post a copy of company policy on the bulletin board and offer to answer any questions employees may have on the subject. Because of the employer's liability under the law, employees should be told that harassment will result in disciplinary action, including termination.

What is harassment?
Q. *How does harassment differ from discrimination?*
A. For all practical purposes they are the same. Harassment is a form of discrimination and is an unlawful practice.

Q. *When do male/female interpersonal relationships on the job constitute harassment?*
A. The best rule to remember is that harassment is present when one or the other individual indicates that advances, attentions, remarks or visual displays are unwanted and should be ended.

Q. *How do you handle situations where two employees are dating, going steady, etc.?*
A. This has nothing to do with harassment. It is possible that employees working together may be romantically attracted to each other and as long as this relationship does not interfere with their individual job performances, it is not a matter of company concern.

Handling complaints
Q. *What do you do in a situation where an employee complains of harassment but gives only general information and will not reveal specific names or events?*
A. You should record the complaint. In the absence of more complete details, conduct a low-key investigation to determine the possible basis for the complaint. Follow up with the employee to report on the actions taken. As a normal rule, such complaints should be viewed as an early warning signal. An employee may not want to stir up trouble for another employee but if no changes occur, he/she may feel compelled to file a specific complaint. If there is any possibility that harassment is involved, one way to defuse this situation is to remind all employees in the work group of the company's policy.

Q. *What do you do when you receive a complaint from an employee you think is mad at another employee and is trying to get them in trouble?*
A. Accept the complaint; do not make assumptions. Each complaint should be considered bona fide until you have the results of a company investigation.

Off-the-job harassment
Q. *What do you do about a complaint of harassment that is occurring off the job?*
A. As a general rule, the company should not become involved with the private lives of employees. However, supervisory personnel may be viewed as company representatives when off the job, depending upon the circumstances. If the complaint alleges supervisory harassment, the company should look into the matter. If the harassment is occurring between peer employees, the company normally should not become involved. In such cases, special attention should be paid to the working relationship of the involved employees to ensure that there is no carry-over harassment at the work site.

False accusations

Q. *What does the employer do if he/she determines that an employee has made a false accusation?*

A. Process it as you would any other employee dispute. Do not accuse the employee of lying unless you have undisputed evidence. It is best to tell the complaining employee you were unable to substantiate the claim and will take no further actions unless he/she can provide more evidence. Failure to prove the accusation does not mean that in some cases it didn't happen. Remember, document each case carefully and maintain your records. The complaining employee has up to one year to file a complaint with the Department of Fair Employment and Housing (DFEH).

Use of ethnic and other slurs

Q. *Should employees be permitted to use ethnic, racial or commonly used slurs where it has been a common practice to use these terms in a give-and-take manner?*

A. Some employees may tolerate this practice because they don't want to "rock the boat" but that does not mean that they might not be deeply offended by such language. This practice should not be permitted and is totally unacceptable.

Non-company employees

Q. *Are contractors' employees and other non-company workers at the work site covered by the company's harassment guidelines?*

A. Yes. They are expected to meet the same behavioral standards as company employees.

Procedure

Q. *Can an employee file a civil lawsuit against a supervisor, co-worker or employer directly without first filing with the Department of Fair Employment and Housing (DFEH)?*

A. Yes. Individuals can file for personal liability under various state and federal statutes for actions such as assault, battery, emotional distress, etc. In addition, under a 1991 decision of the California Supreme Court, employees are no longer required to exhaust DFEH administrative remedies before filing a lawsuit over sex or race discrimination since such discrimination also is specifically prohibited by the California Constitution.

Impact of harassment

Q. *Does harassment have a serious impact on the workforce?*

A. Yes. It has the potential to reduce the effectiveness and productivity of your workforce. It may increase personnel turnover, lower morale or cause some personnel to be intimidated and therefore less motivated. It prevents establishment of a "team attitude" toward the job.

Q. *What is likely to happen in the future regarding this issue?*

A. Even if a company has had very few complaints of harassment in the past, the high visibility of the issue in the newspapers and on television and the recent high dollar court settlements may cause an increase in the number of complaints in the future. For these reasons, it is necessary to make absolutely clear to employees that such improper conduct will not be tolerated.

References

1. 29 C.F.R. §1604.11
2. 29 C.F.R. §1604.11
3. 2 C.C.R. §7287.6(b)
4. *DFEH v. Ring* FEHC No. 85-16 (November 15, 1985).
5. Labor Code §1102.1
6. 29 C.F.R. §1604.11(g)
7. 2 C.C.R. §7287.6(b)(3)
8. EEOC Compliance Manual No. 120
9. *Ellison v. Brady* 924 F2d 872 (9th Cir., 1991).
10. Ibid
11. *Broderick v. Ruder* 685 F Supp. 1269 (D.D.C., 1988).
12. *Fisher v. San Pedro Peninsula Hospital* 214 Cal. App. 3d 590 (Cal Ct. App., 1989).
13. *Robinson v. Jacksonville Shipyards, Inc.* 55 Empl. Prac. Dec 40,535 (M.D. Fla, 1991).
14. *DFEH v. Sigma Circuits, Inc.* FEHC No. 88-14 (July 28, 1988).
15. *Davis v. Tri State Mack Distributors* 57 F.E.P.C. 1025 (E.D. Ark 1991).
16. *Smith v. Bath Iron Works Corp.* 943 F. 2d 164 (1st Cir., 1991).
17. *Paroline v. Unisys Corp.* 900 F. 2d 27 (4th Cir., 1990).
18. Government Code §12950(a)
19. Government Code §12950(b)
20. *Yates v. Avco Corp.* 819 F2d 630 (6th Cir., 1987); *Baker v. Weyerhauser Co.* 903 F2d 1342 (10th Cir, 1990); *Brooms v. Regal Tube Co.* 881 F2d 412 (7th Cir., 1989).

Example

Guidelines Concerning Sexual Harassment Prohibitions

Statement of Principles

Equal opportunity policy states that all managers must ensure equal opportunity in the conduct of all our business activities without regard to an individual's race, color, religion, sex, national origin, age, veteran status, or handicap. Included in this commitment is that there will be an environment free of harassment.

The Equal Employment Opportunity Commission has issued specific guidelines concerning sexual harassment. Essentially, these guidelines state that "unwelcome sexual advances, requests for sexual favors, and other verbal or physical conduct of a sexual nature" will be considered harassment when:

1. "submission to such conduct is made either explicitly or implicitly a term or condition of an individual's employment";

2. "submission to or rejection of such conduct by an individual is used as the basis for an employment decision affecting such individual"; or

3. "such conduct has the purpose or effect of unreasonably interfering with an individual's work performance or creating an intimidating, hostile, or offensive working environment."

The company is in full agreement with the intent of these guidelines and is committed to maintaining a workplace where each employee's privacy and personal dignity are respected and protected from offensive or threatening behavior.

Process for Implementing Guidelines

If any employee believes he or she has been subjected to conduct which may constitute sexual harassment, that employee should immediately report the offensive conduct to his or her immediate supervisor or manager. If a complaint arises because of the action of the employee's supervisor or manager, the aggrieved employee should contact the local EEO Coordinator who, in turn, will advise the employee and consult with the appropriate level of local management to resolve the issues surrounding the complaint. It is imperative that all parties involved in a complaint remain cognizant of the need to maintain strict confidentiality while the complaint is being investigated and evaluated.

After an immediate and confidential investigation of the employee's complaint, the employee will be advised of the results. If there is reasonable evidence that sexual harassment has occurred, the company will take the necessary and appropriate disciplinary action against the offending party. It also should be recognized that because of the serious nature of such a complaint, anyone making a complaint should be certain in his or her mind that sexual harassment has occurred. The company does not condone frivolous complaints. Complaints will be handled in a completely confidential manner with respect for the privacy of all individuals involved. Employees are assured that there will be no retaliation against any employee who makes a complaint with the reasonable belief that sexual harassment has occurred. Managers and supervisors have a responsibility to communicate the company's position on sexual harassment to all employees and will be held accountable for ensuring compliance with these guidelines in their area of responsibility. Managers and supervisors also are encouraged to seek the help of the local EEO coordinator in complying with these guidelines and other matters pertaining to equal employment opportunity.

Example
Sexual Harassment Complaint Procedure

To: All Salaried Supervisors   Date:

From:

Subject: Sexual Harassment — Complaint Procedure

The attached notice regarding corporate policy on sexual harassment has been posted on bulletin boards throughout the plant. It is quite explicit as to the corporation's commitment and management's responsibility in this area. To be specific, it is the responsibility of every supervisor and manager to see that employees are not subjected to any form of sexual harassment. Should a supervisor or any member of management become aware of the occurrence of sexual harassment, it is their responsibility to see that appropriate action is taken in accordance with the following procedure:

1. Any sexual harassment complaint by an employee should be filed with the employee's immediate supervisor. If the complaint happens to be against the employee's supervisor, the complaint should be filed with the Manager of Personnel.

2. The Manager of Personnel should immediately be contacted when a formal sexual harassment complaint is received.

3. The Manager of Personnel will investigate all sexual harassment complaints. This will include, but is not limited to, interviewing the complaining party, supervisors and any other personnel, as required, to obtain sufficient, factual information upon which to make a determination.

4. If at the conclusion of the investigative procedure, it is found that sexual harassment, in fact, has occurred, the Personnel Manager will report his/her findings, along with recommendation to the appropriate management.

5. The complaining party will be advised by the Personnel Manager in the presence of the employee's supervisor and/or department head as to the final disposition of the complaint.

6. Every effort will be made to resolve each complaint within one week after it is received.

If you should have any questions about the corporate policy for sexual harassment, or the procedure for filing complaints, please contact _____, Personnel Manager, at telephone extension ____.

Example
Non-Harassment Policy

1. It is a policy of the company that no individual shall be subjected to harassment on the basis of race, color, religion, sex or national origin.

2. Personnel at all levels of the company have the responsibility to avoid any act or actions, implied or explicit, that may suggest harassment.

3. Management will investigate complaints or allegations of harassment, or improper verbal or physical conduct, to determine if the conduct is interfering with the employee's work performance or creating an intimidating, hostile or offensive work environment. If the complaints or allegations are factual, appropriate corrective action is to be taken.

4. Pursuant to this policy, management and supervisory employees who recommend or authorize actions affecting other employees, will not:

    (a) Use their authority to harass employees.

    (b) Take a personnel action, or fail to take a personnel action as a reprisal against an employee for resisting or reporting any act of harassment.

    (c) Condone any harassment, either verbal or physical, of an employee or employees toward another employee.

Chapter 8
Pregnancy Discrimination

Pregnancy or Maternity Leave

The 1978 amendments to Title VII of the Civil Rights Act (also known as the Pregnancy Discrimination Act),[1] specifically provide that sex discrimination includes discrimination on the basis of pregnancy. That is, a pregnant employee is to be treated the same as any other employee, and when a female employee becomes unable to work due to pregnancy, childbirth or related medical conditions, her disability is to be treated on the same basis as other disabilities.

The California Fair Employment and Housing Act also prohibits discrimination in employment based on pregnancy, childbirth or related medical conditions.[2] However, unlike the federal act, state law requires all employers of five or more employees to grant pregnant employees maternity leave of up to four months, for the time they are medically certified as disabled due to pregnancy, childbirth or related medical conditions.[3] Such leave must be allowed to pregnant employees without regard to any company leave policy applicable to other disabilities. This four-month requirement has been upheld by the U.S. Supreme Court,[4] which ruled that a state law can require more advantageous treatment for pregnant employees than for other employees (male or female) without discriminating against those other employees.

California Pregnancy Law

General

California laws concerning employment, training or a leave of absence for pregnant employees are more liberal than federal laws. All employers having five or more employees are subject to the California Fair Employment and Housing Commission's (FEHC) regulations on pregnant employees, as well as other regulations issued by the Commission. In general, state law requires the employer to treat pregnant employees the same as all other disabled employees except as explained herein.

Employers having 15 or more employees also are subject to the pregnancy disability amendment to Title VII of the Civil Rights Act of 1964.[5] Employers having from five to 14 employees and not otherwise subject to federal law are subject to the California law.

Pregnancy is a disability

In general, an employee who is disabled on account of pregnancy is entitled to take a leave of absence which is of the same duration and terms as is available to other temporarily disabled employees except that a pregnancy disability is permitted for up to four months. Whatever pregnancy leave policy the employer adopts must apply equally, including health insurance coverage. An employer of 15 or more employees who provides health insurance to all employees must include a pregnancy benefit in that program.[6]

Pregnancy, leave of absence

Under California law, the employer is required to provide up to four months' unpaid leave of absence for pregnancies, childbirth or related medical conditions upon medical certification of a pregnant employee's inability to continue working (i.e. disability).[7] The FEHC defines a woman as "disabled" if, in the opinion of her doctor or other licensed health care practitioners, she is unable because of pregnancy, childbirth or related medical conditions to perform the essential duties of her job or to perform those duties without undue risk to herself or other persons. During a pregnancy leave, the employee cannot be denied accumulated seniority or other fringe employee benefits, unless all employees covered by the employer's policy for all other temporary disabilities are treated in the same manner.

An employer may require an employee to give reasonable notice of the date such pregnancy leave will begin and its estimated duration, but pregnant employees may not be required either to begin their maternity leave at a pre-set time or to remain on leave for a pre-determined time.

However, an employer may require a pregnant employee to produce medical verification of her continued ability to work or of her ability to return to work, so long as such verification is required in similar circumstances for other disabilities. A job description may be sent to the employee's physician to ensure that he/she fully understands the duties of the job involved, so long as the same practice is followed with other employees when medical verification of continued ability to work is sought.

Effective January 1, 1993, employers of 15 or more employees must provide a pregnant employee upon request with temporary transfer rights to a less strenuous or hazardous position for the duration of her pregnancy, where that transfer can, for the duration of her pregnancy, be reasonably accommodated.[8] State law previously provided that right only to employees of employers of five to 14 persons.

Calculation of pregnancy leave of absence

A pregnant employee is defined by law as being temporarily disabled, and thus subject to state or private disability insurance provisions. The purpose of a pregnancy leave is to hold open the employee's original job until she is able to return to it, within the limits of the pregnancy leave law.

The California pregnancy leave law provides for a four-month leave of absence. The four-month period begins when pregnancy begins, and its use depends upon a doctor's certification of the employee's inability to work (disability). All time lost from work due to pregnancy counts for purposes of counting the four-month period. For example, if the employee suffers from morning sickness during the first trimester of the pregnancy and loses time from work, those lost days count as part of the four-month leave. The interval of time between the employee leaving the job to have her child and the birth of her child also counts as part of the four-month period.

Employers with five to 14 employees (who are covered by state law but not federal law) must also provide up to four months of unpaid disability leave for pregnant employees. However, if such an employer has a regular policy of providing more than six weeks of *paid* leave for disability, that employer is required to provide only six weeks of paid leave under such policy to an employee disabled by normal pregnancy, childbirth or related medical conditions.

If the employer has a policy or practice that provides for more than four months leave of absence for a disabled employee, then a pregnant employee is entitled to the longer disability leave of absence.

Pregnancy, employment, training programs and promotions

California employers of five to 14 employees may neither refuse to employ a qualified applicant nor refuse to select a qualified employee for a training program on the grounds of pregnancy, so long as the employee or applicant can perform the job or complete the training program three months prior to the anticipated date of her pregnancy leave. Employers of 15 or more (who are covered by state and federal law) must follow a strict equal treatment model — e.g., may not refuse to select a qualified pregnant employee for a training program on the basis of that pregnancy.

Pregnancy, job accommodations

An employer must attempt to make reasonable accommodations for a pregnant employee, such as moving her to a less strenuous or less hazardous position for the duration of her pregnancy, if she so requests under the advice of her physician. However, no employer is required to create additional employment which the employer would not otherwise have created. No employer is required to discharge or transfer another employee with more seniority, or promote any employee not qualified to perform the job, in order to make such an accommodation.

An employer may not deny the request of a pregnant employee for a transfer to a less hazardous or strenuous position for the duration of the disability when an employer has a policy, practice or a collective bargaining agreement that requires or allows an employee to be so transferred due to a temporary disability.

Fringe benefits, including payment of health or disability insurance and accumulation of benefits while on maternity leave, must be applied to pregnancy disabilities on the same basis as they are applied to other disabilities.

Pregnancy upon returning to work

Upon completion of an employee's term of pregnancy and upon the employee's return to work, the employer must return the employee to her original job unless the job is no longer available for reasons unrelated to the employee's leave or due to business necessity, i.e., each means of preserving the job for the employee would substantially undermine the employer's ability to operate its business safely and efficiently.[9] If the original job is legitimately not available, the employer must provide the employee with a substantially similar job. The above defenses would also apply to the substantially similar job.

If an employee was accommodated and transferred to a lower-paying job (without loss of income) due to a temporary disability prior to pregnancy leave, the employer must allow the pregnant employee to return to her original job, or if that is unavailable, to a similar job with no loss of pay, benefits or seniority attributable to the job classification at the time she returns.

Fetal protection policies

Policies which identify certain jobs claimed to be especially hazardous to pregnant or fertile women, and exclusion of women from those jobs on that basis, have been found by the U.S. Supreme Court to be an impermissible discrimination against women on the basis of sex.[10] The Court found such a policy neither justified as a business necessity nor a bona fide occupational qualification that was unconcerned with the possible effects of lead exposure to fathers of unconceived children.

Pregnancy, in summary

In January 1987, the U.S. Supreme Court upheld the validity of California's pregnancy discrimination law; therefore, California employers must grant pregnant employees four months' disability leave for the time the woman is actually disabled, and may not terminate such employees for being pregnant or for taking disability leave. This applies to employers having five or more employees.

The subject of pregnancy leave is complex. If the employer has a specific question concerning employment policy on this subject, he/she is advised to contact either the California Chamber's Labor Law Helpline or the Fair Employment and Housing Commission (FEHC), or to seek the opinion of a competent employment law attorney. The FEHC can be reached at (415) 557-2325.

Questions and Answers on Pregnancy Discrimination

The basic principle of the pregnancy discrimination laws is that women affected by pregnancy and related conditions must be treated the same as other applicants and employees on the basis of their ability or inability to work. In the following question-and-answer section, the answer reflects California law.

Provide another job

Q. *If, for pregnancy-related reasons, an employee is unable to perform the functions of her job, does the employer have to provide an alternative job?*

A. An employer is required to treat an employee temporarily unable to perform the functions of her job because of her pregnancy-related conditions in the same manner as it treats other temporarily disabled employees, whether by providing modified tasks, alternative assignments, disability leaves, leaves without pay, etc.

For example, a woman's primary job function may be the operation of a machine, and incidental to that function, she may carry materials to and from the machine. If other employees temporarily unable to lift are relieved of these functions, pregnant employees also unable to lift must be temporarily relieved of the function.

Q. *If a pregnant employee requests a transfer to a less strenuous or less hazardous position, what are the employer's responsibilities?*

A. For employers with a transfer policy or union contract, obviously you must comply. Employers who do not have a company policy must transfer the employee disabled by pregnancy provided that:

1. The employee requests the transfer;
2. The employee's request is based on the advice of her physician; and
3. Such a transfer can be reasonably accommodated. An employer is not required to create additional employment that would not otherwise be created. An employer is not required to discharge or transfer another employee, nor to promote another employee who is not qualified, in order to accommodate a transfer.

Returning to the job

Q. *If an employee takes up to four months' pregnancy leave of absence, must the employer return her to an equivalent job or exactly the same job?*

A. You must return the employee to exactly the same job she held at the time she began her pregnancy leave. However, if there is a business necessity that would justify not making the same job available, the employer may instead offer a job that is similar in terms of pay, location, job content and promotional opportunities.

Q. *Must a pregnant employee be returned to her same job even though, under the employer's policy, men taking disability leaves and non-pregnant women taking disability leaves must return to whatever job happens to be open?*

A. Yes. The U.S. Supreme Court has upheld special treatment in the case of *California Federal Savings v. Guerra*.

Q. *What are the pregnant employee's rights if her disability leave extends beyond four months or if she takes elective leave following the four-month period of disability?*

A. The law requires no right of return. The employee is entitled to the same rights given to other employees who have taken leaves for reasons not related to pregnancy. However, the employee may have additional rights to child care leave in certain circumstances under the state Family Leave Act, effective January 1, 1992 (see Chapter 9).

Q. *Under what circumstances would an employee on a pregnancy leave not be entitled to get back her job?*

A. If the job had been legitimately dissolved for reasons unrelated to her pregnancy or for business necessity, or if her pregnancy leave exceeded four months (except as noted above).

How to determine if the pregnant employee is able to work

Q. *What procedures may an employer use to determine whether to place on leave as unable to work a pregnant employee who claims she is able to work, or deny leave to a pregnant employee who claims she is disabled from work?*

A. An employer may not single out pregnancy-related conditions for special procedures in determining an employee's ability to work. The Fair Employment and Housing Commission has made it clear that the employer cannot require a medical opinion outside of the employee's own doctor or licensed health care practitioner. If an employer requires employees to submit a doctor's statement concerning their inability to work before granting leave or paying sick leave benefits, the employer may require employees affected by pregnancy-related conditions to submit such statements.

Length of leave

Q. *Can an employer have a rule which prohibits an employee from returning to work for a pre-determined length of time after childbirth?*

A. No.

Q. *Does an employee automatically get a four-month pregnancy leave?*

A. No. The length of the leave of absence is directly related to her state of health. The four-month period is dependent upon a physician's certification of the employee's inability to work due to pregnancy.

Accounting for time taken under pregnancy leave

Q. *Do the four months of disability leave have to be taken at one time?*

A. No. The leave can be taken before or after birth, or at any period the woman is physically unable to work because of the pregnancy or pregnancy-related condition. Periods of leave may be totaled in computing the up to four months required.

Q. *Can periodic absences for pregnancy-related illness of limited duration taken prior to an actual leave be subtracted from the four months of disability leave for pregnancy to which a woman is entitled?*

A. Yes. However, if the employer does not subtract sick leave from other kinds of disability leave, it would not be proper to do so from pregnancy leave.

Q. *Can a pregnant employee be terminated for excessive absenteeism?*

A. If the absenteeism is related to the pregnancy, the employer should make a reasonable effort to accommodate the employee. The absenteeism, if related to pregnancy, may be counted against the four-month leave requirement. The employer is advised to keep a record of days taken off for pregnancy in the event it is challenged at a later date.

Stay off until delivery

Q. *If an employee has been absent from work as a result of a pregnancy-related condition and recovers, may her employer require her to remain on leave until after her baby is born?*

A. No. An employee must be permitted to work at all times during pregnancy when she is able to perform her job.

Status during leave

Q. *May an employer's policy concerning the accrual and crediting of seniority during absences for medical conditions be different for employees affected by pregnancy-related conditions than for other employees?*

A. No. An employer's seniority policy must be the same for employees absent for pregnancy-related reasons as for those absent for other medical reasons.

Fringe benefits

Q. *For purposes of calculating such matters as vacations and pay increases, may an employer credit time spent on leave for pregnancy-related reasons differently than time spent on leave for other reasons?*

A. No. An employer's policy on crediting time for the purpose of calculating such matters as vacations and pay increases cannot treat employees on leave for pregnancy-related reasons less favorably than employees on leave for other reasons. For example, if employees on leave for medical reasons are credited with the time spent on leave when computing entitlement to vacation or pay raises, an employee on leave for pregnancy-related disability is entitled to the same kind of time credit.

Q. *Must I pay an employee for her entire pregnancy leave?*

A. This depends upon your company policy covering a disability leave of absence. A pregnancy leave must be handled in the same way an employer would handle any disability leave of absence. If the employer has a company (or insurance coverage) policy that pays an employee up to six weeks for a disability leave, then each pregnancy leave of absence must receive exactly the same benefit. The employee may be permitted to take accrued vacation time or sick leave before taking any remaining unpaid leave. The state's disability insurance benefits, however, would be paid to the employee on pregnancy leave in conjunction with any other benefits paid by the employer as a matter of employer policy.

Q. *If an employer provides benefits to employees on leave, such as the purchase of disability insurance, payment of premiums for health, life or other insurance,* continued payments into pension, saving or profit-sharing plans, must the same benefits be provided for those on leave for pregnancy-related conditions?

A. Yes. The employer must provide the same benefits for those on leave for a pregnancy-related disability as for those on leave for other disabilities.

Q. *Can an employee who is absent due to a pregnancy-related disability be required to exhaust vacation benefits before receiving sick leave pay or disability benefits?*

A. No. If employees who are absent because of other disabilities receive sick leave pay or disability benefits without any requirement that they first exhaust vacation benefits, the employer cannot impose this requirement on an employee absent for a pregnancy-related disability.

Q. *If an employee is on pregnancy leave, must the employer continue to pay premiums on a health insurance benefits policy?*

A. Unless the employer pays health insurance premiums for other employees on disability leave, there is no requirement that the employer continue to pay health insurance benefits for an employee on pregnancy leave. However, it is proper to offer the pregnant employee the opportunity to pay her own health insurance premiums during this period.

Hiring

Q. *Must an employer hire a woman who is medically unable, because of a pregnancy-related condition, to perform a necessary function of a job?*

A. An employer cannot refuse to hire a woman because of her pregnancy-related condition so long as she is able to perform the major functions necessary to the job. Nor can an employer refuse to hire her because of its preferences against pregnant workers or the preferences of co-workers, clients or customers.

Promotions/training during pregnancy leave

Q. *If a pregnant employee is soon to go on a pregnancy leave of absence, must the employer consider her as a candidate for a promotion or a training program?*

A. Yes, provided the employee is qualified and is able to enter the training program according to pre-determined dates.

Only marrieds protected?

Q. *May an employer limit disability benefits for pregnancy-related conditions only to married employees?*

A. No.

All female workforce

Q. *If an employer has an all-female workforce or job classification, must benefits be provided for pregnancy-related conditions?*

A. Yes. If benefits are provided for other conditions, they also must be provided for pregnancy-related conditions.

Income maintenance

Q. *For what length of time must an employer who provides income maintenance benefits for temporary disabilities provide such benefits for pregnancy-related disabilities?*

A. Benefits should be provided for as long as the employee is unable to work for medical reasons unless some other limitation is set for all other temporary disabilities, in which case pregnancy-related disabilities should be treated the same as other temporary disabilities.

Long-term disability

Q. *Must an employer who provides benefits for long-term or permanent disabilities provide such benefits for pregnancy-related conditions?*

A. Yes. Benefits for long-term or permanent disabilities resulting from pregnancy-related conditions must be provided to the same extent that such benefits are provided for other conditions which result in long-term or permanent disability.

Child care leave

Q. *Must an employer grant leave to a female employee for child care purposes after she is medically able to return to work following leave necessitated by pregnancy, childbirth or related medical conditions?*

A. While leave for child care purposes is not covered by the Pregnancy Discrimination Act, ordinary Title VII principles would require that leave for child care purposes be granted on the same basis as leaves granted to employees for other non-medical reasons. In addition, effective January 1, 1992, California employers with 50 or more employees are required to grant a request by any employee with more than one year's service to take up to four months unpaid leave in a 24-month period for family care responsibilities, including the birth or adoption of a child, or to care for a child who has a serious health condition. See Chapter 9 of this handbook for further information in this area.

State laws

Q. *If state law requires an employer to provide disability insurance for a specified period before and after childbirth, does compliance with the state law fulfill the employer's obligation under the Pregnancy Discrimination Act?*

A. Not necessarily. It is an employer's obligation to treat employees temporarily disabled by pregnancy in the same manner as employees affected by other temporary disabilities. Therefore, any restrictions imposed by the state or federal government on benefits for pregnancy-related disabilities, but not for other disabilities, do not excuse the employer from treating the individuals in both groups of employees the same. If, for example, state law requires an employer to pay a maximum of 26 weeks of benefits for disabilities other than pregnancy-related ones but only six weeks for pregnancy-related disabilities, the employer must provide benefits for the additional weeks to an employee disabled by pregnancy-related conditions, up to the maximum provided other disabled employees.

Spouses

Q. *Must an employer provide the same level of health insurance coverage for the pregnancy-related medical conditions of the spouses of male employees as it provides for its female employees?*

A. Yes.

Dependent coverage

Q. *May an employer offer optional dependent coverage that excludes pregnancy-related medical conditions or less coverage for pregnancy-related medical conditions where the total premium for the optional coverage is paid by the employee?*

A. No. Pregnancy-related medical conditions must be treated the same as other medical conditions under any health or disability insurance or sick leave plan available in connection with employment, regardless of who pays the premiums.

Medical expenses

Q. *On what basis should an employee be reimbursed for medical expenses arising from pregnancy, childbirth or related conditions?*

A. Pregnancy-related expenses should be reimbursed in the same manner as are expenses incurred for other medical conditions. Therefore, whether a plan reimburses the employees on a fixed basis, or a percentage of reasonable and customary charge basis, the same basis should be used for reimbursement of expenses incurred for pregnancy-related conditions. Furthermore, if medical costs for pregnancy-related conditions increase, re-evaluation of the reimbursement level should be conducted in the same manner as are cost re-evaluations of increases for other medical conditions.

Coverage provided by a health insurance program for other conditions must be provided for pregnancy-related conditions except for California employers of five to 14 employees (who are covered by the Fair Employment and Housing Act but not by Title VII of the Civil Rights Act). For example, if a plan provides major medical coverage, pregnancy-related conditions must be so covered. Similarly, if a plan covers the cost of a private room for other conditions, the plan must cover the cost of a private room for pregnancy-related conditions. Finally, where a health insurance plan covers office visits to physicians, pre-natal and post-natal visits must be included in such coverage.

Insurance protection

Q. *May an employer limit payment of costs for pregnancy-related medical conditions to a specified dollar amount set forth in an insurance policy, collective bargaining agreement or other statement of benefits to which an employee is entitled?*

A. The amounts payable for the costs incurred for pregnancy-related conditions can be limited only to the same extent as are costs for other conditions. Maximum recoverable dollar amounts may be specified for pregnancy-related conditions if such amounts are similarly specified for other conditions, and so long as the specified amounts in all instances cover the same proportion of actual costs. If, in addition to the scheduled amount for other procedures, additional costs are paid for either directly or indirectly by the employer, the employer also must make such additional payments for pregnancy-related procedures.

Q. *Where an employer provides its employees a choice among several health insurance plans, must coverage for pregnancy-related conditons be offered in all of the plans?*

A. Yes. Each of the plans must cover pregnancy-related conditions. For example, an employee with a single coverage policy cannot be forced to purchase a more expensive family coverage policy in order to receive coverage for her own pregnancy-related condition.

Deductible

Q. *May an employer impose a different deductible for payment of costs for pregnancy-related medical conditions than for costs of other medical conditions?*

A. No. Neither an additional deductible, an increase in the usual deductible, nor a larger deductible can be imposed for coverage for pregnancy-related medical costs, whether as a condition for inclusion of pregnancy-related costs in the policy or for payment of the costs when incurred. Thus, if pregnancy-related costs are the first incurred under the policy, the employee is required to pay only the same deductible as would otherwise be required had other medical costs been the first incurred. Once this deductible has been paid, no additional deductible can be required for other medical procedures. If the usual deductible already has been paid for other medical procedures, no additional deductible can be required when pregnancy-related costs are later incurred.

Pre-existing condition
Q. *If a health insurance plan excludes the payment of benefits for any conditions existing at the time the insured's coverage becomes effective (pre-existing condition clause), can benefits be denied for medical costs arising from a pregnancy existing at the time the coverage became effective?*

A. Yes. However, such benefits cannot be denied unless the pre-existing condition clause also excludes benefits for other pre-existing conditions in the same way.

Insurance after termination
Q. *If an employer's insurance plan provides benefits after the insured's employment has ended, i.e., extended benefits, for costs connected with pregnancy and delivery where conception occurred while the insured was working for the employer, but not for the costs of any other medical condition that began before employment was terminated, may an employer: 1) continue to pay these extended benefits for pregnancy-related medical conditions but not for other medical conditions, or 2) terminate these benefits for pregnancy-related conditions?*

A. Where a health insurance plan currently provides extended benefits for other medical conditions on a less favorable basis than for pregnancy-related medical conditions, extended benefits must be provided for other medical conditions on the same basis as for pregnancy-related medical conditions. Therefore, an employer can neither continue to provide less benefits for other medical conditions nor reduce benefits currently paid for pregnancy-related medical conditions.

Extended benefits under different conditions
Q. *Where an employer's health insurance plan currently requires total disability as a prerequisite for payment of extended benefits for other medical conditions but not for pregnancy-related costs, may the employer now require total disability for payment of benefits for pregnancy-related medical conditions as well?*

A. Since extended benefits cannot be reduced in order to come into compliance with pregnancy discrimination laws, a more stringent prerequisite for payment of extended benefits for pregnancy-related medical conditions, such as a requirement for total disability, cannot be imposed. Thus, in this instance, to comply with the act, the employer must treat other medical conditions as pregnancy-related conditions are treated.

Self-insurance
Q. *Can an employer self-insure benefits for pregnancy-related conditions if it does not self-insure benefits for other medical conditions?*

A. Yes, so long as the benefits are the same. In measuring whether benefits are the same, factors other than the dollar coverage paid should be considered. Such factors include the range of choice of physicians and hospitals, and the processing and promptness of claim payment.

Abortion
Q. *Can an employer discharge, refuse to hire or otherwise discriminate against a woman because she has had or is contemplating having an abortion?*

A. No. An employer cannot discriminate in its employment practices against a woman who has had or is contemplating having an abortion.

Abortion and fringe benefits
Q. *Is an employer required to provide fringe benefits for abortions if fringe benefits are provided for other medical conditions?*

A. All fringe benefits other than health insurance, such as sick leave, which are provided for other medical conditions, must be provided for abortions. Health insurance, however, need be provided for abortions only where the life of the woman would be endangered if the fetus were carried to term or where medical complications arise from an abortion.

Abortion and complications
Q. *If complications arise during the course of an abortion, as for instance excessive hemorrhaging, must an employer's health insurance plan cover the additional cost due to the complications of the abortion?*

A. Yes. The plan is required to pay those additional costs attributable to the complications of the abortion. However, the employer is not required to pay for the abortion itself, except where the life of the mother would be endangered if the fetus were carried to term, or where medical complications have arisen from the abortion.

Abortion and insurance
Q. *May an employer elect to provide insurance coverage for abortions?*

A. Yes. The pregnancy discrimination laws specifically provide that an employer is not precluded from providing benefits for abortions whether directly or through a collective bargaining agreement. If an employer decides to cover the costs of abortion, the employer must do so in the same manner and to the same degree as it covers other medical conditions.

Suggested Policy Guidelines for Employers

Although the pregnancy discrimination laws have been on the books for many years, many employers still have a maternity leave policy different from that for a ruptured apppendix, pneumonia, etc. Here are general guidelines to keep you out of trouble:

Don't refuse to hire or promote just because the individual is pregnant. Physical inability to do the immediate job is another matter.

Don't have a mandatory maternity leave for a pre-determined period. Time off from the job because of physical inability to do the work due to pregnancy or pregnancy-related illness, both before and after birth, should be based on a medical statement of her doctor. If an employer does not have a sick leave policy at all, there is no need to establish one just for pregnancy.

Don't limit or deny medical benefits for pregnancy under your group health insurance program if medical benefits for other illnesses or diseases are not denied or limited.

You may ask an employee to notify you of pregnancy as soon as possible to help you plan work arrangements during her absence due to pregnancy.

You can hire a temporary replacement for an employee on maternity leave. However, an employee on a pregnancy leave must be returned to her original job if she has returned within the requisite four-month leave period.

An employee (with or without group insurance weekly benefits) on pregnancy leave, based on a medical statement that she is physically unable to work, is ineligible for unemployment insurance. She is, however, eligible for state disability insurance.

If you allow the employee to switch from a sick leave to a personal leave (for the purposes of child rearing) after the doctor has cleared her to return to work, you could face a discrimination charge if you refuse personal leave requests to other employees for other reasons. In addition, effective January 1, 1992, employers with 50 or more employees must comply with the state Family Leave Act, allowing unpaid leaves of up to four months for family care, including leave to care for a child who has a serious health condition. See Chapter 9 of this handbook for further information concerning the Family Leave Act.

References

1. 42 U.S.C. §2000(e)(k)(1978)
2. Government Code §12926(j), 12940(a) and 12945
3. Government Code §12945(b)(2)
4. *California Federal Savings and Loan Association v. Guerra* 479 U.S. 272 (1987)
5. 42 U.S.C. §2000(e) et. seq. (1964)
6. See, e.g. *Newport News Shipbuilding and Dry Dock Co. v. EEOC* 462 U.S. 699 (1983)
7. Government Code §12945(b)(2)
8. Government Code §12945(c)(2)
9. See, e.g. *Robinson v. DFEH* 2 Cal 4th 226 (1992)
10. *UAW v. Johnston Controls, Inc.* 113 L.Ed. 2d 158 (1991)

Chapter 9
The Family Rights Act of 1991

Effective January 1, 1992, state law requires employers with more than 50 employees within California[A] to grant a request by any employee who has more than one year of continuous service and is eligible for other benefits, to take up to four months of unpaid leave in a 24-month period for family care responsibilities. Employees granted such leave are guaranteeed employment in the same or comparable position upon termination of the leave.[1]

Purpose and Reasons for Leave

The purpose of this law is to provide covered employees the right to take time off from work for the birth or adoption of a child, or for the serious health condition of their child, parent or spouse, without jeopardizing their job, provided that such leave does not cause undue hardship to the employer's operation.[B] "Child" includes biological, adopted, foster, stepchild and adult dependent child,[C] and "parent" means biological, foster, adoptive, stepparent or legal guardian, but not parent-in-law or grandparent.[D]

Under this law, the employee may elect, or the employer may require the employee to substitute, accrued vacation leave or other accrued time off during this period, or any other paid or unpaid leave negotiated with the employer. Employees cannot be required to use sick leave during the family leave unless mutually agreed by the employer and employee.[2]

Benefits Eligibility and Payment

During the leave, employees continue to be eligible for health plans, retirement and pension plans, and supplemental unemployment benefit plans to the same extent and under the same conditions as applied to unpaid leaves taken for any purpose other than family leave. If such other leaves do not exist, the employee is still eligible for the benefits set forth above.[E] The employer may require the employee to pay health and welfare benefit plan premiums during the leave to the same extent and under the same conditions as applied to other unpaid leaves, so long as this is consistent with the employee benefit plan.[F] However, the non-payment of premiums by the employee does not constitute a break in service for purposes of longevity, any seniority system or any employee benefit plan.[3]

For purposes of pension and retirement plans, an employer is not required to make plan payments for an employee during the leave, and the leave is not required to be counted for purposes of accrual under the plan. However, an employee covered by a pension may continue to make contributions in accordance with the terms of the plan during the period of the leave.[4]

Note: Numbered footnotes refer to the law; alphabetical footnotes refer to proposed regulations that had not been finalized at the time this handbook was published.

During the leave, the employee retains employee status with the employer, and the leave does not constitute a break in service for purposes of longevity, seniority or any employee benefit plan. The employee returning from leave, therefore, returns with no less seniority than the employee had when the leave commenced, for purposes for layoff, recall, promotion, job assignment and seniority-related benefits such as vacation.[5]

Procedure

If an employee's need for leave under this law is foreseeable, the employee is required to provide the employer with reasonable advance notice of the need for the leave.[6] An employer may not, however, deny a family care leave, the need for which is an emergency or is otherwise unforeseeable, on the basis that the employee did not provide advance notice of the need for the leave.[G] If the need for the leave is foreseeable due to planned medical treatment or supervision, the employee is required to make reasonable efforts to schedule the treatment or supervision to avoid disruption of the operations of the employer, subject to approval of the health care provider of the individual requiring the treatment or supervision.[7]

An employer may require that an employee's request for leave to care for a child, spouse or parent who has a serious health condition be supported by a certification issued by the health care provider of the individual requiring care. That certification need not identify the serious health condition involved, but must include all of the following:

1. The date, if known, on which the serious health condition commenced;
2. The probable duration of the condition;
3. An estimate of the amount of time the health provider believes the employee needs to care for the individual requiring the care;
4. A statement that a serious health condition warrants the participation of a family member to provide care during the treatment or supervision of the individual requiring care.[8]

"Serious health condition" means an illness, impairment, or physical or mental condition of a child, parent or spouse, which warrants the participation of a family member to provide care or supervision during treatment in a hospital, hospice or residential health care facility, or continuing treatment or supervision by a health care provider.[H]

Upon the expiration of the time estimated by the health care provider for such activity, the employer may require the employee to obtain recertification in accordance with the above paragraph, if additional leave is required.

Interaction with Pregnancy Disability Leave

The family leave provisions are construed separately from those involving pregnancy disability leave.[9] However, leave taken pursuant to family leave provisions for the birth of a child may not be more than one month when used in conjunction with the maximum leave under the pregnancy leave provisions, unless the employer and employee agree otherwise.[10] An employee's request for more than five months of combined pregnancy disability/family care leave for the birth of a child is rebuttably assumed to be an undue hardship upon the employer's operations.[I]

Limitations

Family leave may be taken in one or more periods, but shall not exceed a total of four months within a 24-month period from the date the leave commenced, unless otherwise agreed to by the employer and employee. An employer is not required to grant an employee family care leave for any period in which the child's other parent also is taking family care leave from employment or is unemployed and available to care for the child; or in a manner which would allow the employee and the other parent of the child family care leave totaling more than four months during a 24-month period.[11] However, an employer may not refuse a father's request for family care leave for the first two of these reasons solely because the mother is out on pregnancy disability leave at the time the father wishes to take the leave.[J]

An employer may refuse to grant a request for family care if:

1. The refusal is necessary to prevent an undue hardship on the employer's operation;[12] or
2. Leave is requested by a salaried exempt employee who, on the date the family care leave is made, is either one of the five highest paid employees, or is among the top 10 percent of the company's employees in terms of gross salary, whichever group encompasses the greater number of persons employed by the employer at the same location.[13]

Undue Hardship

"Undue hardship" means substantial impairment to an employer's ability to operate the business safely, efficiently or economically. Factors to be considered in determining the existence of undue hardship include:

1. The overall size of the establishment or facility, work area, or classification at or in which the employee requesting the leave works; that is, number of employees, the size of budget, and other such matters;
2. The overall number of employees, number and type of facilities, and size of budget;
3. The type of the establishment's or facility's operation, including the composition and structure of the workplace, the employee's work area and/or classification;
4. The type of the employer's operation, including the composition and structure of the workforce;
5. The feasibility of filling the position with a temporary employee or holding the position open during the period of the requested family care leave.[K]

If granting the leave as requested would produce undue hardship, the employer must offer the employee a leave of shorter duration than the leave requested which is not an undue hardship. There is no other reasonable accommodation duty. However, the employer must consider alternative means suggested by the employee, including modified work schedules, changes in work locations, part-time work, job-sharing or informal time off.[L]

Protections Against Discrimination

The family care leave law is administered by the Department of Fair Employment and Housing (DFEH) and the Fair Employment and Housing Commission (FEHC). It is a violation of the Fair Employment and Housing Act for an employer or appointing authority to suspend, discharge, expel or discriminate against any individual because of:

1. The individual's exercise of the right to family care leave; or
2. An individual's giving information or testimony as to his/her own family care leave, or another person's family care leave, in any inquiry or proceeding related to an employee's right to family care leave.[14]

An employer also may not refuse to honor a guarantee of reinstatement to the same or comparable position for an employee who complies with the provisions of the statute, unless that same or comparable position has ceased to exist due to legitimate business reasons unrelated to the employee's family care leave.[M] Even in that situation, the employer must make reasonable accommodation by alternative means that will not cause undue hardship on the employer's operations, including offering the employee another position that is available and for which the employee is qualified.[N]

Notice Requirements

Covered employers are required to provide employees with notice of their right to request family care leave. Such notice must be posted in conspicuous places customarily used to notify employees, and a description of family care leave must be included in the next edition of any employee handbook which includes personal leaves available to its employees, if such handbook exists. If the employer's establishment contains 10 percent or more of persons whose primary language is other than English, the notice shall be translated into that language and posted as well.[O]

Suggested Notice

The following notice suggested for posting by the Fair Employment and Housing Commission contains only the minimum requirements of the law. Covered employers may develop their own notice or use this text, unless it does not accurately reflect their company policy.

Family Care Leave

Under the California Family Rights Act of 1991, if you have more than one year of continuous service with us and are eligible for at least one employee benefit, you have a right to an unpaid family care leave of up to four months in a 24-month period for the birth or adoption of your child or for the serious health condition of your child, parent or spouse. Granting this leave contains a guarantee of reinstatement to the same or to a comparable position at the end of the leave, subject to any defense allowed under the law. If possible, you must provide at least 30 calendar days written advance notice for foreseeable events (such as the expected birth of a child or planned medical treatment of a family member). For events which are unforeseeable 30 days in advance, we need you to notify us, preferably as soon as you learn of the need for the leave, but in any event no later than five working days from learning of the need for the leave.

Failure to comply with these notice rules is grounds for, and may result in, denial or deferral of the requested leave until you comply with this notice policy.

We may require certification from the health care provider of your child, parent or spouse who has a serious health condition before allowing you a leave to take care of that family member.

Any family care leave taken must be for at least two weeks, except that you may request a shorter leave (of anywhere from one day to two weeks) on any two occasions during a 24-month period or for planned medical treatments, such as chemotherapy, of a family member. If you are taking a leave for the birth or adoption of a child, you must initiate the leave within one year of the birth or adoption. If you are pregnant, you have certain rights to take a pregnancy disability leave in addition to family care leave; you should check regarding your individual situation. There are certain exceptions to eligibility for a family care leave and we are legally permitted to deny a request for leave under certain conditions. Also, taking a family care leave may affect certain of your benefits and your seniority date.

If you want more information regarding your eligibility for a leave and/or the impact of the leave on your seniority and benefits, please contact
_____.

References

1.	Government Code §12945.2	A.	Proposed regulation §7297.1(c)
2.	Government Code §12945.2(d)	B.	Proposed regulation §7297.0(b)
3.	Government Code §12945.2(e)	C.	Proposed regulation §7297.1(b)
4.	Government Code §12945.2(e)	D.	Proposed regulation §7297.1(j)
5.	Government Code §12945.2(f)	E.	Proposed regulation §7297.6(c)
6.	Government Code §12945.2(g)	F.	Proposed regulation §7297.6(b)
7.	Government Code §12945.2(h)	G.	Proposed regulation §7297.5
8.	Government Code §12945.2(i)	H.	Proposed regulation §7297.1(e)
9.	Government Code §12945	I.	Proposed regulation §7297.7(c)
10.	Government Code §12945.2(l)	J.	Proposed regulation §7297.2(B)
11.	Government Code §12945.2(o)	K.	Proposed regulation §7297.1(o)
12.	Government Code §12945.2(p)	L.	Proposed regulation §7297.2(3)
13.	Government Code §12945.2(q)	M.	Proposed regulation §7297.3(b)
14.	Government Code §12945.2(j)	N.	Proposed regulation §7297.3(b)(2)
15.	Government Code §12945.2(6)	O.	Proposed regulation §7297.10

Note: Numbered footnotes refer to the law; alphabetical footnotes refer to proposed regulations that had not been finalized at the time this handbook was published.

Chapter 10
The Americans with Disabilities Act and State Regulation of Disability Discrimination

Overview

The Americans with Disabilities Act (ADA), which was signed into law in July 1990, requires practically all businesses to make their facilities accessible to disabled employees and customers, and requires businesses with 15 or more employees to accommodate disabled job candidates in hiring, firing, benefits and other terms, conditions and privileges of employment.[1]

The impact of the law upon business cannot be overstated. It has the potential to change the face of the nation with regard to treatment of persons with disabilities. It will change the way most businesses conduct their employment practices and determine the actions they must take to make their facilities accessible to all people.

As this important statute takes effect in stages over the next three years, companies must cope with requirements ranging from highly detailed specifications on the width of retail store aisles to such vague standards as "readily achievable," "undue hardship" and "reasonable accommodation." In addition, recent regulations issued by the enforcement agency for the act, the Equal Opportunity Employment Commission, provide that each determination concerning the existence of impermissible discrimination, reasonable accommodation, undue hardship, etc., will be made on a case-by-case basis. The lack of specificity in these standards could make it even more difficult for employers to comply before court cases determine the meaning of those standards.

Employers presently governed by California's Fair Employment and Housing Act (FEHA) should already be in substantial compliance with many provisions of the ADA. However, there are some differences: the public accommodation provisions of the ADA which are absent from the FEHA but covered to some degree in the Civil Code, will indirectly affect many employers; FEHA allows jury trials, while the ADA does not. Also, the ADA does not preempt the FEHA to the extent that the FEHA provides greater or equal protection of the rights of the disabled worker. In addition, employers with federal government contracts of $2,500 or more, or who receive federal financial assistance, will be governed by both the Federal Rehabilitation Act of 1973 and the ADA (which incorporates many of the standards set forth in the Rehabilitation Act).

Effective January 1, 1993, the FEHA, like the ADA, adds individuals with mental disabilities to the classes protected by that statute. The new law also expands the definitions of "public accommodations" and "full and equal access" under the Civil Code, requires licensing boards to "reasonably accommodate" an individual's disability, expands requirements regarding devices and interpreters for disabled persons in court proceedings, and requires that regulations adopted by the state architect for access and usability of public facilities by disabled persons impose no lower standards of usability and accessibility than those specified under the ADA.[2]

The ADA differs from existing civil rights laws in many ways. First, the beneficiaries of the law are an exceptionally diverse and broad-based group. The generic definition of "disability" in the ADA encompasses a wide range of physical and mental conditions. Covered disabilities include not only the well-known disabilities (such as visual or hearing impairments, or loss of limbs), and medical conditions (e.g., cancer, epilepsy, heart disease and contagious diseases), but also learning disabilities and various psychiatric conditions. Moreover, the ADA covers individuals who have recovered from a prior disability, such as a recovered cancer patient, as well as those who are not disabled but are regarded as having a disability, such as a burn victim with cosmetic disfigurement.

Second, the ADA does not merely prohibit discrimination against people with disabilities. It imposes additional affirmative obligations upon businesses to accommodate the needs of people with disabilities and to facilitate their economic independence.

Compliance with the ADA will not be easy because the scope of the new law is so unclear. Although Congress mandated an accessible America, it did not require that accessibility be purchased regardless of cost. To ease the financial burden of complying with the ADA, Congress provided a limited tax break so businesses could make physical alterations when necessary for employment and public accommodation situations. Businesses with less than $1 million in gross receipts or with fewer than 30 full-time employees will be eligible for a tax credit. These small businesses will have to pay the first $250 of any accommodation cost. Above $250, the employer would qualify for a 50 percent, non-refundable credit up to $5,000. Costs above $5,000 qualify for a tax deduction up to $15,000. All businesses not fitting into the less than $1 million/fewer than 30 full-time employees category, are limited to the $15,000 tax deduction. Expenditures that qualify for these tax breaks include, but are not limited to: removing architectural, communication, transportation or other physical barriers, buying or modifying needed equipment, and providing technical assistance for employers and employees to comply with the act.

Many employers are unaware of the sweeping nature of the ADA. Below are the basic details and key provisions that companies should be aware of as they prepare to implement the disabilities law. For further and more detailed information, the California Chamber has recently published *ADA: 10 Steps to Compliance*, which contains detailed step-by-step procedures to assure compliance with the ADA. To order call 1-800-331-8877.

Introduction

ADA consists of five titles. This chapter will focus on Titles I and III, and the requirements on employers, since the other three titles generally do not address issues relevant to employers.

Title I provides that employers, employment agencies, labor organizations or joint labor-management committees may not discriminate against any qualified individual with a disability. This includes job applicants, the hiring procedure, promotions and employee terminations. It also includes job training, an employee's wages, and terms and conditions of employment.

Title III provides that no person can be discriminated against or prevented from equal enjoyment of goods, services, facilities and accommodations of any place of public accommodation operated by the private sector because he/she is disabled. This includes hotels, restaurants, theaters, retail sales, schools, service establishments, etc. It focuses in particular on the construction of places that may have the potential for being places of employment or public access, and requires these places to be physically accessible to persons with disabilities.

Title I: Employment Provisions of ADA
Who Is Considered Disabled?

1. A person who has a physical or mental impairment that substantially limits one or more of the major life activities;

2. A person who has a record of such an impairment;

3. Being regarded as having such an impairment.[3]

Examples of physical or mental impairments include, but are not limited to, such contagious and non-contagious diseases and conditions as orthopedic, visual, speech and hearing impairments; cerebral palsy, epilepsy, muscular dystrophy, multiple sclerosis, cancer, heart disease, diabetes, mental retardation, emotional illness, specific learning disabilities, HIV disease, tuberculosis, specific learning disabilities, drug addiction and alcoholism. Homosexuality, bisexuality and related conditions and practices are not physical or mental impairments under the ADA.

Impairments that substantially limit "major life activities" include inability or difficulty in caring for oneself, performing manual tasks, walking, seeing, hearing, speaking, breathing, learning, working, or participating in community activities. Individuals with a record of impairment include those having a history of, or have been misclassified as having, a mental or physical impairment that substantially limits one or more major life activities. The law also prohibits discrimination against an individual who is being treated as if he/she were disabled.[4]

Auxiliary Aids and Services

Auxiliary aids and services include the following:

1. Qualified interpreters or other effective methods of making orally delivered materials available to individuals with hearing impairments;

2. Qualified readers, taped texts or other effective methods of making visually delivered materials available to individuals with visual impairments;

3. Sign language interpreters, assistive listening headsets, television decoders, telecommunication devices for the deaf (TDDs), and brailled materials;

4. Eliminating architectural barriers that constitute access blocks to the disabled;

5. Modifying equipment or devices making it possible for certain qualified disabled persons to operate them;

6. Other similar devices and actions.[5]

Auxiliary aids that would result in an undue burden or in a fundamental alteration in the nature of the employer's goods or services are not required by the law. However, a public accommodation must still furnish another auxiliary aid, if available, that does not result in a fundamental alteration or an undue burden.

When Does the ADA Take Effect?

Title I, "Employment Section," took effect on July 26, 1992, for all employers having 25 or more employees for each working day in each of 20 or more calendar weeks in the current or preceding year. For employers having 15 or more employees for each working day in each of 20 or more calendar weeks in the current or preceeding calendar year, the ADA becomes effective on July 26, 1994.[6]

Title III, "Public Accommodations," took effect on January 26, 1992. However, for employers having fewer than 25 employees and annual gross receipts of less than $1 million, no civil action will be brought for violation of the ADA's prohibitions regarding existing public accommodations. After July 26, 1992, the public accommodations requirement of the ADA must be completed. For employers having 15 or more employees and annual gross receipts in excess of $500,000, the ADA takes effect on July 26, 1994.

Purposes of the ADA

Congress found that there are approximately 43 million Americans who have one or more physical or mental disabilities. The purpose of the ADA is to promote and expand employment opportunities in the public and private sectors for handicapped individuals. The ADA contains two primary objectives:

1. All employers having 15 or more employees are under the jurisdiction of the ADA. The ADA prohibits all employers from discriminating against handicapped individuals and requires these employers to take actions to employ and promote qualified handicapped persons.

2. The ADA prohibits qualified handicapped individuals from being denied the benefits of, being excluded from participation in, or being subjected to, discrimination because they are handicapped. This includes programs or activities receiving federal financial assistance. The U.S. Supreme Court has interpreted this to be applicable to an employer's practices whether or not the purpose of the federal financial assistance is to provide employment. Further, the section is interpreted to apply to the entire employer even though the benefiting institution has only a specific program receiving federal funds.

    The employer cannot discriminate against a disabled person with respect to job applications, hiring procedures, promotions, job compensation, job training, discharge or other matters relating to employment.[7]

To Whom Does the ADA Apply?

The ADA will apply to all employers engaged in industry affecting commerce and having 25 or more employees for each working day in each of 20 or more calendar weeks in the current or preceding calendar year from July 26, 1992 to July 26, 1994. After July 26, 1994 all employers having 15 or more employees for each working day in each of 20 or more calendar work weeks for the current or preceding calendar year will be covered by the law.[8] However, California is one of many states that has already enacted statutes that prohibit all private and non-federal government employers from discriminating against disabled applicants or employees if they have five or more employees.

Exempt from ADA are private membership clubs (other than labor organizations) exempt from taxation by the Internal Revenue Code, Section 501(c).[9] Such organizations are not exempt from the disability discrimination provisions of the Fair Employment and Housing Act, unless they are religious, non-profit organizations.

What Does "Disability" Mean?

Disability is defined as a physical or mental impairment that substantially limits one or more of the major life activities of an individual, or an individual who has a record of an impairment or is regarded as having such an impairment.[10] Examples of a "record of such impairment" include recovered cancer victims and recovered alcoholics. Persons "regarded as having a disability" include, for example, a victim of disfiguring burns who might be shunned as impaired.

Specifically excluded from the definition of "disability" are transvestism, transsexualism, pedophilia, voyeurism, exhibitionism, gender identity disorders, compulsive gambling, kleptomania or pyromania, and psychoactive substance use disorders resulting from current illegal use of drugs.[11]

What Is a "Qualified" Individual with a Disability?

A qualified individual having a disability means an individual with a disability who, with or without reasonable accommodation, can perform the essential functions of the employment position that the disabled person desires.[12] An employer is not required to hire or retain an individual who is not qualified to perform a job.

There are two basic steps in determining whether an individual is "qualified" under the ADA. The first is to determine if the individual meets the necessary prerequisities for the job, such as education, work experience, training, skills, licenses and other job-related requirements. If he/she meets all the job requirements other than those he/she cannot meet due to the disability, the second step is for the employer to determine if the individual can perform the essential functions of the job, with or without reasonable accomodation. Before interviewing applicants, consideration should be given to what functions of a job are essential and to a prepared written job description. The written description is considered evidence of the essential functions of the job, if the employer has prepared the job description before advertising the position or interviewing job applicants.

Employment Protections

The equal employment protections of the law cover all aspects of the work relationship, including hiring, discharge, training, benefits, promotion, transfer, and other terms, conditions and privileges of employment.

Under the law, a disabled candidate is considered qualified to be hired or promoted if he or she can carry out the "essential functions" of the job, with or without "reasonable accommodation." An employer may have to offer training, or such aids as readers or interpreters, if these steps would enhance employment opportunities and not cause "undue hardship" to the company.

What Does "Reasonable Accommodation" Mean?

A "reasonable accommodation" is any modification or adjustment in a job, an employment practice, or the work environment that allows an individual with a disability to enjoy an equal employment opportunity. The reasonable accommodation obligation is an ongoing duty, and may arise anytime a person's disability or job changes. The ADA does not require an employer to make any modification, adjustment or change in job or policy that an employer can demonstrate would fundamentally alter the essential functions of the job in question.

The term reasonable accommodation may include:

1. Providing personal assistants or attendants to help a qualified individual with a disability perform an essential job function;

2. Making existing job facilities used by employees readily accessible to and usable by disabled individuals;

3. Job restructuring, part-time or modified work schedules, reassignment to a vacant position, acquiring or modifying equipment or devices, modifying examinations, training materials or policies, providing qualified readers or interpreters, and other similar accommodations.[13]

The term "qualification standards" may include a requirement that an individual does not pose a direct threat to the health or safety of other workers in the workplace.

These requirements do not prohibit a religious corporation, association, educational institution or society from giving preference in employment to its own members. Religious organizations may even require that all applicants and employees conform to the religious tenets of the organization.

What Are "Essential Functions" of the Job?

The key factor in determining whether the employer needs to equally consider qualified disabled persons for job openings and promotions is whether the disabled person can perform the "essential functions" of the job. A job function may be considered essential if it constitutes the fundamental job duties of the position or if the reason the job exists is to perform that function. It is imperative for an employer to determine these essential functions, both as the criteria for deciding the ability of the disabled person to perform the job and as a defense against any subsequent claim of discrimination.[14] To determine if a function is essential, consideration should be given to, at minimum, the following factors:

1. Does the job exist to perform this function?

2. Who else is available to perform this function?

3. What level of expertise or skill is required to perform this function?

4. What is the experience of previous or current employees in this job?

5. What is the amount of time spent performing this function?

6. What are the consequences of failing to perform this function?

7. What is stated in the job description and help wanted ads?

Because determining "essential functions" is one of the least clear provisions of disabilities law, an employer should, as a matter of policy, take the following steps in determining these "essential functions."

Document all important job functions.
In the best of all worlds, an employer should maintain current detailed job descriptions that set forth each important job function of each position. Pre-established essential functions avoid the appearance that an employer is merely rationalizing the rejection of an individual with a disability.

Be accurate and realistic.
Job descriptions or definitions should describe the actual duties of the position rather than the "ideal" set of duties. Individuals who wish to inflate their importance to the company may exaggerate the extent of their duties or those of their subordinates, and may not be a reliable source for a description of essential job functions. Job descriptions that easily can be called into question by those who know the workplace are of little or no value.

Stay current.
Many jobs change rapidly. Job descriptions should be reviewed and updated periodically to ensure their accuracy.

Be flexible.
In describing the essential functions of a job, employers should be flexible and should not take a "that is the way it always has been done" attitude. Tasks that easily can be transferred to another person and are not necessarily the heart of the job are unlikely to constitute "essential" elements. Employers who are able to pare their jobs down to core elements are more likely to prevail in litigation that those who insist that every traditional element of every job is "essential."

Review job descriptions with employees
It is always a good idea for employees to understand exactly what is expected of them. The essential functions of a job should be reviewed with employees to solicit their input and increase accuracy. Document employee agreement with the description of essential job functions.

The ADA does not limit an employer's ability to establish or change the content, nature or functions of the job. The employer has the right to establish what a job is and what functions are required to perform it. The ADA simply requires that the qualifications of an individual with a disability are evaluated in relation to its essential functions.

What Does "Undue Hardship" Mean?

The concept of "undue hardship" includes any action that is unduly costly, extensive, or substantial to a particular employer, or which would fundamentally alter the nature of the operation of the business. The Equal Employment Opportunity Commission will determine only on a case-by-case basis whether a particular accomodation will impose an undue hardship. In general, a larger employer would be expected to undertake greater efforts and expense to make an accommodation than a smaller employer.

Factors to be considered in determining the existence of an undue hardship include:

1. The overall size of the establishment or facility and the employer; that is, number of employees, size of budget and other such matters;

2. The type of the establishment's or facility's operation, including the composition and structure of the workplace and the work force;

3. The nature and cost of the accommodation involved;

4. The availability of state, federal or local tax incentives; and

5. The amount of assistance available from other agencies or organizations, including the California Department of Rehabilitation, the U.S. Department of Health and Human Services and other private and public agencies concerned with the physically handicapped.[15]

What is a "Direct Threat"?

An employer is not required to hire a candidate posing a "direct threat" to the health and safety of co-workers or the employer.

"Direct threat" means a significant risk to the health or safety of the individual or of others that cannot be eliminated by reasonable accommodation. However, an employer must determine whether a reasonable accommodation would mitigate or eliminate the possiblity of harm.

The determination that an individual with a disability will pose a "direct threat" to the safety of others must be made on a case-by-case basis, and an employer must identify specific behavior on the applicant's part that will constitute the threat. The risk must be current, not speculative and remote, and based on reasonable medical judgment or other objective evidence, not on subjective perceptions, irrational fears or stereotypes. The employer should be careful to assure that assessments of direct threat are based on current medical knowledge or other reliable evidence, rather than relying on generalized or frequently mistaken assumptions about the risks associated with certain disabilities.

Medical Examinations

An employer may require a medical examination only after making an offer of employment, but may condition a job offer on the successful results of a medical examination if all entering employees also are required to undergo a medical examination. A medical examination may not be required for the purpose of determining whether the individual has a disability or the severity of a disability unless it is clearly job-related. An employer may not inquire at the pre-offer stage about an applicant's workers' compensation history. Medical exams for the purpose of determining the individual's state of health can be used to determine if the job applicant or employee can perform job-related functions consistent with business necessity.[16] Neither increases in workers' compensation premiums nor medical benefit costs constitute a legitimate basis for denying a job opportunity to a qualified disabled person.

Supervisors, managers and safety personnel should be informed of job restrictions related to a disability, especially when job accommodations are required. Such persons should also be informed of the confidentiality of medical records produced by such examinations.

Drugs and Alcohol

The term "qualified individual with a disability" shall not include any applicant or employee who is using illegal drugs when the employer enforces a drug-free workplace policy. However, the ADA protects an individual who has successfully completed a supervised drug rehabilitation program and is no longer using illegal drugs; or who is participating in a supervised rehabilitation program and not using illegal drugs; or who is erroneously regarded as using illegal drugs. It is not in violation of the ADA for an employer to adopt and administer reasonable policies to prevent drug use, possession or sale in the workplace, nor are drug tests to determine illegal use of drugs considered to be medical examinations under the ADA.[17]

Infectious and Communicable Diseases

An employer can refuse to assign a food handling duties to employees with a communicable or infectious disease that can be transmitted to others through the handling of food, if the risk cannot be eliminated by reasonable accommodation.[18] Determinations of what constitutes "infectious and communicable diseases" are published by the State Department of Health on a twice yearly basis.

ADA and Workers' Compensation

Individuals whose work-related injury results in an impairment that substantially limits a major life activity, creates a record of impairment, or causes the individual to be regarded as having such an impairment, are covered by the ADA, so long as the individual is qualified for the position and is able to perform the job with or without reasonable accomodation. Workers' compensation coverage does not automatically establish that the person is protected by the ADA.

An employer may not refuse to allow an individual with a disability to return to work even if he/she is not fully recovered from the work-related injury, unless the employer can show either that the individual cannot perform the essential functions of the job with or without reasonable accommodation, or that the individual would pose a direct threat to himself/herself or others that could not be reasonably accommodated.

The ADA does not require an employer to create "light duty" positions unless the "heavy duty" tasks are marginal job functions which could be reallocated to co-workers as part of the "reasonable accomodation" process. However, a past practice of creating "light duty" positions may result in an obligation to offer such an accomodation to the injured worker with a disability.

Discriminatory Acts

Discrimination on the basis of disability is established by showing that an employment practice or a public accommodation denies, in whole or in part, an employment benefit or public access to an individual because he/she is disabled. The ADA does not require a plaintiff to prove that the discrimination in employment was based solely on the disability.[19]

An employer covered by the ADA may not discriminate against a qualified individual with a disability because of the disability in job application procedures, hiring, advancement, discharge, compensation, job training and other terms, conditions and privileges of employment.[20]

Examples of discriminatory acts include:

1. Limiting, segregating or classifying a job applicant or employee in a way that adversely affects his/her opportunities because of a disability.

2. Participating in a contractual or other arrangement that has the effect of subjecting a qualified applicant or employee with a disability to discrimination prohibited by law. This includes employers, job referral agencies, labor unions, and apprenticeship programs.

3. Utilizing standards, criteria or administrative methods that:

— have the effect of discriminating on the basis of disability.

— perpetuate the discrimination of others who are subject to common administrative control.

4. Excluding or otherwise denying equal jobs or benefits to a qualified individual because of a known disability of an individual with whom the qualified individual is known to associate.

5. Not making reasonable accommodations to the known physical or mental limitations of a qualified applicant or employee having a disability unless the employer can demonstrate that the accommodation would impose an undue hardship on the employer.

6. Using qualification standards, employment tests or other selection criteria that screen out a disabled applicant or employee, unless the standard, test or other selection criteria can be shown to be job-related and is consistent with business necessity.

7. Failure to select and administer tests concerning employment in an effective manner to ensure that the tests accurately reflect the skills, aptitude or factor being tested when administered to an applicant or employee having a disability that impairs sensors, manual or speaking skills.[21]

Employer Defenses

If an employee alleges discrimination because of the application of a qualifying standard, test or selection criteria that leads to denial of a job, the employer must be able to demonstrate that the standard, test or selection criteria is job-related and consistent with business necessity and that job performance cannot be accomplished by reasonable accommodation.

It is a permissible defense for an employer to demonstrate that, after reasonable accommodation has been made, the applicant or employee cannot perform the essential job functions of the position in question: 1) because of his/her disability; 2) in a manner which would not endanger his/her health or safety because the job imposes an imminent and substantial degree of risk to either the applicant or employee or to others to a greater extent than if a non-handicapped individual performed the job. However, it is no defense to assert that the handicapped individual has a condition or disease with a future risk, so long as the condition/disease neither interferes with his/her job performance now nor will do so over a reasonable length of time.

Remedies and Enforcement

The ADA adopts all of the powers, remedies and procedures set forth in Title VII of the Civil Rights Act and, like most other federal discrimination statutes, is administered by the Equal Employment Opportunity Commission. Available remedies designed to prevent future employer discrimination and to make "whole" the individual or class subject to the discrimination, include reinstatement, back-pay, and reasonable attorney's fees and costs.

The 1991 Civil Rights Act significantly increased remedies available under the ADA, including compensatory and punitive damages for willful or intentional violations, and a right to jury trials that was previously not available. The ADA also encourages informal resolution of claims through mediation and arbitration.

Recommendations to Employers

If the employer believes that a disabled person cannot perform essential job functions even after reasonable accommodations, the employer should:

1. Base such a decision only on competent medical testimony.

2. Be sure that medical testimony is based on a clear understanding of the job to be performed. (Provide a valid job description.)

3. Be sure that the future risk to one's health is substantial and imminent.

4. Be sure to document all efforts at reasonable accommodations and the reasons why no options are considered feasible.

Recruiting Activities

Employers engaged in recruiting activities must consider individuals with a disability and place them on an equal basis with non-disabled applicants. For example:

1. The employer cannot advertise a job in any way that may discourage a disabled applicant.

2. The employer must accept all applications for evaluation.

3. The employer cannot ask any applicant a question concerning a physical condition personally or on the application that is not connected with the job requirements.

4. The employer may condition an offer of employment on the results of a medical examination in order to determine the applicant's fitness for the job in question. However, all employees for the position must be subjected to the same examination. If the applicant is declared disqualified, the applicant may submit independent medical opinions to be considered prior to a final determination.

5. The medical records of disabled employees should be kept in a place separate from the main file for employees. It is a good idea, however, to advise managers and/or supervisory persons of the work or duty restrictions placed on a disabled employee so that the accommodations required by his/her disability can be made in the workplace, or to provide first aid and personnel safety where necessary.

Applications and Job Tests

1. The employer must accept and consider applications from disabled persons equally with non-disabled persons.

2. Both the Equal Employment Opportunity Commission and Department of Fair Employment and Housing will closely scrutinize the job-relatedness of any tests for job applicants or job promotion given to an individual with a disability that are not given to a non-disabled person or that are not job-related.

3. The employer may give job-related tests that accurately measure the applicant's job skills or aptitude. Reasonable accommodation must be given a disabled applicant when he/she takes the test.

4. Job testing sites must be accessible to all applicants and must accommodate all disabled applicants. For example, blind applicants might be given tests in Braille or have a person read for them or simply be given an oral examination. Quadriplegic individuals should have someone write the answers or be given an oral examination. Applicants that have a hearing impairment might be provided with the services of an interpreter.

Qualification Standards

The ADA does not prohibit an employer from establishing job-related qualification standards, including education, skills, work experience, and physical and mental standards necessary for job performance, health and safety. However, employers may not use those standards to screen out individuals on the basis of a disability unless those standards are consistent with business necessity. Thus, even a qualification standard related to an essential job function may not be used to exclude an individual with a disability if he/she could satisfy the standard with reasonable accommodation.

Both qualification standards and job-related physical requirements for a position are allowed, so long as the employer can establish that the criteria of those standards and requirements are necessary and substantially related to an employee's ability to perform the essential functions of the job.

Employee Selection

An employer cannot deny employment or employment benefits because of the prospective need to make reasonable accommodation to a disabled applicant.

Tests, both written and physical, must be shown to be job-related, or show that better job screening procedures are not available. Tests must accurately reflect the applicant's job skills, aptitude and ability to perform the job.

Posting a Notice of ADA Required

All employers, employment agencies, labor organizations and others covered by the ADA must post a notice in an accessible format to applicants, employees or members describing the applicable provisions of the ADA.[22] The recently modified Equal Employment Opportunity Commission poster containing ADA requirements, like all required employer posters, is available from the California Chamber. To order call 1-800-331-8877.

Title III: Public Accommodations and Services by Private Sector

Title III of the ADA requires public accommodations to be accessible to people with disabilities in these areas:

1. Non-discrimination by businesses serving the public in the goods, services, facilities, privileges, advantages and accommodations they provide.[23]

2. The ADA requires both affirmative efforts by businesses to remove physical barriers to the full and equal enjoyment of goods and services by individuals with disabilities, and prohibits a vast array of conduct that inhibits such equal enjoyment. These rules affect not only the physical layout of facilities open to the public, but also the policies, procedures and practices businesses utilize in providing goods and services to the public.

3. Mandatory accessibility and usability in all newly constructed public accommodations and commercial facilities and those facilities that undergo structural alterations.

4. Where facilities renovate primary function areas (e.g., lobby or main employee spaces of a bank, the dining room or lobby of a restaurant), the path of travel to that area, and to restrooms, telephones and drinking fountains served by that area, must be made accessible to people with disabilities, unless the cost of accessibility changes is disproportionate to the alteration. All newly constructed accommodations in commercial facilities must comply with rigorous standards of accessibility and usability.[24]

Whom Does This Cover?

1. Restaurants, bars, theaters, concert halls, auditoriums, stadiums or other places for entertainment, exhibition or place of public gathering.

2. Grocery stores, hardware, clothing and other stores, shopping centers or other sales or rental establishments.

3. Laundromats, banks, beauty shops, funeral parlors, gas stations, lawyers, accountants, pharmacies, business offices, hospitals and other service establishments.

4. Museums, libraries, galleries or other places of public display.

5. Parks, zoos and recreation areas.

6. Nurseries, schools and other places of education.

7. Terminals, depots or other stations used for public transportation.

8. Gymnasiums, health spas, bowling alleys, golf courses or other places for exercise or recreation.[25]

9. In addition, commercial facilities such as warehouses, factories, office buildings and other facilities, which are open to the general public, must comply with the access requirements of Title III when they alter their buildings or engage in new construction.

They need not comply with other requirements of Title III that govern full and equal access to goods and services and readily achievable removal of barriers from existing buildings.

Who Is Not Covered Under Title III?

1. Private clubs or establishments exempt under Title II of the Civil Rights Act of 1964.

2. Religious organizations or entities controlled by religious organizations.

3. Private schools controlled by religious organizations.

4. Small, owner-occupied inns with five or fewer rental rooms.[26]

Acts of Discrimination

The ADA broadly prohibits discrimination against individuals on the basis of "disability in the full and equal enjoyment of the goods, services, facilities, privileges, advantages, and accommodations of any place of public accommodation by any person who owns, leases (or leases to) or operates a place of public accommodation." It also prohibits exclusion and segregation of individuals with disabilities, and the denial of equal opportunities enjoyed by others based on, among other things, presumptions, patronizing attitudes, fears and stereotypes about individuals with disabilities.[27]

Basically, the standards prohibit all actions that result in discrimination, whether intentional or inadvertent, against disabled individuals by denying them access to goods and services.

Acts of discrimination include:

1. Physical facilities that screen out any individual with a disability, and which prevent him/her from equally enjoying services and facilities of the accommodations being offered.

2. Failure to make reasonable modifications in policies, procedures or practices to afford goods, services, facilities and advantages to individuals with disabilities, unless it can be demonstrated that such accommodations would fundamentally alter the nature of services, facilities, goods, advantages, etc.

3. Attempts to identify unnecessarily the existence of a disability.

4. Failure to provide appropriate accommodation to ensure that no disabled individual is excluded or treated differently than other individuals, unless the entity can demonstrate that taking such steps would fundamentally alter the nature of the facility and services offered or would result in an undue burden.

5. Failure to remove architectural and/or communication barriers that are structural in nature in existing facilities and transportation barriers, such as vehicles and rail passenger cars, where such removal is readily achievable.

6. Failure to design and construct facilities that are readily usable by disabled persons, except where it can be demonstrated that it is structurally impracticable to meet requirements.

7. Failure to alter a facility for use by disabled persons.[28]

Buildings

New buildings containing places of business to be occupied on or after January 26, 1993, must be readily accessible to disabled persons.

Alterations to existing buildings or places of business depend upon the size, cost and nature of the alteration. Essentially, the building must be readily accessible by individuals who are disabled. The cost and scope of altering the facility should be proportional to the overall cost of alterations.

Typical building alterations would be wider aisles, ramps for access, toilet facilities for use by the disabled, or possibly hydraulic lifts. Transportation vehicles should have seats for the disabled, access to vehicles when loading, accessible luggage racks, etc. (See the Self-Audit Facility Accessibility Checklist below for further details.)

Readily accessible means that employees and customers are able to readily enter and exit the place of business. This includes accessible parking places, accessible entrances, bathrooms, water fountains, etc. that provide access to goods, services, facilities, programs, checkout lanes, etc.

Facilities that have fewer than three stories or less than 3,000 square feet per story are not required to have an elevator. This exemption does not apply to shopping centers, professional offices or health care providers.

Both the landlord who owns the building that houses public accommodation, and the tenant who owns or operates that public accommodation, are responsible for ADA compliance. This responsibility can be allocated between the landlord and tenant by lease or other contract.

Self-Audit Facility Accessibility Checklist

Parking lot

❑ Is there an off-street parking area adjacent to the building?

❑ Is the parking lot surface hard and smooth?

❑ Are there parking spaces wide enough to allow a car door to be opened to full extension (approximately 12' wide)?

❑ Are there parking spaces identified specifically for the handicapped?

❑ If there are curbs, wheel stops or parking barriers within the parking area, has a curb cut, ramp or passageway been provided to eliminate these barriers?

Building access

❑ Are walkways at least 5' wide with smooth, hard surfaces (no sand or gravel), free of deep cracks, ruts or sudden changes in level?

❑ Is the most accessible entrance to the building one which avoids unsafe traffic crossings from the parking area to the building entrance?

❑ Is the approach to the entrance door on ground level?

❑ If there are steps in the travel path or approach to the building entrance, has a ramp been provided to eliminate this barrier?

❑ If there are steps, is there a sturdy handrail in the center or either side of the stairs extending 12" beyond the top and bottom step?

❑ Are the ramps a minimum of 3' wide and built so that the grade does not exceed a 1:12 ratio? That is, for every foot in length it gains no more than 1" in height.

❑ If there is a turnstile or revolving door, is there a standard door adjacent to the revolving one for use by handicapped persons?

Building entrance

❑ Is the doorway at least 32" clear width?

❑ Are thresholds and door saddles flush with floor or no higher than 1/2" off the floor?

❑ Is the door automatic?

❑ Can doors be opened using no more than 8 pounds pressure (operating pressure)?

❑ Have lever-type door handles, which are easy to grasp and depress, been used in place of knob-type hardware?

❑ If there are steps or interior level changes, have ramps been provided to eliminate these barriers?

❑ If there are steps, is there a sturdy handrail in the center or either side of the stairs extending 12" beyond the top and bottom step?

Elevator or lift

❑ If the building is multi-story, is there an elevator or lift which provides access to all essential areas?

❑ If there are any steps or interior level changes between essential areas which are not served by an elevator, have ramps been provided to eliminate these barriers?

❑ Is the control panel located no more than 48" to the highest call button?

❑ Does the elevator have at least one handrail for balance and support?

❑ Have floor designation markers with raised characters been used to aid the visually impaired? (These should be mounted to the left of the call button.)

❑ Have audible signals for people with visual impairment been used to indicate direction (one for up, two for down) and to identify floors as they are being passed?

Restrooms

❑ Would a person need to go up or down steps to reach the restroom or toilet?

❑ If there are steps, does each flight of stairs have a sturdy handrail in the center or on either side?

Is the restroom entrance doorway at least 32" wide (including clearance by privacy screen)?

Are thresholds and door saddles flush or no higher than 1/2" to the floor?

❑   Is there enough space within the restroom to allow a wheelchair to turn around (approximately a 5' diameter)?

❑   Is the width of the toilet stall door opening at least 32"?

❑   Are toilet stalls and urinals equipped with grab bars?

❑   Does the stall door open outwards?

❑   Has the door been replaced with a privacy curtain?

❑   Are sinks, dispensers and mirrors low enough for use by a person in a wheelchair (Bottom of mirrors no higher than 40"; dispensers and controls 48" to highest operable part)?

❑   Is the accessible restroom toilet stall door clearly identified?

Telephones

❑   Is the public phone mounted low enough to be used by persons in wheelchairs (the coin slot 48" from the floor)?

❑   If located inside a phone booth, is the opening into the booth at least 30" wide?

❑   Would a person have to go up or down steps to use the telephone?

❑   Have volume control handsets been used to aid persons with hearing impairments?

❑   Have tactile instructions been used to aid persons with visual impairments?

Wall-mounted controls

❑   Are all vital wall controls (light switches, door knobs, elevator controls, etc.) located within the reach of handicapped individuals (approximately 48" or less from the floor)?

❑   Are all emergency equipment (fire alarms, instruction panels, fire extinguishers, etc.) located within the reach of handicapped individuals (approximately 48" or less from the floor)?

❑   Have nameplates with raised characters been used to identify controls and communicate vital instructions to persons with visual impairments?

❑   Have Braille markers been used to identify controls and communicate instructions to persons with visual impairments?

Water fountains

❑   Are the water fountains low enough to be used by persons in wheelchairs (bubblers a maximum of 36" from floor)?

❑ Are there any barriers, such as steps, around or leading to the water fountain?

Visually impaired

❑ Have Braille markers or relief graphics been used to communicate important information to people with visual handicaps?

❑ Has textured paint or change in surface texture been used to alert people with visual limitations to curb cuts, sudden level changes or other vital information important

Information and Assistance

The California Chamber has recently published a step-by-step guide to compliance with both the discrimination and public accommodation provisions of the ADA, entitled ***ADA: 10 Steps to Compliance.*** Also available is IBM-compatible graphical interface software that helps you identify "essential functions" of your job positions and write ADA-ready job descriptions quickly. The California Chamber has also developed two training videos: ***ADA: What Every Manager Must Know*** and ***ADA: Interviewing Dos and Don'ts*** to help you familiarize your managers and supervisors with the requirements of the ADA. To order any or all of these important materials, please call 1-800-331-8877.

The President's Committee on Employment of People with Disabilities, a federal office, offers technical help and management consulting on the subject and runs a speakers' bureau. Write to the committee at Suite 636, 1111 20th St., N.W., Washington D.C. 20036-3470; or call (202) 653-5044.

Job Accommodation Network (JAN), a branch of the President's Committee on Employment of People with Disabilities, offers free consulting for employers who face specific challenges in accommodating disabled individuals in the workplace. Technical experts counsel small firms. Call JAN's hotline at 1-800-JAN-7234.

The Architectural and Transportation Barriers Compliance Board offers copies of the access standards it developed for the law. Call 1-800-USA-ABLE.

The Office on the Americans with Disabilities Act, which is part of the U.S. Department of Justice, operates an information line about the disabilities law. Call (202) 514-0301.

Common Questions and Answers About the ADA

Q. *Who is a person with a disability?*
A. Deciding who is protected by the ADA is a difficult task. Generally, most individuals who are materially hampered in everyday life by their physical or mental conditions will be considered "disabled" within the meaning of the law. In the absence of a specific exclusion from coverage, or a condition that more closely resembles a mere physical characteristic rather than an impairment, the safe assumption is that an individual is disabled within the meaning of the ADA.

Q. *What businesses are covered under the ADA?*
A. The ADA's employment obligations ultimately will apply to employers who have 15 or more workers. The act's public accommodation provisions extend to virtually all privately owned businesses that provide goods and services to customers, clients or visitors. In California, employment obligations apply to employers with five or more employees under the state act.

Q. *Do I have to hire someone simply because they have a disability?*

A. No. The general rule of the ADA precludes an employer from discriminating against a "qualified individual with a disability" who can perform the "essential functions of the job." If an applicant cannot perform these functions, or another applicant is more qualified for the job, the employer reserves the right to hire the most qualified applicant.

Q. *What are the essential functions of a job?*

A. The ADA does not provide a clear definition of "essential," and little practical guidance exists for employers confronted with the difficult task of determining whether a function is or is not essential. The legislative history of the ADA says that the term means job tasks that are "fundamental and not marginal." Of course, a vast range of possibilities stands between the two extremes of "fundamental" and "marginal." The ADA does provide that "consideration" should be given to an employer's judgment in determining the essential functions of a job.

Q. *What is a reasonable accommodation?*

A. A "reasonable accommodation" is defined by the act as follows: (1) making existing facilities used by employees readily accessible to and usable by individuals with disabilities; and (2) job restructuring including hours, vacant positions, equipment (necessary as aids), policies and procedures that are reasonable and achievable. The list is not exhaustive, but designed to provide general guidance as to the nature of the obligation. An employer does not have to provide an accommodation if it would result in "undue hardship."

Q. *What is undue hardship?*

A. "Undue hardship" is difficult to define, and like many of these variables, subject to different standards in different situations. In general, though, "undue hardship" would be present when an action requires significant difficulty or expense to the employer. Congressional reports make it clear that employers need not undertake actions that are unduly costly, extensive, substantial and/or disruptive. Obviously, the size and financial resources of the employer are important in determining what would impose an "undue hardship."

Q. *Who pays for an accommodation?*

A. The responsibility of providing an accommodation rests with the employer, as long as it does not create an "undue hardship." If there is an undue harship, an employer must first provide the disabled applicant with an opportunity to pay for the accommodation himself/herself before disqualifying the applicant from the job.

Q. *Are persons infected with AIDS covered by the ADA?*

A. Under the ADA, a person suffering from a contagious disease is considered disabled. An employer may limit the job activities of such an individual only if he/she can demonstrate that the contagious disease constitutes "a significant risk to the health or safety of others that cannot be eliminated by reasonable accommodation."

Q. *Are persons who illegally use drugs and/or alcohol considered disabled under the ADA and how does the law relate to the requirements of the Drug-Free Workplace Act of 1988?*

A. First, the ADA establishes that an employee's current illegal use of drugs may disqualify him/her from holding a position. Also, employers may require that employees not use or be under the influence of alcohol or not use illegal drugs in the

111

workplace. Additionally, employers may hold an employee who is a drug user or alcoholic to the same qualification standards for employment or job performance and conduct required of other employees, even if the employee's unsatisfactory performance or conduct is related to his or her substance abuse. Finally, employers may require that employees comply with the provisions of the Drug-Free Workplace Act of 1988, which prohibits the unlawful manufacture, distribution, dispensation, possession or use of a controlled substance in the workplace for employers that receive federal funds.

Q. *If I hire someone with a disability and they do not work out, can I dismiss him/her without possible charges being filed?*

A. No one can ever be sure whether charges will be filed. However, there is no requirement in the ADA that an employer keep an incompetent or unproductive employee. It is important, though, to document the reasons for dismissal.

Q. *Is an employer obligated to provide health insurance to an employee with a disability?*

A. A qualified applicant cannot be denied insurance by the employer if the employer provides insurance to all employees. Pre-existing condition clauses are valid, but only if applicable to everyone. Employers can limit the scope of coverage and possibly the number of procedures or treatments (such as a limit on the number of X-rays in a year for each employee), but any such limitation must apply to every employee equally.

Q. *What about the attitudes and effects upon my other employees?*

A. One of the specific reasons for the adoption of the ADA is to eliminate strereotypes and incorrect assumptions about individuals with disabilities. The attitudes of co-workers are an integral part of any workplace, and the introduction of employees with disabilities may pose immediate reactions. But employees with disabilities have the same rights to employment opportunities as employees without disabilites. The employer has the responsibility of making sure that the workplace is free of discrimination against employees with disabilities.

Q. *Can an employer rely on a collective bargaining agreement in denying a reasonable accommodation?*

A. In certain situations, yes. If a collective bargaining agreement reserves certain jobs for employees with a given amount of seniority, it may be considered as a factor in determining whether it is a reasonable accommodation to assign an employee with a disability — but without seniority — to the job. If the collective bargaining agreement has listed job tasks and requirements, these can be used in determining whether tasks are essential functions.

Q. *Is a tax break available for those who provide accommodations to the disabled?*

A. In the 1990 Budget Reconciliation Act, Congress did provide limited tax relief to those who accommodate the disabled. For businesses with less than $1 million in gross receipts or fewer than 30 full-time employees, a tax credit is available. For all other businesses, a tax deduction is available.

Summary: Public Accommodation Provisions
of the Americans with Disabilities Act

Areas for Consideration	Requirements	Defenses/Exceptions
Eligibility Criteria	Eligibility criteria that screen out or tend to screen out disabled individuals from full and equal enjoyment are prohibited.	Eligibility criteria necessary for the provision of the goods and services provided. Direct threat to the health and safety of others that cannot otherwise be eliminated.
Policies, Practices and Procedures	Failure to make reasonable modifications in policies, practices or procedures that are necessary to afford goods and services to disabled individuals.	Modification would fundamentally alter the nature of the goods and services provided. Direct threat defense.
Auxiliary Aids and Services	Failure to take steps necessary to ensure that no individual with a disability is excluded, denied services, segregated, or otherwise treated differently due to the absence of an auxiliary aid or service.	Providing auxiliary aid would: (1) fundamentally alter the nature of the goods and services provided or (2) would result in undue burden. Direct threat defense.
Architectural and Communications Barriers in Existing Facilities	Remove where readily achievable.	Not readily achievable. Direct threat defense.
Alternative Methods	Supply where necessary and readily achievable.	Not readily achievable. Direct threat defense.
Alterations in Existing Facilities	Alterations not affecting areas containing a primary function: altered portions must be readily accessible and usable by individuals with disabilities, to the maximum extent feasible. Alterations affecting areas containing a primary function: path of travel to the altered area and the restrooms, telephones and drinking fountains serving the remodeled area also must be readily accessible and usable, to the maximum extent feasible.	Exception for installation of elevators in facilities that have less than three stories or that have less than 3,000 square feet per story. Disproportionate expense in some cases.
New Construction	Readily accessible and usable.	Structurally impracticable.

113

References

1. 29 U.S.C. 102(a)
2. Chapter 913, Acts of the 1992 General Assembly
3. 29 U.S.C. 101(2)
4. *School Board of Nassau County v. Arline* 480 U.S. 273 (1987).
5. 29 U.S.C. 101(1)(a)
6. 29 U.S.C. 101(5)(a)
7. 29 U.S.C. 102
8. 29 U.S.C. 101(5)(a)
9. 29 U.S.C. 101(5)(B)(ii)
10. 29 U.S.C. 101(2)
11. 29 U.S.C. 101(8)
12. 29 U.S.C. 104(a)
13. 29 U.S.C. 101(9)
14. 29 U.S.C. 101(8)
15. 29 U.S.C. 101(10)
16. 29 U.S.C. 102(c)
17. 29 U.S.C. 104
18. 29 U.S.C. 103(d)
19. 29 U.S.C. 102(b)
20. 29 U.S.C. 102(a)
21. 29 U.S.C. 102(b)
22. 29 U.S.C. 105
23. 42 U.S.C. 302(a); 42 U.S.C. 302 (b)(1)(A)
24. 42 U.S.C. 303
25. 42 U.S.C. 301(7)
26. 42 U.S.C. 307
27. 42 U.S.C. 302(b)(2)
28. 42 U.S.C. 302(b)(2)

Chapter 11
AIDS in the Workplace: An Employer's Response

Background

Acquired Immune Deficiency Syndrome (AIDS) is an epidemic of mammoth proportions. AIDS also raises many practical and legal issues for employers. Major AIDS employment issues may be divided into three general categories:

1. Employment discrimination against employees or applicants with AIDS, with AIDS-Related Complex (ARC) or who are asymptomatic carriers of Human Immune Deficiency Virus (HIV);
2. Employees who are exposed to HIV virus in the workplace, and
3. Employees who refuse to work with or around individuals who carry HIV.

According to the U.S. Department of Public Health, HIV is not transmitted through casual workplace contact. Federal public health authorities have noted repeatedly that workers infected with HIV generally need not be restricted from using telephones, toilets, office equipment and eating facilities.

These same authorities have identified sexual contact, prenatal transmission, sharing of contaminated needles and direct contact with blood or bodily fluids as the primary modes of transmission of the virus.

The primary legal recourse to individuals suffering from AIDS who are subjected to adverse employment decisions is protection against disability discrimination.[1] In addition, such individuals may sue based on other forms of employment discrimination, invasion of privacy, defamation, as well as AIDS-specific statutes that provide employee rights to sue.[2]

Effective January 1, 1993, California law considers AIDS a protected disability within the meaning of the California Fair Employment and Housing Act (FEHA), as is an HIV-positive diagnosis or being perceived as having AIDS. California case law had previously found AIDS to be a protected disability under federal law.[3] Association with persons having AIDS also is protected. AIDS also is a qualifying disability within the scope of both the Americans with Disabilities Act[4] and the Vocational Rehabilitation Act of 1973.[5] The new state law also allows local jurisdictions with an anti-AIDS/HIV discrimination unit as of March 1, 1991, to bring suit against any employer named in a complaint filed with the Department of Fair Employment and Housing over alleged discrimination due to AIDS or HIV-positive diagnosis.[6]

In addition to prohibiting disability discrimination on the basis of mental or physical disability, the FEHA also prohibits discrimination based on an employee's "medical condition," which includes any health impairment associated with a diagnosis of cancer.[7] Since persons diagnosed with AIDS often experience certain cancers, discrimination charges might also be brought on the basis of medical condition by those diagnosed with AIDS.

Employment Discrimination

The Americans with Disabilities Act (ADA) and the Vocational Rehabilitation Act of 1973 are the main federal statutes that prohibit handicap discrimination in employment. Section 503 of the Rehabilitation Act requires federal contractors and subcontractors to take affirmative action "to employ and advance in employment qualified individuals with handicaps" to carry out federal contracts. Section 504 of the Rehabilitation Act applies to employers that are not recipients of federal financial assistance or federal contractors. See Chapter 10 for a discussion on the employment requirements of the Americans with Disabilities Act.

Both the ADA and the Rehabilitation Act define a disabled individual as "any person who:

1. "Has a physical or mental impairment that substantially limits one or more of such person's major life activities,
2. "Has a record of such impairment, or
3. "Is regarded as having such an impairment."[8]

These acts generally prohibit discrimination against individuals who are otherwise qualified to perform the essential functions of a job.[9] The employer also is required to make reasonable accommodation to such individuals if such accommodation would allow the individual to perform the job and does not cause undue hardship upon the employer.

The courts have indicated a tendency to interpret the acts' coverages broadly when dealing with potentially contagious diseases. For example, the U.S. Supreme Court held that tuberculosis was a protected handicap under the Rehabilitation Act and that the communicable nature of a disease does not, in and of itself, remove it from the Rehabilitation Act's definition of a handicap.[10] In another case, AIDS was determined to be a protected handicap under the Rehabilitation Act and there was no credible medical evidence of a "significant risk" of spreading the disease to others which could justify removal of a schoolteacher from the classroom.[11]

Under the Rehabilitation Act, the term handicapped individual does not include an individual who has a current contagious disease or infection and who, by reason of such disease or infection, would constitute a direct threat to the health and safety of other individuals or who by reason of the current contagious disease or infection, is unable to perform the duties of the job.[12]

AIDS Legislation

A second type of legal protection available to persons with AIDS is included in statutes that have been passed by a number of states and municipalities specifically prohibiting discrimination in employment on the basis of AIDS. In addition, a number of states, such as California, Florida, Wisconsin and Massachusetts, prohibit employers from requiring HIV testing as a condition of employment. Moreover, California employers may not reject or terminate from employment, nor deny coverage under an insurance policy to, or discriminate in any way against, individuals exposed to the AIDS virus. Blood tests may not be used in any instance to determine insurability or suitability for employment.[13] Finally, since employer policies that discriminate against persons with AIDS arguably have an adverse impact upon men, such policies may violate prohibitions against gender-based discrimination.

It also is possible for persons with AIDS to bring legal action based on a number of common-law (non-statutory) causes of action. Legal actions that fall under this area include suits based on the growing number of exceptions to the traditional employment-at-will theory. Lawsuits alleging violation of public policy and contract rights are the primary types of employment-at-will actions that may be expected.

In addition, individuals may bring suit for violations of privacy rights and for defamation, especially where an individual was terminated for having AIDS where, in actuality, he/she does not suffer from the condition.

Routine Testing of Applicants and/or Employees for HIV Virus

Neither federal nor state statutes prohibit pre-employment inquiries or physicals that are directly related to an individual's ability to perform the job functions at issue. Similarly, if an inquiry or test is taken to determine whether an individual poses an occupation hazard within the workplace, this too, might be defensible from an employer's standpoint.

However, employees or applicants may not be rejected for or terminated from employment because of exposure to the AIDS virus, absent a showing that an employee cannot perform the essential job functions of the position after reasonable accommodation in a manner that would not endanger his/her health or safety, or the health or safety of others.[14] Based upon present knowledge, an employee with AIDS who remains at work will not endanger the health or safety of others because AIDS is neither considered to be highly contagious nor believed to be transmitted by any type of casual contact.

In general, because of the difficulty of establishing a job-related reason for undertaking HIV testing in the majority of workplace situations, coupled with the significant legal issues that arise from such a program, employers have not engaged in general testing programs. One federal district court has, however, held that a hospital did not violate the Federal Rehabilitation Act when it discharged a male nurse whose roommate had AIDS, after the nurse refused to take an HIV test. This decision must be viewed narrowly and has been subject to significant debate.

Workers Exposed to AIDS in the Workplace

Whether a worker is at risk of exposure to AIDS in the workplace is, in essence, a medical question. While the medical community has not definitively identified all the potential modes of transmission of the virus, the Centers for Disease Control (CDC) position, as set forth in its guidelines, is that current epidemiological evidence implicates only blood products, semen and breast milk in the transmission of the AIDS virus. The CDC, based on conclusions of studies of non-sexual household contacts of AIDS patients, has indicated that casual contact should not result in infection. **According to the CDC, there is no known risk of transmission to co-workers or others in a normal work environment.** Except in a work environment where direct exposure to blood or other bodily fluids occurs on a regular or frequent basis, or where the individual has another contagious opportunistic infection, there is no known risk of infection, according to the CDC.

To the extent that an employee may come into contact with blood or bodily fluids, the U.S. Occupational Safety and Health Administration (OSHA) and the U.S. Department of Health and Human Services have issued guidelines for appropriate workplace precautions. Any employer potentially covered by this type of circumstance should be following the OSHA guidelines. In fact, almost any employer that has a first aid program should be aware of the OSHA guidelines and should be following them for procedures that could result in exposure to blood or bodily fluids. Employers in health and human services, in particular, should make sure that their personnel take all appropriate precautions to avoid any unnecessary contacts with HIV virus that could lead to infection.

Employer Liability

If a worker contracts HIV virus or AIDS as a result of a workplace exposure, workers' compensation statutes normally cover such a situation. These statutes usually constitute an employee's sole remedy if the employee has contracted a particular occupational disease as a result of a workplace exposure. Claims relating to other infectious diseases, such as hepatitis and tuberculosis, have been recognized under a number of state workers' compensation statutes.

Individuals may be able to circumvent workers' compensation where it is established that the employer was aware of a risk of infection and intentionally disregarded the problem by failing to adequately disclose needed information to employees and to take appropriate remedial measures. If an employee can establish an intentional or deliberate wrong, infected employees may succeed in a suit for additional damages above and beyond workers' compensation remedies. Finally, it also may be possible to bring criminal action against employers who knowingly expose employees to potentially fatal conditions in the workplace without precautions or warnings.

Employees Who Refuse to Work with Persons with AIDS

The federal Occupational Safety and Health Act (OSHA) specifies that employers shall furnish to each employee "employment and a place of employment which are free from recognized hazards that are causing or likely to cause death or serious harm" to the employee. At a minimum, employers should follow the precautions established by OSHA and other reputable bodies to the extent that such precautions apply to their facility. To refuse an employee the precautions recommended by OSHA clearly subjects the employer to potential OSHA liability.

Section 7 of the National Labor Relations Act[15] provides that employees have the right to engage in protected concerted (collective) activity for mutual aid and protection. Protest of dangerous conditions may be protected if it is concerted and if the employees have a good-faith subjective belief of the hazards, even if they are wrong. Recent National Labor Relations Board case law suggests, however, that the reasonable person approach should be used in determining whether there is reason to believe a hazard is present.

In a unionized environment, employers should not legally implement policies relating to AIDS in the workplace without first bargaining with the collective bargaining representative concerning such terms and conditions of employment. The NLRB, for example, has held that employers must bargain before requiring employees to take physical examinations or drug tests.

Commonly Asked Questions and Answers

Q. *What is AIDS?*

A. AIDS is a disease that is diagnosed on the basis of specific criteria established by the Centers for Disease Control. While a number of factors can lead to a diagnosis of AIDS, the most common infections include pneumocystis carini pneumonia (a rare form of pneumonia); Kaposi's sarcoma (a rare form of skin cancer) and AIDS dementia (central nervous system involvement). These so-called "opportunistic infections" occur as the result of the body's immune system being attacked by the HIV virus.

Q. *What is the difference between an employee who tests positive for the HIV virus and an employee who has Aids-Related Complex versus an employee who has AIDS?*

A. HIV is a virus that attacks the body's immune system. The virus, however, is capable of remaining dormant for many years. Accordingly, an individual may actively carry HIV virus and have no symptoms of disease. Individuals with AIDS-Related Complex (ARC) suffer some of the symptoms foretelling a possible onset of AIDS but do not have full-blown AIDS. Finally, individuals with AIDS have been clinically diagnosed as having the disease pursuant to Centers for Disease Control standards.

Q. *Is there a test that determines whether someone has AIDS or ARC? How do you test for the virus?*

A. There is no current test for AIDS. There also is currently no commercially available test for HIV virus. Rather, current commercially available tests look for antibodies that the body develops in response to HIV infection. Although positive HIV antibody tests are strong indicators of active HIV virus, they are not diagnostic tests for AIDS and cannot predict whether an individual will develop ARC or AIDS.

Q. *How is AIDS transmitted?*

A. According to the guidelines published by the Centers for Disease Control and the U.S. Department of Public Health, AIDS is not contracted through casual workplace contact. Generally, AIDS is transmitted through sexual contact, sharing of contaminated needles or by blood or other bodily fluids that penetrate the mucus membrane of the body.

Q. *Is there a cure or vaccine for AIDS? When can we expect one?*

A. There is currently no cure or vaccine for AIDS, and it is difficult to predict when such a vaccine or cure may be available.

Q. *What laws protect an employee with AIDS, ARC or HIV virus from being discriminated against in employment?*

A. Both the Americans with Disabilities Act and the Federal Rehabilitation Act prohibit discrimination on the basis of AIDS. Such discrimination also is prohibited under the state Fair Employment and Housing Act and the Health and Safety Code.

Q. *What is an employer's lawful response if other employees refuse to work with an employee who has AIDS or has tested positive?*

A. Unless there is some valid reason for an individual refusing to work around someone with AIDS (such as the individual having an immune-suppressed condition or concerns regarding exposure to pregnant employees) and the individual has been properly educated about the lack of risk of transmission (assuming a normal work environment, not an operating room or a place where blood and bodily fluids exist in large quantities), generally it may be lawful for an employer to engage in a progressive discipline process against an individual who refuses to work around people with AIDS. It is strongly suggested that counseling and progressive discipline be used as opposed to any summary disciplinary action.

Q. *What is an employer's lawful response if an employee who is diagnosed as having AIDS is continuously sick and misses work?*

A. Statutes prohibiting discrimination on the basis of mental or physical disability do not require employers to continue to employ individuals who are disabled, but who are unable to perform the duties of the job with or without reasonable accommodation. Accordingly, if an individual is unable to work because of AIDS or any other condition, and there is no reasonable accommodation that can be made, the individual should be treated like any other completely disabled employee. In other words, if the employer has current full-time disability policies or other benefits available to individuals who are unable to work, such policies should be enforced. In a nutshell, an individual who is disabled as a result of AIDS should be treated like any other disabled employee.

Q. *What is an employer's response if an employee tests positive or displays symptoms of AIDS, but has not fully developed AIDS?*

A. This should be reviewed on a case-by-case basis. No uniform decision is applicable to a question of this breadth. Generally, however, if the individual does not pose a direct threat to the safety and health of others and is otherwise able to perform the essential functions of the job, disability discrimination issues would likely exist if termination were undertaken. In some cases, however, both the employee and the employer agree to a reassignment of the employee. The key is to treat individuals who are displaying symptoms of AIDS, but are otherwise able to work, with compassion and sensitivity. By so doing, it is hoped that they also will show a degree of understanding toward the employer's economy and business interests that will allow the parties to reach an amicable resolution.

Q. *What is an employer's response if it determines that an employee is in a high-risk group but has not tested positive for AIDS?*

A. Individuals in high-risk groups who have tested negative for HIV antibody are not likely carriers at the present time. Nonetheless, if the employer terminates the individual because it believes the employee is at high risk of contracting the HIV virus in the future, discrimination on the basis of a perceived disability issues obviously exist. Generally, however, there would be no reason not to continue to employ an individual who is in a high-risk group but has not tested positive for HIV virus.

Q. *How do you accommodate an employee with AIDS?*

A. There are many ways to accommodate employees with AIDS, as there are with any other individual who may be suffering from a disabling or contagious condition. Common sense should prevail in the employer's approach to such accommodation.

Q: *Can you require, as part of a pre-employment physical, that an applicant be tested for AIDS?*

A: It is not generally recommended that HIV testing be undertaken for applicants for employment. Disability discrimination statutes allow pre-employment testing only where it is related to an individual's ability to perform the job for which an offer of employment has been made. The question, obviously, once again arises as to whether testing for AIDS has such a job-related purpose.

Q. *Are there any restrictions on testing for AIDS? Federal? State laws?*

A. No federal law currently exists relating to AIDS testing. California law prohibits AIDS testing as a condition of employment, and further prohibits blood tests from being used in any instance to determine insurability or suitability for employment.

Q. *Can you treat an employee with AIDS or Aids-Related Complex any differently if the employee works in a factory, hospital, restaurant, hotel, airline?*

A. Individuals who work in certain high-risk occupations arguably may be treated differently than the majority of employees with respect to AIDS and AIDS-related conditions. For example, employers may have a better argument that there is a direct or significant risk to the safety and health of others for hospital employees who are involved in invasive procedures where there is potential for direct blood-to-blood contact with a patient. A case-by-case approach with appropriate medical and legal advice must, however, be followed.

Q. *What about policies for union employers? Must you bargain with the union about an AIDS policy?*

A. Yes, any policy that affects terms and conditions of employment regarding AIDS is subject to bargaining and requires negotiation unless the union has waived its right to so bargain.

Q. *What should a company with a first aid department or a plant nurse, either full-time or temporary, do in view of the AIDS epidemic? Are there special precautions that must be followed? What is the law?*

A. Follow established universal precautionary procedures and engage in educational programs for employees and supervisors.

Q. *Who in an organization has the right to know the results of an AIDS test? The employee? Health service? The employee's supervisor? Other employees?*

A. This depends on the state in which one operates. In California, consent must be provided before an HIV test result can be disclosed to any third party.

References

1. Chapter 912, Acts of the 1992 General Assembly
2. Health and Safety Code §199.21
3. *Raytheon Company v. FEHC* 212 Cal App 3d 1242 (1989)
4. 29 U.S.C. §101(2)
5. 29 U.S.C. §793 and 794
6. Government Code §12965(b)
7. Government Code §12940(a)(2) and 12926(f)
8. 29 U.S.C. §101(2)
9. 29 U.S.C. §101(8)
10. *School Board of Nassau County, Florida v. Arline* 480 U.S. 273 (1987)
11. *Chalk v. United States District Court, Central District* 840 F2d 701 (9th Cir. 1988)
12. 29 U.S.C. §793
13. Health and Safety Code §199.21
14. 29 U.S.C. §101(9)
15. 29 U.S.C. §158, et seq.

Chapter 12
The Civil Rights Act of 1991

Introduction

In November 1991, the President signed into law the Civil Rights Act of 1991.[1] This major piece of legislation amends both Title VII of the Civil Rights Act of 1964[2] and Section 1981 of the Civil Rights Act of 1866.[3] It significantly expands employee rights which had been narrowed by the U.S. Supreme Court in fewer than seven Supreme Court decisions, across the entire spectrum of employment practices and decisions, ranging from the interview process to termination criteria. It also allows jury trials and punitive damages where they were previously unavailable.

All of the major federal laws regarding discrimination in the workplace, including all aspects of the 1964 Civil Rights Act, the Age Discrimination in Employment Act[4]; the Americans with Disabilities Act[5]; and the Rehabilitation Act of 1973[6] are affected by the new law.

Under all of these statutes, the principal form of relief available to plaintiffs suing thereunder was limited to backpay, frontpay, attorney's fees, and injunctive relief, except Section 1981 claims in actions for national origin and race discrimination, which also allowed compensatory and punitive damages. Until 1989, the general legal principles and remedial frameworks of these laws were relatively well-settled. However, during the next three years, the U.S. Supreme Court issued seven controversial decisions that significantly altered employment law and tipped the scale in favor of the employer. Those cases, which served as the catalyst for enactment of the new Civil Rights Act, decided a range of issues:

1. Narrowing the coverage of Section 1981 to discrimination that occurred in the hiring process[7];
2. Limiting the time to challenge an intentionally discriminatory seniority system to the period when the system was adopted, not when it adversely affected an individual[8];
3. Allowing challenges to a consent decree to remedy employment discrimination years after court approval of that consent decree[9];
4. Easing the employer's burden of proof in mixed-motive discrimination cases[10];
5. Making it significantly more difficult for plaintiffs to prove adverse impact in discrimination cases[11];
6. Refusal by the Court to apply Title VII protections to Americans working outside of the United States[12];
7. Limiting recovery of expert witness fees in discrimination cases.[13]

Each of these decisions greatly narrowed previously accepted legal remedies available to plaintiffs in employment discrimination cases, and became the subject of heated controversy in political and legal circles. They were viewed by both legal scholars and many advocates of both employers and employees as overly restrictive in their interpretation of legislative language and congressional intent in the passage of these laws.

The 1991 Civil Rights Act overturns, in whole or in part, the aforementioned seven Supreme Court decisions. The most dramatic impact of the Act, however, is the creation of the right to jury trials and awards of compensatory and punitive damages to successful plaintiffs suing employers under Title VII, the ADA, or the Rehabilitation Act.

The 1991 Civil Rights Act relaxes certain burdens of proof, thus providing new incentives for plaintiffs and their attorneys to file discrimination claims. Moreover, those new claims may be more difficult and expensive to defend, as employers face the specter of jury trials and large damage awards to successful plaintiffs — a requirement that previously did not exist under the ADA or Title VII. It is likely, therefore, that a greater number of discrimination claims will be filed in the immediate future.

Substantive Provisions of the 1991 Civil Rights Act
Compensatory and Punitive Damages in Cases of Intentional Discrimination

The Civil Rights Act expands the right of plaintiffs to compensatory and punitive damages and allows those claiming intentional discrimination or harassment based on sex, race, religion, national origin or color under Title VII, or disability under the ADA or Rehabilitation Act, to obtain compensatory and punitive damages measured by the size of the employer's workforce up to a maximum of $300,000. These compensatory or punitive damages do not include backpay or frontpay, fringe benefits, and interest on backpay or frontpay — traditional equitable remedies previously available.

The compensatory and punitive damages are as follows:

Number of Employees	Damages Limitation
1 - 14	no damages recoverable (employers of fewer than 15 employees are not covered by these acts, but are covered by the state Fair Employment and Housing Act).
15 - 100	$50,000
101 - 200	$100,000
201 - 500	$200,000
500+	$300,000[14]

Such compensatory or punitive damages are allowed under the Act only in cases where the employer has engaged in intentional "disparate treatment" discrimination. Where "adverse impact" discrimination is found, punitive and compensatory damages are not allowed. Adverse impact cases are those in which the employer has followed an employment policy or practice which applies to all employees, but has a harsh or adverse affect upon a certain category of employees.[15]

In addition, plaintiffs suing under these statutes for compensatory or punitive damages will have the right to jury trials, and courts are prohibited from informing juries about the legal limits on punitive and compensatory damage awards.

Adverse Impact Cases — Burden of Proof

Before 1989, courts held that Title VII prohibited business policies or practices that disproportionately excluded "protected classes" of employees, even if such policies or practices were neutral and applied equally to all employees.[16] Under that decision, employers could defend against adverse impact claims by demonstrating that the exclusionary policy or practice constituted a "business necessity." So long as the employers could establish that the practice bore a demonstrable relationship to successful performance on the job, it was not ruled as discriminatory under Title VII.

In 1989, however, the Supreme Court made it more difficult for plaintiffs to prevail by changing the standards of "business necessity" to one of "business justification."[17] The Court held that employers were not required to establish that such a policy or practice was "essential" or "indispensable" to its business operations.

The 1991 Civil Rights Act returns to the prior standard by requiring that employers establish business necessity. In addition, the burden of proof now shifts to the employer to demonstrate that the practice is job-related and consistent with business necessity, if the plaintiff initially shows that the practice had an adverse impact on protected categories. A plaintiff may still prevail on the adverse impact claim if he/she demonstrates that an alternative and effective business practice exists which would have a less discriminatory effect, and the employer refuses to adopt the alternative practice.[18]

"Mixed Motive" Cases

The 1991 Civil Rights Act clarifies, in "mixed motive" cases, Title VII's prohibitions against impermissible consideration of race, color, religion, sex or national origin in any employment decision. It overturns the Court's ruling that if an employer happened to consider an individual's protected class status in an employment decision, the employer would not necessarily be found to have violated Title VII as long as other non-discriminatory reasons also existed to justify the employer's conduct.[19]

The Act prevents employers from considering as a "motivating factor" any impermissible discriminatory criteria in any employment decision, even if the employer can demonstrate that other non-discriminatory factors also motivated the decision. If the plaintiff shows that a prohibited factor based upon protected class status played a motivating role in the employer's decision, the burden shifts to the employer to prove that it would have taken the same action in the absence of the impermissible motivating factor. If the employer proves the same action would have been taken despite the discriminatory motive, the court may not award damages or require reinstatement, hiring or promotion.

Prohibition Against All Types of Discrimination in Contracts

The 1991 Civil Rights Act expands Section 1981 to cover all acts of on-the-job discrimination, not just bias that may occur in the hiring process. In so doing, it reverses the Court's determination that the right to enter into contract applies only to the formation stages of the employment contract and not to discrimination arising after the individual is hired.[20]

Reimbursement of Expert Witness Fees

The 1991 Civil Rights Act also reverses the Court's decision that a provision allowing successful civil rights plaintiffs to recover legal fees did not include the cost of hiring expert witnesses.[21] The only limit to reimbursement by employers to prevailing plaintiffs is that such fees must be "reasonable." This award provision applies to Title VII, the ADA, the Rehabilitation Act and Section 1981.

Extension of Time for Seniority System Challenges

The 1991 Civil Rights Act further expands rights under Title VII for challenging seniority systems. It overturns the Court's decision that the statute of limitations for challenging the impact of intentionally discriminatory seniority systems under Title VII begins to run at the point when the system was adopted. That finding was contrary to the prior requirement that the limitations period did not begin to run until the aggrieved party had sustained harm. The Act provides that a seniority system that intentionally discriminates, regardless of whether such discrimination is apparent, may be challenged when the system is adopted, when an individual becomes subject to it, or when an individual is first injured by its application.[22]

Application of Discrimination Laws Outside of United States

The 1991 Civil Rights Act also reverses the Court's prior holding that Title VII does not apply to U.S. citizens working for U.S. companies abroad. Both Title VII and the ADA now apply to such workers, unless compliance would violate the laws of the foreign country where the workplace is located.[23]

Employment Test Adjustments

The 1991 Civil Rights Act also prohibits what has been termed "race-norming" of employment tests, specifically providing that an employer cannot adjust, alter or use different cut-off scores for such tests on the basis of an employee's or applicant's protected class status.[24]

"Glass-Ceiling" Commission

Advocates for women's and minority groups have long argued that there is an invisible "glass-ceiling" which prevents women and minorities from achieving senior ranks at upper management levels. The 1991 Civil Rights Act establishes the "Glass-Ceiling" Commission consisting of 21 members appointed by Congress and the President. The commission's duty is to conduct studies and prepare recommendations in an effort to eliminate artificial barriers to the advancement of women and minorities, and to increase the opportunities for the advancement of women and minorities to management and decision-making positions.[25] The commission will conduct basic research into practices, policies and manners in which management and decision-making positions are filled; comparative research of business and industries in which women and minorities are promoted to management and decision-making positions and those in which women are not promoted; and research on programs and practices that have led to the advancement of women and minorities to management and decision-making positions, including training programs, developmental programs, reward programs, employment benefit structures, rotational assignments, and family leave policy.

Encouragement of Alternative Dispute Resolution Procedures

While the 1991 Civil Rights Act does not mandate the use of alternative means of dispute resolutions, it does encourage parties to use alternatives to the court system in resolving disputes that arise under the Act.[26] The law specifically encourages the following forms of dispute resolution: settlement negotiations, conciliation, facilitation, mediation, fact finding, mini-trial and arbitration. Given the uncertainty and potential high costs of jury trials, employers and employees are encouraged to consider using of such forms of alternative dispute resolution.

Affirmative Action

The 1991 Civil Rights Act was not intended to affect the affirmative action obligations of federal contractors and subcontractors found in Executive Order 11246.[27]

References

1. Public Law 102-166
2. 42 U.S.C. Section 2000(e) et seq.
3. 42 U.S.C. Section 1981
4. 29 U.S.C. Section 621 et seq.
5. Public Law 101-336
6. 29 U.S.C. Section 791 et seq.
7. *Patterson v. McLean Credit Union* 491 U.S. 164 (1989)
8. *Lorance v. AT & T Technologies, Inc.* 490 U.S. 900 (1989)
9. *Martin v. Wilks* 480 U.S. 755 (1989)
10. *Price Waterhouse v. Hopkins* 490 U.S. 228 (1989)
11. *Wards Cove Packing Co., Inc. v. Atonio* 490 U.S. 642 (1989)
12. *EEOC v. Arabian American Oil Company* 111 S.Ct. 1227 (1991)
13. *West Virginia University Hospital, Inc. v. Casey* 113 L.Ed. 2nd 68 (1991)
14. Civil Rights Act Section 102
15. Civil Rights Act Section 102
16. *Griggs v. Duke Power Company* 401 U.S. 494 (1971)
17. *Wards Coal Packing Co., Inc. v. Atonio* 490 U.S. 642 (1989)
18. Civil Rights Act Section 105
19. *Price Waterhouse v. Hopkins* 490 U.S. 228 (1989)
20. *Patterson v. McLean Credit Union* 491 U.S. 164 (1989)
21. Civil Rights Act Section 113
22. Civil Rights Act Section 112
23. Civil Rights Act Section 109
24. Civil Rights Act Section 106
25. Civil Rights Act Section 202-203
26. Civil Rights Act Section 118
27. Civil Rights Act Section 116

Chapter 13
Resolving Discrimination Claims Through Arbitration

Introduction

Since the late 1970s, employers have kept a watchful eye over the steady expansion of employee rights and the accompanying shrinkage of employers' discretion in disciplining and terminating employees. New laws and court decisions expanding employee rights have caused an unprecedented rise in employee litigation against employers. During a three-year period ending in early 1992, California juries issued nearly 125 wrongful termination/discrimination case decisions, more than half of which ended in plaintiff's verdicts. Jury awards for individual plaintiffs ranged as high as $15 million. These figures, coupled with the extensive time and spiraling costs of litigation in these cases even before trial, have produced heightened interest in other ways of avoiding employee lawsuits, particularly in wrongful termination and discrimination actions. One of those alternatives is arbitration.

Among litigation alternatives to the existing system of trial by jury, arbitration is perhaps the most familiar and popular. The use of arbitration in non-union, employment-related work disputes has received a significant boost from a recent Supreme Court decision, *Gilmer v. Interstate/Johnson Lane Corporation.*[1] In that case, which will be discussed more fully below, the Court held that an employee who signed an agreement requiring arbitration of any dispute arising out of his employment or his termination was not entitled to a jury trial of his federal age discrimination claim. The Court's decision suggests that courts may compel mandatory arbitration even of statutory employment claims, subject to the following conditions:

1. The parties have agreed to submit that type of dispute to arbitration;
2. The arbitration agreement does not restrict the arbitrator's authority to award remedies that would have been available to the employee under the statute had the claim been brought in court; and
3. Certain procedural safeguards are met, unless the employee demonstrates that the statute in question does not provide for waiver of the judicial forum.

As a practical matter, by using arbitration rather than the court system, the employee simply is trading one forum for hearing the dispute (the court system) for another (the arbitrator).

In a parallel development, both of the two most recent comprehensive federal employment statutes, the Americans With Disabilities Act of 1990,[2] and the Civil Rights Act of 1991,[3] specifically encourage alternative dispute resolution procedures, including arbitration, to resolve disputes occuring under those statutes.

Background

By definition, arbitration normally is the final and binding settlement of disputes between parties by a method voluntarily agreed upon by the parties themselves, including selection of the person to serve as arbitrator. Arbitration has long been associated both with the settlement of union-management disputes and as an alternative to litigation within the business community. Although arbitration began during the latter part of the 19th century, its popularity grew following World War II. By the late 1950s, arbitration had become a viable means of dispute resolution in the employment arena, usually as part of an employer and union collective bargaining agreement. The most common form found in most collective bargaining agreements is referred to as "grievance arbitration," whereby, as an alternative to having the collective bargaining agreement enforced in a court, the parties agree to the alternative system of arbitration to resolve their disputes over the meaning and interpretation of that agreement.

Recent Change in Legal Framework

For years, employers generally assumed that a 1974 Supreme Court decision[4] precluded resorting to arbitration in disputes involving employment statutes such as the Civil Rights Act and the Age Discrimination in Employment Act. In that case, *Alexander V. Gardner-Denver Co.*, the court determined that an adverse decision concerning a non-discrimination clause in a collective bargaining agreement did not foreclose an employee's right to a new trial under Title VII of the Civil Rights Act.[5]

In the *Gilmer* case, however, the Supreme Court held for the first time that an agreement to arbitrate an employment discrimination claim — in this case, an age discrimination claim under the Age Discrimination in Employment Act (ADEA) — is enforceable under the Federal Arbitration Act[6] and bars the employee's right to initiate legal action for alleged age discrimination. In essence, the Court held that the right to a judicial forum for trial of a federal age discrimination claim may be waived by the employee.

Gilmer involved the Court's interpretation of an agreement Gilmer had been required to sign as a condition of employment in order to register as a securities representative with the New York Stock Exchange. That registration application provided that the employee agreed to arbitrate any dispute arising between him and his employer, pursuant to the rules of the New York Stock Exchange, including any dispute arising out of the registered representative's employment or termination of that employment.

In rejecting Gilmer's contention that subjecting an age discrimination claim under the ADEA to compulsory arbitration would be inconsistent with the purposes and provisions of that statute, the Court held as follows:

1. Parties may agree to arbitrate statutory claims and have their agreement enforced pursuant to the Federal Arbitration Act, unless Congress in enacting the statute in question evinced an intent not to allow the waiver of a judicial forum.
2. There was no showing that Congress in enacting the ADEA meant to preclude arbitration of age discrimination claims.
3. Deferral was appropriate because only a change in forum was involved and not an abrogation of any substantive rights of the employee.

4. The arbitration agreement specifically included statutory claims within its scope.
5. The adequacy of the arbitration procedures provided under the New York Stock Exchange rules were sufficient to protect the employee's statutory rights since they:
   — provided for resolution by a neutral arbitration panel;
   — allowed for limited document production and information requests, depositions and subpoenas;
   — provided broad authority to the arbitrator to establish equitable relief, such as reinstatement and the award of monetary damages.

Most importantly, the Court held that the fact that the arbitration agreement was contained in the application Gilmer was required to sign as a condition of employment was no impediment to enforcement. The Court found that "mere inequality of bargaining power. . . is not sufficient reason to hold that arbitration agreements are never enforceable in the employment context."[7]

It is clear that the Court, by its decision in *Gilmer*, reaffirmed its intention to encourage arbitration as an alternate means of dispute resolution in an ever-increasing variety of situations. The Court had expressed that preference in numerous previous cases not involving employment law considerations.[8]

California Arbitration Act

In contrast to the Federal Arbitration Act, the California Arbitration Act expressly applies to employment agreements[9] and contains detailed provisions about the conduct of arbitration hearings, discovery provisions, representation by counsel, use of depositions in lieu of testimony at hearings, issuance of subpoenas, payment of expenses, and correction of the arbitrator's award.[10] Like the policy favoring arbitration under federal law, the California Arbitration Act expresses a strong public policy favoring arbitration in California.[11] That policy is intended to promote a "speedy and final disposition of disputes, by arbitrators of the parties' own choice, in a quasi-judicial manner as a substitute for the formalized and oftentime expensive court proceedings."[12]

The California Arbitration Act has been applied to compel arbitration of contractual disputes under collective bargaining agreements and a wide variety of commercial agreements. Although there is no case authority on this point, there are significant reasons for concluding that agreements to arbitrate statutory claims such as discrimination disputes under the Fair Employment and Housing Act should not be denied enforcement merely because a statutory claim is involved. First, the Act expresses state policy favoring arbitration of disputes. Second, it does not limit the types of controversy that may be included in a written agreement to arbitrate and made enforceable pursuant to the terms of that statute.[13] Third, the large majority of California discrimination statutes do not make a judicial forum for determination of claims non-waivable. In fact, the Fair Employment and Housing Act not only does not compel such claims to be resolved in an administrative or judicial forum, but rather contemplates other ways of resolving disputes, such as conferences, conciliation and persuasion.[14] In other words, the Legislature has expressed a preference for resolving such claims without litigation.

Enforcement of Agreements to Arbitrate in Employment Contracts

An arbitration agreement may be denied enforcement if grounds exist for revoking it.[15] Therefore, a fundamental issue that employers must consider carefully when implementing an arbitration policy is the risk that a standard provision of an employer's employment agreement requiring employees to arbitrate employment-related disputes may be denied enforcement on the grounds that the employee did not freely and voluntarily enter into such an agreement. Courts in California have held that an agreement to arbitrate may be enforced provided that:

1.   Its terms do not exceed the expectations of the weaker or "adhering" party; and
2.   Its terms are not unconscionable.[16]

To be enforceable, a standardized arbitration agreement:

1.   Must not exceed the reasonable expectations of the employee as the weaker party;
2.   Must satisfy minimum levels of integrity in its procedures; and
3.   Must not, in its substantive provisions, overly favor the employer.

To meet the "reasonable expectations" requirement, employers should give employees adequate and reasonable notice of the meaning and exact scope of the arbitration agreement and its consequences.[17]

Advantages of Arbitration Over Litigation

There are compelling reasons for employers to prefer final and binding arbitration over a judicial forum for wrongful discharge claims and other employment disputes. Arbitration claims among its advantages the expertise of specialized, experienced employment law professionals who understand the applicable law and the realities of the workplace, who have decided similar disputes, and who are relatively insulated from community pressures and attitudes that tend to influence juries. In addition, unlike a jury trial, both arbitration as a private dispute resolution mechanism and the arbitrator's award generally are treated as confidential unless the parties agree otherwise.

Other major advantages include the significant saving of time, expense and trouble. Arbitration can and does resolve disputes more quickly than litigation. The average time between the filing of a grievance in collective bargaining and the ultimate arbitration decision is less than one year, compared to the costly prolonged technical procedures of court, where frequent continuances and appeal of judgments can lead to significant additional years and costs of litigation. Without a jury present, the hearing usually is conducted expeditiously, and arbitrators tend to render decisions significantly more quickly than judges burdened by an ever-increasing workload. Moreover, a court may vacate an arbitrator's award only on very narrow grounds, such as where the award was procured by fraud, or the arbitrator exceeded his/her jurisdiction by deciding an issue not submitted for decision. Thus, unlike in court, where appeals from judgments often are routine, arbitration tends to be final. These advantages to employers also accrue to employees, who may have similar concerns regarding time, expense and hassle.

Finally, although some might claim that the finality of arbitration is a disadvantage to employers, the opposite is true. Arbitrators know that issuing decisions either extreme in nature or without basis will result in refusal by similarly situated parties to select that arbitrator in the future. Thus, there is institutional pressure for arbitrators to render only reasonable and well-supported decisions.

Securing the Arbitration Agreement

Arbitration requires an agreement of the affected parties to submit their dispute to arbitration. Quite often, the use of arbitration clauses in employment contracts and policies offers a means of securing in advance the employee's consent to binding arbitration to resolve any dispute between the employer and the employee, especially disputes regarding termination of employment, which may trigger large claims for damages. Once a dispute has occurred, it often is difficult or impossible to persuade an employee to agree to arbitrate a controversy, particularly since by that time he/she may be represented by counsel and be contemplating the prospect of a large recovery in litigation.

If the employer determines to use arbitration, notice of the arbitration requirements should be provided to applicants for employment by way of the employment application and/or the offer of employment letter from the employer. These documents should clearly state that employment-related disputes will be subject to binding arbitration and incorporate by clear reference a separate document containing the actual arbitration agreement and arbitration procedures.[18] A disclaimer clearly explaining that the prospective employee foregoes his/her right to pursue legal action on any claim within the scope of the arbitration agreement should preface the arbitration agreement and procedures.

A more difficult question is whether an employer can require existing employees to arbitrate any employment-related disputes. Unlike the applicant or newly hired employee— who agrees at the outset of his/her employment relationship that binding arbitration of enumerated employment-related disputes shall be a condition of employment—existing employees have been hired without that expectation. Unilateral imposition of a binding arbitration policy would thus be more susceptible to being challenged as unconscionable because, arguably, the addition of this policy was beyond the expectations of existing employees and was not separately bargained with each employee, as was the case with the applicant/newly hired employee.

One way to reduce this risk is to ask each employee to sign an agreement acknowledging the binding arbitration policy and its provisions, and providing some sort of monetary or related inducement to the employee for such an agreement. Employees who then sign such agreements would be similarly situated to newly hired employees, and the risk of the courts finding an unconscionable contract would be correspondingly reduced.

If an employer decides not to enter into individual contracts with its current employees, the employer may simply add the arbitration policy to its existing employee handbook or personnel manual, announce the adoption of the arbitration policy to its affected employees, provide a written summary outlining the basic points of the policy in clear and concise language, disseminate copies of the complete policy/procedures to all employees, and have each employee sign an acknowledgment of receipt of the handbook or manual containing the new policy. Although these measures would be more susceptible to challenge than an individual written agreement with the employee, they do help establish that the policy was not concealed from the employees and was not a covert attempt to deny them their substantive rights. In addition, so long as the procedures themselves are fair and equitable, it is likely that a court would find the binding arbitration policy enforceable. Moreover, the more the courts view binding arbitration as merely changing the forum for enforcing statutory rights from the courts to the arbitrator, the greater the likelihood that such arbitration policies for existing employees will be viewed as enforceable.

It is vitally important that the employer give careful consideration to how it will present its arbitration policy to its employees. The employer also should carefully explain the benefits of arbitration to the employee before implementing the arbitration policy or executing the arbitration agreement.

The benefits of arbitration are not one-sided, and are significant for the employee as well. In talking about arbitration to employees, the employer should emphasize that employees give up no substantive rights by arbitrating rather than litigating employment disputes, but rather are selecting a different, less expensive and less time-consuming forum for resolving those disputes. In arbitration, the employee, like the employer, may have legal representation. Arbitration has major benefits for employees as well as employers, in that it is relatively fast and informal, and generally simpler than judicial procedures and therefore much less costly.

Following is a typical clause providing for agreement to arbitration of employment-related disputes:

> Any controversy or claim arising out of or relating to the employee's employment with the employer, or the termination of that employment, will be settled by binding arbitration. Judgment upon the award rendered by the arbitrator may be entered in any court having jurisdiction over the matter.

The employer should be aware that the language above constitutes the broadest form of an arbitration agreement, and may encompass matters the employer does not wish to submit to arbitration. If an employer wishes to restrict arbitration to certain disputes, or to disputes related only to an employee's termination from employment, the language of the agreement should reflect that limitation.

Sources of Arbitrators and Arbitration Proceedings

It is important in arbitration proceedings that a neutral body be designated for both selection of the arbitrator and a description of the procedures to be used. Because of the bar against unconscionable contracts of adhesion, if the arbitration agreement is presented to the employee on a "take-it-or-leave-it" basis, and/or if the designated arbitration tribunal is viewed as biased against the employee, the employee may later be able to have the agreement voided in court.[19]

The American Arbitration Association is a nationwide organization used for alternative dispute resolution in various types of disputes. It has rules governing such matters as the format and scheduling of initial pleadings, filing fees, selection of the arbitrator(s), availability of discovery, hearing procedures, and other related matters. Similar related organizations providing arbitration expertise are the Federal Mediation and Conciliation Service and the California State Mediation and Conciliation Service. The state agency has offices in San Francisco, Los Angeles, San Diego and Fresno.

Considerations in Determining Whether to Use Arbitration

Before adopting a policy requiring arbitration of employment disputes, the employer should carefully analyze whether adopting of such a policy makes sense economically and in terms of its employment relations. Some factors to consider in making this analysis are as follows:

1. What is the company's history on employment disputes, both in number, time and cost?
2. What would be the effect on employment relations with the company's employees and on employee morale?
3. Will the employer be disadvantaged by the relatively simpler arbitration proceedings?
4. Will the time and cost of handling potentially more claims offset the savings the company would achieve by avoiding judicial litigation of fewer claims?

Considerations in Drafting Arbitration Agreements

Once an employer adopts a policy requiring arbitration of employment disputes, an arbitration agreement should be drafted, defining not only what will be arbitrated but also how covered disputes will be arbitrated. In drafting that agreement, the employer should consider the following issues:

1. *What type of disputes will be subject to arbitration? Will claims be limited only to those arising from termination of employment, or should all employment-related disputes be arbitrated?* In making that determination, the employer should consider how the claim will be resolved in the absence of arbitration, the relative time and expense involved in arbitration versus other available proceedings, and the economic exposure to the employer should the employee prevail. In most cases, more will be at stake in an employment termination than in disputes that arise while the employee is still on the job.

2. *Which employees will be covered? Will only new employees hired after the arbitration policy is in place be subject to its provisions, or will it apply to all employees? Will the policy cover only managers and supervisors, or only rank-and-file employees, or both?* Selecting a sampling of employees might provide the employer with a first experience with arbitration before applying it to all employees.

3. *What time limits should govern bringing any claim to arbitration? Should the employee have a shorter time in which to request arbitration than he/she would have in civil actions in court in the same type of claim?* If a significantly shorter time is allowed than the employee would otherwise have, the agreement may be challenged in court as unconscionable.

4. *What does the employee do to request arbitration? To whom should the request be made?* At a minimum, the request should be in writing and contain a short statement of the claim.

5. *Will the arbitration agreement require the parties to attempt some sort of voluntary settlement dispute informally with the assistance of an outside neutral party before*

proceeding to arbitration? It might be advisable for the parties to have a mediation step before arbitration, wherein a mutually selected mediator is brought in to attempt to help the parties resolve the dispute voluntarily, and failing that, to provide an informal opinion concerning his/her view of the ultimate outcome of the claim.

6. *How will the arbitrator be selected?* Under the most common procedure, the moving party submits, with the request for arbitration, a request for a list of an odd number of experienced professional arbitrators from either the California State Mediation and Conciliation Service, the American Arbitration Association, or the Federal Mediation and Conciliation Service. These sources also provide extensive background descriptions of the arbitrators listed. The parties alternately strike names from the list until only one name remains.

7. *What procedures will govern the conduct of the arbitration hearing, any pre-hearing discovery or motions, and enforcement of the arbitrator's award?* The more closely the arbitration procedures are modeled on comprehensive statutes such as the California Arbitration Act, the more likely they are to be viewed fair by the court.

8. *What restrictions, if any, will apply on the remedies obtainable in arbitration?* The more restricted the remedy as compared to what the employee might obtain in court on the same claim, the more vulnerable the agreement may be to attack as unconscionable.

9. *How will the cost of arbitration, including the arbitrator's fee, be allocated?* The normal method of allocating costs is for the company and the employee to each pay half. It might be advisable for the employer to pick up the majority of the arbitrator's costs, because if the cost of arbitration becomes too onerous, the arbitration policy could be challenged on the grounds that it imposes financial burdens that an employee going to court with a lawyer paid on a contingency fee basis would not have to bear.

10. *Should arbitration be mandatory or only optional?*

11. *Should the arbitrator be empowered to rule on motions for summary judgment or to dismiss? If so, what rules should govern the decision on motions (e.g., federal rules of civil procedure)?*

Other Forms of Alternative Dispute Resolution

In addition to arbitration, employers also may use other forms of dispute resolution as an alternative to litigation. The following is a review of some of the more common procedures.

Mediation

Mediation involves a neutral third party who facilitates settlement discussions between the parties. The mediator does not have the authority to render a decision or to decide factual disputes. But through the mediator's ability to question extreme positions, to flush out hidden agendas, to develop alternative approaches to the same problem, etc., mediation can be greatly successful in voluntarily resolving disputes between employers and employees. When requested, the mediator also may express his/her opinions based upon the parties' discussions, but those opinions are not binding upon the parties.

Early Neutral Evaluation

Early neutral evaluation involves a case evaluation session early in the life of the possible litigation. The evaluation normally is presided over by a mediator or advisory arbitrator. At the session, the parties and their lawyers present their positions, and the evaluator attempts to reduce the scope of the dispute by identifying areas of agreement between the parties, assessing the strengths and weaknesses of the case, and helping the parties develope a plan for sharing information and potentially resolving the case on their own.

Other Alternatives

Other more formalized programs also exist in the traditional court process. Those include such functions as judicial arbitration, summary jury trials, and mini trials. Each of these procedures becomes becomes progressively more formalized and expensive, but still might be explored as a less costly and time-consuming alternative to litigation.

Conclusion

Given the extensive costs, time involved and uncertainty of litigation, coupled with the overwhelming backlog of litigation on the courts' dockets, arbitration of employment-related disputes, including those involving statutory claims, is likely to be the coming trend in employment relations. Employers should strongly consider the possibility of invoking or agreeing to arbitration procedures in employment matters, including employment contracts. Employers are strongly advised to consult legal counsel before implementing any arbitration agreement.

References

1. *Gilmer v. Interstate/Johnson Lane Corp.*, 111 S.Ct. 1647 (1991)
2. 42 U.S.C. Section 12212 et seq.
3. 42 U.S.C. Section 118
4. *Alexander v. Gardner-Denver Co.*, 415 U.S. 36 (1974)
5. 415 U.S. at 60
6. 9 U.S.C. Section 1 et seq.
7. 111 S.Ct. at 1655
8. See e.g., *Rodriguez de Quijas v. Shearson/American Express Inc.*, 490 U.S. 477, 481 (1989)
9. Code of Civil Procedure Section 1280(a)
10. Code of Civil Procedure Section 1282 et seq.
11. *Grunwald-Marx, Inc. v. Los Angeles Joint Board, Amalgated Clothing Workers Union*, 192 Cal. App. 2d 268, 276-77 (1961)
12. *Accito v. Matmor Canning Co.*, 128 Cal. App. 2d 631 (1954); *Utah Construction Co. v. Western Pacific Railway Co.*, 174 Cal. 156, 159 (1917); *Turner v. Cox*, 196 Cal. App. 2d 596, 602-3 (1961); *Lauria v. Soriano*, 180 Cal. App. 2d 163, 170 (1960)
13. Code of Civil Procedure Section 1281
14. Government Code Section 12963.7(a)
15. Code of Civil Procedure Section 1281; 9 U.S.C. Section 2
16. *Graham v. Scissor-Tail, Inc.*, 28 Cal. 3d 807 (1981)
17. *Graham v. Scissor-Tail, Inc.*, 28 Cal. 3d 807 (1981); *Hope v. Superior Court*, 122 Cal. App. 3d 147, 154 (1981)
18. *Chan v. Drexel Burnham Lambert, Inc.*, 178 Cal. App. 3d 632, 641 (1986)
19. *Graham v. Scissor Tail, Inc.*, 28 Cal. 3d 807 (1981)

Chapter 14

Recent EEO Court Decisions

ssment

9t. es "reasonable woman" test for Title VII sexual harassment claim
The : rt of Appeals reinstated a previously dismissed sexual harassment lawsuit
filed by voman who received "love letters" from a male colleague. The court said
that in ga. r a hostile work environment affects plaintiff's psychological well-being,
Title VII re. sonable woman" standard. The court faulted the trial judge for treating
the man's am. ions and love letters as isolated and trivial, even though the plaintiff
regarded his at. s as shocking and frightening and his letters as bizarre. The court held that a
sex-blind reasonable person standard tends to be male-biased and tends to systematically ignore
the experiences of women. The court noted that the reasonable woman standard does not
establish a higher level of protection for women than men but instead enables women to
participate in the workplace on an equal footing with men. The court further noted that the
employer's remedy of offering the plaintiff a transfer to another office in another city was not
reasonable under Title VII. This remedy is akin to punishing the victim for the harasser's
conduct. Moreover, the court said that the record was devoid of any showing that the
management reprimanded the harasser, placed him on probation or otherwise warned him that his
conduct would result in suspension or discharge. The employer had merely transferred the
harasser, temporarily, to another office. The court suggested that to avoid liability for failing to
remedy a hostile environment, employers may have to remove the offending employee from the
workplace. The court reversed the district court's decision that the plaintiff did not allege a *prima
facie* case of sexual harassment, but remanded the case to the district court so that it could fully
explore the facts concerning the employer's decision to return the harasser to the plaintiff's
workplace. *Ellison v. Brady,* 924 F.2d 872 (9th Cir. 1991).

Court dismisses sexual harassment claim on basis of omissions from application
An employee brought a Title VII sexual harassment action after she quit her job as a part-time
security officer, because of harassment by a customer who contracted with her employer,
Pinkerton's, for security guards. The harassment allegedly included indecent exposure, sexual
propositions, a visit to the employee at her home and unwelcome physical contact. In its defense,
Pinkerton's demonstrated that the employee's employment application omitted vital information
— she had not listed a number of her prior residences; she answered "no" to a question about
hospitalization for mental illness even though she had been hospitalized for two days after a
suicide attempt; she denied she used any narcotic or illegal drugs, even though she had used
speed, marijuana, and valium; and she denied she had ever been terminated from a job, even
though she had twice been discharged. She also listed only five jobs during the previous 10
years, when in fact she had worked at 12 jobs during that period. The court held that the
employee could not obtain relief under Title VII because she failed to disclose vital information
on her employment application that would have resulted in a refusal to hire or a discharge had the
company been informed earlier of her employment and personal history. *Churchman v.
Pinkerton's, Inc.*, 756 F. Supp. 515 (D.C. Kan. 1991).

Sexual harassment memo immune from slander charge

A memorandum distributed by an employer to inform its workplace that it had terminated an employee for engaging in sexual harassment, and to reemphasize its sexual harassment policy, was found not defamatory. The company terminated a male employee for sexually harassing a female co-worker. Subsequently, a number of concerned employees questioned management about sexual harassment, and a flurry of rumors circulated throughout the plant concerning the employee's termination. In response, the company issued a bulletin to all supervisors explaining why the male employee was terminated, reiterating in detail the company's sexual harassment policy, and instructing supervisors to discuss the contents of the memorandum with all employees. The memorandum did not identify the terminated employee by name, was not distributed to non-supervisory employees, and was not posted on any company bulletin boards. The terminated male employee subsequently sued the company for libel and slander. Although the employee won $100,000 in compensatory damages under Florida libel law, the federal appellate court reversed the jury award and found that the company communication to its employees was protected by a qualified privilege. Not only did co-workers have a legitimate interest in the reasons a fellow employee was terminated, the company had an interest in maintaining employee morale as well as complying with its legal obligation to prohibit sexual harassment in the workplace by affirmatively raising the subject and expressing disapproval of any sexually harassing conduct. *Graziano v. E.I. Du Pont de Nemours & Company*, 818 F.2d 350 (5th Cir., 1987).

Employer liable for sexual harassment claim because of delay in responding to employee's complaints

The 10th Circuit Court of Appeals held that Weyerhaeuser Company discriminated against a female employee by failing to discharge one of the woman's co-workers, a known sexual harasser, until six months after she complained to her supervisor. Upholding a $90,000 jury verdict in a state court action and a separate verdict on the Title VII claim, the 10th Circuit rejected the company's argument that it was not liable because the harasser was not a supervisor and because he was ultimately discharged. Plaintiff established that the harasser should have been terminated long before he was, and that Weyerhaeuser did nothing when it should have acted. The court noted that the co-worker's status as a supervisor was not a critical issue and focused instead on the findings of pervasive sexual harassment of plaintiff which was known or should have been known by Weyerhaeuser. *Baker v. Weyerhaeuser Company*, 903 F.2d 1342 (10th Cir. 1990).

Discharging supervisor for sexual harassment does not bar back pay liability against the company

A female employee filed sexual harassment claims against her employer, charging that a supervisor had sexually harassed numerous female employees and had created a hostile work environment. The company fired the supervisor soon after the employee filed her complaint with the Equal Employment Opportunity Commission (EEOC). However, the EEOC sued the company for back pay on the grounds that the company was aware of the supervisor's conduct and failed to do anything about the unlawful harassment until a complaint was filed. The court found that the back pay award was proper because the company knew of the supervisor's wrongful conduct yet "continued toleration of that behavior." *EEOC v. Gurnee Inn Corp.*, 914 F.2d 815 (7th Cir. 1990).

Mere allegations of a supervisor's romantic involvement with a co-worker are not grounds for sexual harassment claim

The 3rd Circuit Court of Appeals determined that allegations that a supervisor's romantic relationship with a co-worker created an oppressive and inadequate environment were not grounds for a sexual harassment claim absent a showing that the couple's conduct rendered the workplace a sexually charged environment and that fellow workers suffered discrimination because of that environment. The court acknowledged that such an atmosphere could have constituted harassment if sexual discourse displaced standard business procedure in a way that prevented the plaintiff from working in an environment in which she could be evaluated on grounds other than her sexuality. The court said that there was no evidence that the plaintiff's supervisor and co-worker flaunted the romantic nature of their relationship, nor was there evidence that these kinds of relationships were prevalent at the employer's place of business. The court pointed out that a sexual relationship between a supervisor and co-worker could adversely affect the workplace without creating a hostile sexual environment. *Drinkwater v. Union Carbide Corp.*, 904 F.2d 853 (3rd Cir. 1990).

Employee's termination upheld despite sexual harassment by supervisor
The 7th Circuit Court of Appeals held that an employee's retaliatory discharge suit based on sexual harassment was properly dismissed because the employee was terminated for poor work performance and not because she rejected her supervisor's sexual advances. The employee's supervisor made repeated sexual advances toward the employee during her first two weeks of employment. After repeated rejections by the employee, the supervisor ceased his sexual advances. Nine weeks later, the employee was terminated for failure to perform her work obligations. Other female employees corroborated the employee's stories and indicated that other female employees were subjected to the same treatment. Nevertheless, the court found that the supervisor's actions were not continuing, that the discharge was not based on sexual harassment, and that the acts did not rise to a level of conduct actionable under Title VII. The court focused on the employee's inability to perform her basic job requirements and not on the evidence of sexual harassment occurring early in her employment. *Dockter v. Rudolf Wolff Futures, Inc.*, 913 F.2d 456 (7th Cir. 1990).

Hostile work environment constitutes sexual harassment
In its first decision on sexual harassment, the U.S. Supreme Court ruled that a hostile work environment constitutes sexual harassment in violation of Title VII of the 1964 Civil Rights Act, even if the complaining employee has not suffered actual job or earnings loss. The case was brought by a former employee of a bank who alleged that a vice president of the bank sexually harassed her. Although the case is viewed as a setback for employers, the court ruled favorably on two points. The court held that a company would not automatically be liable for sexual harassment by a supervisor, indicating that liability would not be imputed to the company unless the company knew or should have known of the improper conduct. The court also held that courts could permit introduction of the dress style and manner of speech or conduct of the complaining party as proof that the misconduct was consensual. *Meritor Savings Bank v. Vinson, 477 U.S. 57 (1986).*

Although the U.S. Supreme Court said that a company will not automatically be held liable for a supervisor's acts, the Department of Fair Employment and Housing in enforcing California state law does not accept that limitation.

Sex Discrimination

Laying off women based on a belief that they cannot lift heavy items is sex discrimination
The California Fair Employment and Housing Commission (FEHC) found that an employer violated the Fair Employment and Housing Act (FEHA) when it laid off two women in the assembly department of a metal-forming business because changes in the assembly department would require lifting of heavy objects. Concluding that the employees had been discriminated against, the FEHC noted that the women were not given any opportunity to demonstrate whether they would be able to handle the new heavier parts in the assembly department, and that no men were terminated in the assembly department at the time the two women were terminated. *DFEH v. Matthews Metal Prod., Inc.*, FEHC Dec. No. 91-13 (1991).

Exhaustion of state administrative remedies unnecessary in sex discrimination actions
In a major develpment, the California Supreme Court ruled that the Fair Employment and Housing Act (FEHA) is not the exclusive remedy for discrimination claims, and that employees are not required to exhaust the administrative process before filing a common law discrimination suit. Two female physician's assistants filed an action for sexual harassment and infliction of emotional distress claiming their employer had grabbed, fondled and otherwise harassed them sexually. The employer contended that the FEHA was plaintiffs' exclusive remedy and that they had failed to exhaust administrative procedures. The court found that the FEHA does not preempt or preclude other state law claims relating to employment discrimination. The court also held that a victim of sex discrimination is not required to exhaust his/her administrative remedies under the FEHA, except as to claims brought under that act, and that the two plaintiffs were free to file a civil action alleging common law claims. The court also held that plaintiffs' allegations of sexual harassment and discrimination would support a claim of damages for discharge in contravention of public policy. *Rojo v. Kliger*, 52 Cal. 3d 65 (1990)

Accounting firm ordered to provide partnership to woman denied post due in part to sexual stereotyping
A federal district judge ordered the accounting firm Price Waterhouse to provide a partnership to a woman who resigned from the firm six and one half years ago after being denied a post due in part to sexual stereotyping. The holding is the first one in which a court-ordered remedy included placement in a professional partnership for a bias victim. The court rejected Price Waterhouse's contention that it lacked the authority to order such relief. The court explained that if Title VII liability may be premised on denial of partnership, there is no logical reason that the full range of Title VII remedies are not appropriate. The court held that it would be futile to order Price Waterhouse to simply reconsider plaintiff for partnership since the record suggested that the deck was stacked against her. *Hopkins v. Price Waterhouse*, 737 F. Supp. 1202 (D.C 1990), *aff'd*, 920 F.2d 967 (1990).

Fetal protection policy is discriminatory
The U.S. Supreme Court held that an employer fetal protection policy violated Title VII. The court concluded that the exclusion of women with child-bearing capabilities from lead-exposed jobs created a classification based on sex which impermissibly discriminated against women. The court held that the policy could not be justified as a business necessity, nor was it defensible as a bona fide occupational qualification. Finally, the court stated that the employer "could not seek to protect the unconceived children of all its employees," as the policy was unconcerned with the possible effects of lead exposure to the father of an unconceived child. Significantly, five justices of the court expressed the opinion that the BFOQ defense could never justify a sex-specific protection policy, unless a female's reproductive potential actually prevented her from performing job duties. *International Union, UAW v. Johnson Controls, Inc.*, 59 U.S.L.W. 4209 (March 20, 1991).

a California court of appeal. In that case a female applicant was denied employment in a job which required exposure to lead pursuant to the company's fetal protection policy. The court held that the policy constituted categorial discrimination against fertile women and was a blatant, overt violation of the Fair Employment and Housing Act. The court referenced the Occupational Safety and Health Administration's finding that lead exposure to men, as well as women, is hazardous to the unborn and concluded from the evidence that unless a fertile woman becomes pregnant, she stands in precisely the same position with regard to exposure as does a fertile man.

The court held that the policy was not valid pursuant to the BFOQ defense because the company did not establish that fertile women could not efficiently perform jobs involving contact with lead at the company's facility, nor could the company establish that the essence of its business — making lead acid batteries — would be undermined by the employment of fertile women in production positions. The court stated that the issue of safety to potential offspring is best left to the parent and, if need be, to the Legislature. The California Supreme Court declined further review of the policy. *Johnson Controls, Inc. v. FEHC*, 218 Cal. App. 3d 517 (1990).

Law firm ordered to provide partnership to a woman denied a post due to sexual discrimination

A federal district court in Pennsylvania ordered a law firm to place a female employee, Nancy Ezold, in a partnership position. Although the chairman of her department gave Ezold an outstanding review for her work on a complex matter, Ezold was informed by the law firm that she would not be recommended for partnership. Ezold demonstrated that there were disparities in work assignments and that the standards applied to her were stricter than those applied to male associates, many of whom received poorer evaluations and yet were named partners. In addition, at the time that Ezold was informed she had not been named a partner, the law firm's executive committee chairman offered Ezold a conditional partnership in the firm's Domestic Relations Department, often viewed as female-oriented area of law. In an unusual move, the district court ordered the law firm to accept Ezold as a partner. The court looked to the broad authority given to the courts under Title VII to make victims of discrimination whole in order to put the victim in the position she would have been in had there been no discrimination. The law firm has appealed. *Ezold v. Wolf, Block, Schorr & Solis-Cohen*, 56 Fair Empl. Prac. Cas. 580 (E.D. Pa. 1991).

Pregnancy Discrimination

Employer may not second-guess physician's recommendation for pregnancy leave

In a unanimous decision by the California Fair Employment and Housing Commission, ordered a California law firm to pay more than $24,000 in back wages and compensatory damages to a female employee who challenged its pregnancy disability leave policy. The commission found that the law firm violated the Fair Employment and Housing Act by misleading a legal secretary about the time legally available to her for pregnancy disability and by second guessing her physician's recommendation for a longer leave. The commission found the law firm's policy of allowing only six weeks of disability leave for pregnancy illegal, and ordered the firm to adopt a new policy consistent with state law and to instruct its employees in the provisions of the law, allowing for up to four months of disability leave for pregnancy. *DFEH v. Dimino and Card*, FEHC Dec. No. 90-05 (1990).

Prohibiting use of sick leave to extend maternity leave does not violate Pregnancy Discrimination Act

The 6th Circuit Court of Appeals held that an employer did not violate the Pregnancy Discrimination Act (PDA) when it prohibited employees from using accumulated sick leave to extend maternity leave. The court found that a school district's maternity and sick leave policies did not discriminate against disabilities related to pregnancy or treat disabilities related to pregnancy less favorably than other disabilities. The court noted that the impact of the leave policy was not dependent on the biological fact that pregnancy and childbirth cause some period of disability, but on a schoolteacher's choice to forego returning to work, in favor of spending time at home with her newborn child. Such a choice, however, falls outside the scope of the PDA. *Maganuco v. Layden Community High Sch. Dist.* 212, 939 F.2d 440 (6th Cir. 1991).

Early retirement ineligibility based on previous pregnancy leave is discriminatory

The 9th Circuit Court of Appeals held that an early retirement plan that denied eligibility to an employee because of a previously taken pregnancy-related leave discriminated on the basis of sex. Pacific Bell instituted a new early retirement benefit plan for management employees that required 20 years of service to qualify. Employees did not receive credit for time spent on personal leave, including leaves related to pregnancy disabilities. As other types of disability leaves received service credit toward the early-retirement benefit plan, the court found that the plan violated Title VII, the Fair Employment and Housing Act and ERISA. *Pallas v. Pacific Bell*, 940 F.2d 1324 (9th Cir. 1991).

Pregnancy Discrimination Act protects man discharged because of wife's pregnancy

J. Scott Nicol and Jody Nicol were employed as vice presidents at Imagematrix, Inc. The company fired Jody six weeks after it learned that she was pregnant, claiming that she was being fired because of declining sales and cash flow problems. Her husband was fired hours later. Both Scott and Jody filed suit against Imagematrix alleging violations of the Pregnancy Discrimination Act (PDA). The court determined that the company violated the PDA when it fired both Scott and Jody, analogizing to discrimination cases involving interracial relationships where a white employee is discharged because the spouse is black. *Nicol v. Imagematrix, Inc.*, 773 F. Supp. 802 (E.D. Va. 1991).

Firing female employee due to premature infant's costs does not constitute pregnancy discrimination

The 6th Circuit Court of Appeals held that termination of an employee because of excessive health costs did not violate the Pregnancy Discrimination Act (PDA). The PDA prohibits discrimination "because of" pregnancy, defining such discrimination to be the unequal treatment of female employees affected by pregnancy, childbirth or related medical conditions. Fleming was terminated because her prematurely born infant cost the company $80,000 under its self-insured plan. In rejecting the employee's claim, the court distinguished between women affected by pregnancy-related medical conditions and conditions of the resulting offspring. The court found there was no link between the reason for firing Fleming — her child's high medical costs — and Fleming's gender or pregnancy. The court did, however, hold that the company had violated ERISA because it fired an employee in retaliation for using benefits. *Fleming v. Ayers & Assocs.*, 948 F.2d 993 (6th Cir. 1991).

Age Discrimination

Replacing of older worker with younger employee motivated by salary saving does not violate the Age Discrimination in Employment Act

The Second Circuit Court of Appeals held that the Age Discrimination in Employment Act (ADEA) does not prohibit an employer from making employment decisions that relate to an employee's salary, even where high salary and age are related factors in the decision to terminate. The court held that Times-Mirror did not violate the ADEA when it terminated a 54-year-old employee whose yearly salary was $195,000 and replaced him with a 35-year-old employee whose salary was $85,000. The court noted that the position occupied by the terminated employee had recently been stripped of many of its previous responsibilities and that the terminated employee had shown great dissatisfaction with his new responsibilities. As a caveat, the court stated that although employment decisions relating to an employee's salary are not barred by the ADEA, the employer must still review each employee individually on the merits, must not impose a general rule that has a disparate impact on older workers, and must base the decision solely on financial considerations. *Bay v. Times-Mirror Magazines, Inc.*, 936 F.2d 112 (2d Cir. 1991).

Statements that employee is "too old" and "making too much money" are enough to establish age discrimination

A 50-year-old manager was fired from Sears and subsequently brought an age discrimination claim against his former employer. Because the employee had received four disciplinary memoranda in the few months before his firing, the district court found that any evidence of age discrimination was rebutted, and dismissed the case. The 11th Circuit Court of Appeals (Atlanta) reversed the district court and revived the case based on comments that were made to the employee when he received his disciplinary memoranda. The supervisor allegedly told the employee, "Both of us have been around too long and are too old and are making too much money." Based on these comments and allegations that the memoranda were merely pretextual, the court remanded the case for a jury trial. *Alphin v. Sears, Roebuck & Co.*, 940 F.2d 1497 (11th Cir. 1991).

Age Discrimination in Employment Act — bona fide occupational qualification defense

Employers facing age discrimination charges may not be able to rely as heavily on the bona fide occupational qualification (BFOQ) defense as a result of two U.S. Supreme Court decisions. The Age Discrimination in Employment Act (ADEA) allows employers to terminate employees on account of age if age is a "bona fide occupational qualification" necessary for the business operation. But in two recent decisions, the Supreme Court rejected the use of the BFOQ exception as a defense of the employer. In one case, the court held that an airline violated the ADEA by forcing flight engineers to retire at age 60, stating, "The BFOQ exception was in fact meant to be an extremely narrow exception to the general prohibition of age discrimination contained in the ADEA." In the other case, which involved Baltimore firefighters who were required to retire at age 55, the court rejected the city's contention that because Congress had permitted federal agencies to retire firefighters at age 55, age is a BFOQ for all firefighters. *Western Air Lines, Inc. v. Criswell; Johnson v. City of Baltimore.*

"Overqualified" may be a buzzword for age bias

The 2nd Circuit Court of Appeals reinstated the age-discrimination claim of a printing manager who was rejected for 32 other positions with the company when his job was eliminated. The plaintiff was 58 years old and had more than 30 years' experience in the printing industry when he was hired by the company to work in one of its subsidiaries. When the subsidiary was dissolved six months later, the plaintiff was told that he would be given special consideration for jobs in other divisions but would not be guaranteed a job. The plaintiff applied for 32 positions within the corporation but was not offered employment. The company explained that he was overqualified for some jobs and underqualified for others. The court held that denying employment to an older job applicant because he or she has too much experience, training or education is simply a euphemism to mask the real reason for refusal — the applicant is too old. The court concluded that characterizing an applicant as overqualifed may be a "buzzword" for discrimination. *Taggart Inc.*, 924 F.2d 43 (2d Cir. 1991).

Claim for age discrimination under Age Discrimination in Employment Act subject to arbitration
In a very significant ruling, the U.S. Supreme Court held that an employee's age discrimination complaint was subject to binding arbitration, irrespective of the Age Discrimination in Employment Act's (ADEA) comprehensive administrative process of investigation and conciliation of age discrimination claims, and the availability of subsequent legal action. The court found that the employee's pre-employment entry into a mandatory agreement to resolve through arbitration any claim arising out of employment or termination of employment was binding upon the parties, that arbitration could provide a complete remedy in such situations, and that nothing in the ADEA or its legislative history precluded arbitration of such claims. *Gilmer v. Interstate/Johnson Lane Corporation*, 59 U.S.L.W. 4407 (May 13, 1991).

Race and National Origin Discrimination

United States-Japan treaty permits foreign-owned subsidiaries in United States to prefer Japanese citizens for executive positions
The 7th Circuit Court of Appeals (Chicago) held that the Treaty of Friendship, Commerce and Navigation between the United States and Japan permits each country to prefer its own citizens for executive positions on foreign-based subsidiaries. Three United States-born executives alleged that they had been discriminated against on the basis of their citizenship and natural origin in violation of Title VII when the employer, a subsidiary of a Japanese company, laid off several United States-born executives in a reduction in force while retaining all of its executives of Japanese national origin. The court held that the company's discrimination in favor of Japanese citizens temporarily employed in the United States as executives was consistent with the treaty between the United States and Japan. The court noted that the treaty was not inconsistent or prohibited by Title VII. The court also noted that Title VII prohibits discrimination based on national origin but not preferences based on citizenship. The court found that the basis of discrimination against the United States-born executives who brought the claim was not discrimination based on national origin but preference by the company for foreign executives. The court also determined that pursuant to the treaty, Japanese subsidiaries located in the United States have the right to choose citizens of Japan as executives. The court explained that the actual prejudice against the plaintiffs in the case was based on the fact that they were not executives of Matsushita, the parent company, which spearheaded the reorganization. *Fortino v. Quasar Co.*, 950 F.2d 389 (7th Cir. 1991).

Employee told to "speak American" wins national origin discrimination suit
A bank teller who was told he would have to "speak American" and bring in the business of his former countrymen before he could be promoted was awarded $389,000 in damages. Phanna K. Xieng was hired by the Peoples' National Bank of Washington in 1979 as a bank teller. Xieng received positive evaluations while employed at the bank. He often applied for advancement but was denied. On one occasion, he was told that he would be promoted only if he persuaded everyone in Seattle's Cambodian community to bank at Peoples' Bank. On another occasion, he was told that he would not be promoted because he could not "speak American." Xieng filed a

complaint under Washington's anti-discrimination law alleging that the bank had discriminated against him on the basis of his Cambodian national origin by failing to promote him. The bank argued that denial of a promotion based on a foreign accent is not discrimination if the employer has a good faith belief that the lack of communication skills would materially interfere with job performance. The Washington Court of Appeals determined that the bank's subjective standard could easily become a refuge for unlawful national original discrimination. The court noted the Xieng had filled the job for which he had been denied a promotion for eight months, indicating that he was qualified for the job. Other employees also testified that they did not believe his accent materially interfered with his work and that he was often complimented on his accuracy, attention to detail, his pleasant manner and his ability to work well with bank employees and customers. *Xieng v. Peoples' National Bank of Washington*, 821 P.2d 520 (Wash. Ct. App. 1991).

Religious Discrimination

"Best" reasonable accommodation to religious belief is not required
In another of the many recent cases involving the World Wide Church of God, the U.S. Supreme Court held that an employer is not required to provide the specific "accommodation" to religion requested by the employee, as long as it provides a "reasonable accommodation." In this case, the employee worked for a school district which provided three days of paid leave for religious observance and three days of paid leave for "necessary personal business." The plaintiff celebrated more than three church holy days each year, and he asked the school board to allow him to use his paid days for personal business leave to cover his extra religious holidays. The school board refused, but accommodated his religious needs by allowing him time off without pay. The Supreme Court said time off without pay was reasonable accommodation that satisfied the law — unless paid leave was provided for all reasons except religious ones. *Ansonia Board of Education v. Philbrook, No. 85-495.*

Bias finding against peyote user upheld
The Supreme Court upheld the religious discrimination of a Navajo Indian job applicant who was denied a job as a truck driver because he used peyote in religious ceremonies. At his job interview, the applicant informed the company that he had used peyote twice in the previous six months during religious rituals as a member of the Native American Church. Although he met other qualifications for the job, he was told he could not be hired. After the applicant filed religious discrimination claims, the company said they would hire him if he limited peyote use to twice a year, took a week's vacation after each use, and dropped his complaint. The applicant rejected the settlement offer and sued the company. The court found that the company failed in its duty to accommodate the religious beliefs of the job applicant as required by Title VII and could not try later to make up for that failure by offering to settle his discrimination claims. *Nobel-Sysco Food Service Co. v. Toledo,* 110 S.Ct. 2208 (1990).

Transfer to lower pay position is reasonable accommodation of religious belief
The 9th Circuit Court of Appeals held that an individual who was offered a temporary transfer to a lower-rated position that would not require him to work on his sabbath had no claim for religious discrimination under California state law. The employee, who belonged to the Worldwide Church of God, was prohibited by his religious beliefs from working between sundown Friday and sundown Saturday. Originally his religious beliefs did not conflict with his work schedule because he was permitted to work a Sunday to Thursday shift. When the employer began to operate on a five-day work week, a conflict developed. After unsuccessful attempts to accommodate the employee, the employer's only viable option was to transfer him to a lower-paying day shift job. The court found that under the circumstances, the accommodation was reasonable and no basis for a religious bias claim existed. *Cook v. Lindsay Olive Growers,* 911 F.2d 233 (9th Cir. 1990).

Religious proselytizing at work violates employees' civil rights

The Oregon Bureau of Labor and Industries held that an employer's religious proselytizing on the job violated an employee's civil rights. The employer and co-workers harassed the plaintiff because of his lack of a specific religious belief. The employer repeatedly criticized the plaintiff's life style, called him "a sinner who was going to hell" and said that he had to be a good Christian in order to be a good painter. The bureau found that the employer's actions were unwelcome and that his conduct created an intimidating and offensive working environment that violated the state's civil rights law. The bureau held that employers are "prohibited from creating an unwelcome and objectively offensive atmosphere at work that constitutes religious harassment of their employees." *In the Matter of James Miltebeke, Ore Bur of Lab Ind.*, No. 29-90 (February 4, 1991).

Requirement that employee make her job first priority is not religious discrimination under Title VII

The 7th Circuit Court of Appeals held that Blue Cross insurance company did not discriminate against an employee on the basis of religion when it told her during a training seminar that her job should be her first priority. The court rejected the plaintiff's argument that this "requirement" amounted to religious discrimination. The court noted that Title VII does not preclude a company from motivating its work force by asking its employees to make their jobs their top priority unless such a requirement actually conflicts with an employee's religion. Finding no actual conflict with the employee's religion, the court held that the requirement did not violate Title VII. *Beasley v. Health Care Serv. Corp.*, 940 F.2d 1085 (7th Cir. 1991).

Anti-Semitism constitutes religious discrimination

Paul Rosen was offered a position as a Drug Enforcement Administration (DEA) agent contingent upon the completion of a training program. Rosen, who is Jewish, alleged that he was wrongfully dismissed from his position as a trainee on the basis of his religion. As part of his training, Rosen was sent to Georgia. Soon after arriving, Rosen was treated poorly as a result of anti-Jewish animus. One DEA counselor asked Rosen what kind of name "Rosen" was and later stated that since she didn't like the name Rosen, she would call him "Franklin." Another instructor questioned Rosen about whether he enjoyed lox and bagels. This instructor further referred to New York as "Rosen land." Another instructor explained to a class that Jews only care about their money. Another instructor made derogatory comments about the Jewish population in Miami. Rosen's instructors also condoned the anti-Semitic behavior of his DEA classmates. One trainee even called Rosen a "half-breed Jew bastard" and yet the instructor paired Rosen with this individual for certain training exercises.

Rosen discussed his discrimination complaints with a DEA counselor who advised him against taking any formal or public action. When Rosen insisted that his claims be addressed, a DEA official insisted that the problem must be resolved internally. The following day, Rosen was told to report to remedial driving class where he was given some perfunctory instructions and then told to complete a practical driving exam. After only one lap, Rosen was ordered to exit the course. Shortly thereafter, Rosen was removed from class by DEA instructors. They informed Rosen that he was being dismissed from the training program because he was unable to satisfy the DEA's driving requirements. The DEA argued that the ability to drive was an integral DEA requirement. On the basis of this argument, the district court dismissed Rosen's action. On appeal, Rosen conceded that driving was an integral DEA requirement. He contended, however, that he was denied any meaningful opportunity to satisfy this requirement because of religious discrimination. The Court of Appeals agreed and reinstituted his lawsuit against the DEA. *Rosen v. Thornburgh*, 928 F.2d 528 (2d Cir. 1991).

Employer's refusal to hire Muslim is religious bias under Title VII
READS, Inc. a private agency that provides educational services to non-public schools under a contract with the Philadelphia School District, declined to hire Moore for a position as a third grade counselor. During Moore's job interview with READS, she was asked why she wore a head scarf. She replied that her religious belief mandated that her head be covered. The interviewer then told Moore that she could be hired for the counselor's position only if she removed her head covering while she was on the job. The employer contended that removal of the head scarf was necessary because of a Pennsylvania statute known as the "garb law" which prohibits instructional employees from wearing religious attire. The court rejected the employer's argument that Moore's head covering violated the garb law. The court held the Moore's scarf, although worn for religious purposes, would not be perceived by children as an endorsement of religion. The court found that the employer violated Title VII's prohibition against discrimination on the basis of religion. *EEOC v. READS, Inc.*, 759 F. Supp. 1150 (E.D. Pa. 1991).

Court upholds termination of agent for failing to follow orders because of religious beliefs
The 7th Circuit Court of Appeals held that the FBI has no duty to accommodate an agent who refuses to follow an order because of his personal religious and human beliefs. John Ryan, a Roman Catholic FBI agent for over 20 years, brought suit claiming the FBI failed to accommodate his religious beliefs. Ryan was responsible for domestic security and terrorism investigations. He refused an assignment to investigate a peace activist group because of his personal religious and human beliefs. He noted that the group that he was asked to investigate had consistently advocated non-violence. Although a fellow agent volunteered to change assignments with Ryan, he refused. When ordered by another agent to carry out the investigation or face discipline, Ryan again refused. Ryan was charged with insubordination and eventually terminated. The court determined that although Ryan's sincerity in his religious views was unquestioned, the FBI was justified in terminating him for refusal to carry out a lawful order and for refusal to swap assignments with another agent. *Ryan v. United States Department of Justice*, 950 F. 2d 458 (7th Cir. 1991).

Disability Discrimination

Work-related physical handicap claim under Fair Employment and Housing Act is not preempted by the exclusivity provisions of the Workers' Compensation Act
A California court of appeal held that the exclusive remedy provisions of the California Workers' Compensation Act did not bar a civil action under the Fair Employment and Housing Act (FEHA) alleging a physical handicap that arose out of a work-related injury. Relying on the California Supreme Court decision in *Shoemaker v. Meyers*, the court reasoned that discrimination against an employee on the basis of a physical handicap did not stem from risks reasonably deemed to be part of the compensation bargain between the employee and employer. The court therefore held that a civil action for discrimination is not the kind of claim preempted by the Workers' Compensation Act. *Hartman v. Mathis & Bolinger Furniture Co.*, 1 Cal. App. 4th 1338 (1991).

Obesity is not a handicap
The Supreme Court of Pennsylvania ruled that the state's anti-discrimination law did not protect an employee who lost a job because he was obese. The employee, DeMarco, was told that the job position required him to lose 37 pounds in 19 weeks. When DeMarco failed to lose the weight, he was suspended without pay. He was called back to work two months later when the city discontinued its use of a height/weight table. DeMarco filed a complaint with the Pennsylvania Human Relations Commission arguing that he was a victim of employment discrimination based

on obesity. The state law in question provides that it is unlawful employment practice to consider a non-job-related handicap or disability in making employment decisions. The court held that obesity is not a physiological disorder, cosmetic disfigurement or anatomical loss, and thus, DeMarco was not handicapped or disabled under the statute. *Civil Serv. Comm'n of the City Pittsburgh v. Pennsylvania*, 591 A.2d 281 (Pa. 1991).

Court says acrophobia does not rise to level of a handicap

A federal court of appeals has ruled that fear of heights is not a handicap that deserves protection under the Federal Rehabilitation Act of 1973. The job for which the acrophobiac had been hired (and from which he had been terminated) required him to climb stairways and ladders for routine maintenance and in emergencies. He said he could not do the work unless some kind of "accommodation" was made for his acrophobia. The court referred to this particular situation as an "isolated mismatch of employer and employee." Continuing, the court said that it would debase the high purpose of the the statute if protection available to the "truly handicapped" could be claimed by anyone whose disability was "minor" and whose relative severity of impairment is widely shared. The court drolly observed that to regard such common conditions as protected handicaps "would stand the Act on its head." *Forrisi v. Bowen, 4th Cir. 1985.*

Sexual Orientation Discrimination

Employment test questioning religious beliefs and sexual orientation violates right to privacy and Fair Employment and Housing Act

As part of an application process, a company required applicants for security officer positions to pass a psychological screening test, which was intended to eliminate emotionally unstable applicants. The test included questions concerning the applicants' religious beliefs and sexual orientation. While the company never saw the answers to the questions, it did make hiring decisions based on recommendations made by the consulting firm that graded the test. A group of applicants filed a class action suit against the company for violation of the California Constitution's right to privacy and for violation of the Fair Employment and Housing Act. The court required the company to show a nexus between the questions on the test and future job performance. The court found that the company was not able to establish that a person's religious beliefs or sexual orientation had any bearing on emotional stability or the ability of a person to perform the duties of a security officer position. *Soroka v. Dayton Hudson Corp.* 235 Cal. App. 3d 654 (1991).

Discrimination on the basis of perceived homosexuality falls within constitutionally protected interests

A federal district court in Kansas held that a refusal to hire on the basis of perceived sexual orientation constituted a violation of the individual's rights under Section 1983 of the Civil Rights Act of 1871. Jantz filed a Section 1983 action alleging a violation of his right to equal protection after he was denied a teaching position. Jantz testified that the principal did not hire him because he had "homosexual tendencies." The court, in allowing the case to proceed to the jury, found that sexual orientation is a trait that is not subject to voluntary control or change. The court compared discrimination on the basis of perceived homosexuality with racial bias, which is invidious and based on stereotypes. The court held that homosexuality, or even perceived homosexuality, fell within the sphere of constitutionally protected interests. *Jantz v. Muci*, 759 F. Supp. 1543 (D. Kan. 1991).

Discharge from the Army based on sexual orientation does not violate the First Amendment but may violate the Equal Protection Clause
The 9th Circuit Court of Appeals held that the discharge of a female homosexual Army Reserve officer did not violate her right to free speech under the First Amendment of the U.S. Constitution. The court reasoned that she was not discharged from the Army because she admitted to being homosexual. It was her homosexuality, not her speech, that gave rise to her discharge. The court determined, however, that her discharge may have violated her rights under the Equal Protection Clause of the U.S. Constitution. The standard applied by the court in determining whether the plaintiff's discharge constituted a violation of her equal protection rights was whether the reasons cited by the Army for her discharge were rationally related to the Army's permissible goals. The court concluded that the record was insufficient to supply a rational basis for the officer's discharge. *Pruitt v. Cheney*, 943 F.2d 989 (9th Cir. 1991).

Homosexual awarded $7.8 million in a wrongful discharge case
A high-ranking official conducting AIDS research was awarded $7.8 million for his termination following the discovery of a memorandum outlining rules for a "safe sex" homosexual party he was planning to have at his home. The court determined that the company violated its own procedures for disciplinary action when it failed to provide the employee an opportunity to correct the inappropriate behavior involved in having sexually explicit materials on the job. The court also found that the employee had been fired "solely because he is a sexually active homosexual." The court noted that the company engaged in extensive fabrications regarding the employee's job performance and abilities to justify his termination. *Collins v. Shell Oil Co.*, 56 Fair Empl. Prac. Cas. 440 (1991).

AIDS Discrimination

Termination of HIV-positive firefighter does not constitute discrimination
The 11th Circuit Court of Appeals held that the termination of an HIV-positive firefighter who refused to accept light duty work did not constitute unlawful handicap discrimination or a violation of the firefighter's due process or equal protection rights. The court concluded that the firefighter's reassignment to light duty was based on the department's concern that continued rescue operations might result in the transmission of the HIV virus. The court further held that the termination, rather than being based on discrimination against a person because he is HIV-positive, resulted from the employee's insubordination in refusing to perform the light duty work. *Severino v. North For Myers Fire Control Dist.*, 935 F.2d 1179 (11th Cir. 1991).

Court allows hospital to suspend surgeon with AIDS
A New Jersey state court held that a hospital was justified in terminating the surgical privileges of a doctor with the AIDS virus. In his suit under New Jersey's discrimination laws, the doctor alleged that he suffered both emotional and financial harm from revocation of his surgical privileges as well as from the breach of confidentiality of his diagnosis. Within hours of being diagnosed with the AIDS virus, the doctor received numerous phone calls from colleagues and patients concerned for his welfare. Although the court ruled that the doctor was protected by the New Jersey law against discrimination, it found that the hospital demonstrated that the termination of surgical privileges was justified in light of the hospital's need to protect patients from harm. The court ruled, however, that the hospital breached its duty of confidentiality by failing to ensure that the doctor's AIDS diagnosis would not become a matter of public knowledge. The hospital was required to pay damages for the breach of the doctor's confidentiality. *Behringer v. Medical Ctr. at Princeton*, 592 A.2d 1251 (N.J. Super. 1991).

Local ordinance banning AIDS discrimination is not preempted by Fair Employment and Housing Act
Contra Costa county in California passed an ordinance that prohibits discrimination against persons with AIDS or AIDS-related conditions, persons carrying HIV antibodies, persons perceived as having AIDS-associated conditions, persons believed to be at risk of contracting AIDS, and persons believed to associate with persons who have AIDS. The stated purpose of the ordinance was to combat the AIDS epidemic by promoting HIV testing. Local citizens brought suit against the county, attempting to declare that the ordinance was preempted by the Fair Employment and Housing Act (FEHA). However, a California court of appeal held that since the ordinance's purpose was to combat the AIDS epidemic by promoting HIV testing, it was not preempted by the FEHA, the primary purpose of which is to prohibit employment discrimination. *Citizens for Uniform Laws v. County of Contra Costa*, 233 Cal. App. 3d 1468 (1991).

Immigration Discrimination

Ignorance of immigration law is no excuse for discrimination
In the first full trial based on a complaint of discrimination against a U.S. citizen under the Immigration Reform and Control Act of 1986 (IRCA), an administrative law judge (ALJ) ruled that a company's "good faith efforts" to comply with the law did not excuse its refusal to hire an applicant who could not produce a green card. The ALJ rejected the company's claim that it failed to hire the applicant because of its confusion over the documentation requirements of IRCA. The ALJ ordered the company to pay civil fines and lost pay to the applicant totaling nearly $10,000. The plaintiff, a U.S. citizen born in Puerto Rico, applied for an unskilled position as a packer. When asked to produce documentation proving her authorization to work in the United States, she offered a Social Security card, a voter registration card and a birth certificate. The company official interviewing the plaintiff asked for a green card, which is given to permanent resident aliens but not U.S. citizens. Plaintiff insisted that she was a U.S. citizen and that she did not have to produce a green card. The company official claimed he could not hire her without seeing a green card. In its defense, the company pleaded ignorance of all IRCA's complicated requirements. By trying to comply with the law, which requires employers to check the identity and work authorization of all new hires, the company said it inadvertently violated the law's discrimination provision. That provision prohibits discrimination against authorized workers on the grounds of their national origin or citizenship status. *U.S. v. Marcel Watch Corp.*, OCAHO No. 8920085 (March 26, 1990).

Veteran's Status Discrimination

Employer may not reject reservist's request for leave based on length of proposed absence
In a unanimous opinion, the U.S. Supreme Court ruled that the Veteran's Reemployment Rights Act (VRRA) did not place a time limit on the protections it provides to reservists who request leave of absence for military service. The court found that a veteran of the Alabama National Guard was entitled to reemployment rights at a hospital after a three-year leave. The hospital had denied the reservist's request on the ground that the request was unreasonable. The court held that VRRA does not place any time limit on the amount of leave an employee may take. The court noted that Congress deliberately did not include qualifications or limitations on the reemployment rights of veterans and found that the VRRA grants enlistees at least four years of reemployment protection, with the possibility of an extension to five years or more. *King v. St. Vincent's Hosp.*, 112 S. Ct. 570 (1991).

Workers' Compensation Discrimination

Public policy discharge claims must be based on statute or the Constitution
In a major new development, the California Supreme Court ruled that claims of discharge in violation of public policy must be based upon a statutory or constitutional provision. The plaintiff claimed that he had been constructively discharged for supporting a co-worker's claim of sexual harassment and refusing to alter testimony provided to the Department of Fair Employment and Housing (DFEH). The court determined that California Government Code Section 12975, which makes it a misdemeanor to willfully interfere with a DFEH investigation, supported the plaintiff's public policy claim. The court specifically rejected an argument that judges should be able to declare public policy in the absence of a statute or constitutionally provision. Upholding a $1.34 million jury verdict, the court also determined that public policy wrongful discharge claims are not preempted by the exclusive remedy provisions of the Workers' Compensation Act. *Gantt v. Sentry Ins. Co.*, 1 Cal. 4th 1083 (1992).

Workers' compensation preemption does not bar whistleblower claim
A California court of appeal held that an employee's claim of wrongful discharge in violation of public policy based on a state law which protects whistleblowers was not preempted by the Workers' Compensation Act. Jack Shoemaker, an investigator for the Department of Health Services, had been assigned to investigate alleged wrongdoing within his department. After he began investigating, his superiors ordered him to curtail his inquiries and not to share his findings with law enforcement agencies. Following complaints to the department in an unrelated matter, Shoemaker's supervisors demanded written answers and explanations from him. When he asserted his right to counsel, Shoemaker was fired for insubordination. He then filed a suit for wrongful termination in violation of public policy and infliction of emotional distress. The court upheld Shoemaker's wrongful discharge claim based on the state's whistleblower statute, holding that it was intended to provide a remedy in addition to that granted under the workers' compensation statute. *Shoemaker v. Myers*, 2 Cal. App. 4th 1407 (1992).

Arbitration and Discrimination Laws

Supreme Court says age discrimination claim can be subject to arbitration
The U.S. Supreme Court determined that an employee's age discrimination claim was subject to binding arbitration. When the plaintiff was hired in 1981, he was required to register as a securities representative with the New York Stock Exchange. The registration application mandated arbitration for any claim arising out of the employment relationship. When the plaintiff was discharged in 1987, he filed an age discrimination suit in federal court. The company, in turn, filed a motion to compel arbitration. The Supreme Court held that the Age Discrimination in Employment Act (ADEA) does not prohibit age discrimination claims from being resolved through arbitration rather than under the ADEA in this factual circumstance. The court further found that arbitration of age discrimination claims is consistent with the Equal Employment Opportunity Commission's enforcement responsibilities and does not hinder the ADEA's purpose. *Gilmer v. Interstate/Johnson Lane Corp.*, 111 S. Ct. 1647 (1991).

Employee bound to arbitrate Title VII claim under employment application provision
The 9th Circuit Court of Appeals recently held that an employee who filled out an employment application that contained an arbitration clause was obligated to arbitrate her Title VII claim alleging sexual harassment and gender discrimination. Despite having signed the application, the plaintiff brought a Title VII action in federal court against her employer. She contended that the arbitration agreement in the employment application was a contract of adhesion and that Title VII claims are not subject to arbitration. Relying on the 1991 Supreme Court decision in *Gilmer v.*

Interstate/Johnson Lane Corp., the 9th Circuit determined that the plaintiff failed to show that Congress intended to prohibit arbitration of Title VII suits. The court noted that the agreement between the plaintiff and her employer was privately negotiated, like the agreement in *Gilmer*, and that the Age Discrimination in Employment Act and Title VII are similar in their aims and substantive provisions. The 9th Circuit declined to rule on the issue of whether the application was a contract of adhesion, finding that this was a factual issue best left to the district court on remand. *Mago v. Shearson Lehman Hutton, Inc.*, 956 F.2d 932 (9th Cir. 1992).

Federal Arbitration Act does not bar arbitration of age discrimination and wrongful discharge claims by worker engaged in interstate/foreign commerce

The 3rd Circuit Court of Appeals (Philadelphia) held that age discrimination and wrongful discharge claims filed by a former partner at an accounting firm were subject to compulsory arbitration. George Dancu was hired by the accounting firm in 1980 and in 1985 joined the partnership as a principal. The partnership agreement contained an arbitration clause requiring arbitration of any claims or controversies arising out of the agreement. In 1989, the company asked Dancu to withdraw from the partnership. He left and later filed an age discrimination claim with the Equal Employment Opportunity Commission (EEOC). The EEOC declined to review the merits of Dancu's case, reasoning that he was a partner of the firm and thus not covered by the ADEA. Dancu then filed a federal suit alleging ADEA violations and wrongful discharge. The company argued that the exclusive forum for Dancu's claim was arbitration and that the arbitration exclusions under the Federal Arbitration Act (FAA) for workers engaged in foreign or interstate commerce was not applicable. The court held that the FAA exclusion applied only to workers engaged in the transportation industry. Because Dancu was not involved in interstate transportation, the arbitration agreement was held valid and enforceable. *Dancu v. Coopers & Lybrand*, 778 F. Supp. 832 (E.D. Pa. 1991).

Chapter 15
Exhibits and Publications

Exhibits

1. Federal equal employment poster

2. Equal employment opportunity policy (example)

3. State fair employment poster

4. Policy on employment of physically and mentally handicapped, disabled veterans and Vietnam era veterans (example)

5. Suggested family leave poster (California employers of 50 or more employees only)

6. EEOC guidelines on discrimination because of sex

Publications

1. Discrimination is Against the Law

2. Guide to Respondents

3. Guide to Complainants

4. Employment Discrimination Based on Mental or Physical Disability

5. Sexual Harassment

6. Pregnancy Discrimination Fact Sheet

7. Your Right to Freedom from Violence

Note: All the above publications can be obtained by writing to:

Department of Fair Employment and Housing
2014 "T" Street, Suite 210
Sacramento, CA 95814-2919

Exhibit 1

EQUAL EMPLOYMENT OPPORTUNITY IS THE LAW

Private Employment, State and Local Governments, Educational Institutions

Race, Color, Religion, Sex, National Origin:
Title VII of the Civil Rights Act of 1964, as amended, prohibits discrimination in hiring, promotion, discharge, pay, fringe benefits, and other aspects of employment, on the basis of race, color, religion, sex or national origin.

The law covers applicants to and employees of most private employers, state and local governments and public or private educational institutions. Employment agencies, labor unions and apprenticeship programs also are covered.

Age:
The Age Discrimination in Employment Act of 1967, as amended, prohibits age discrimination and protects applicants and employees 40 years of age or older from discrimination on account of age in hiring, promotion, discharge, compensation, terms, conditions, or privileges of employment. the law covers applicants to and employees of most private employers, state and local governments, educational institutions, employment agencies and labor organizations.

Sex (Wages):
In addition to sex discrimination prohibited by Title VII of the Civil Rights Act (see above), the Equal Pay Act of 1963, as amended, prohibits sex discrimination in payment of wages to women and men performing substantially equal work in the same establishment. The law covers applicants to and employees of most private employers, state and local governments and educational institutions. Labor organizations cannot cause employers to violate the law. Many employers not covered by Title VII, because of size, are covered by the Equal Pay Act.

Disability:
The Americans with Disabilities Act of 1990, as amended, prohibits discrimination on the basis of disability, and protects qualified applicants and employees with disabilities from discrimination in hiring, promotion, discharge, pay, job training, fringe benefits, and other aspects of employment. The law also requires that covered entities provide qualified applicants and employees with disabilities with reasonable accommodations that do not impose undue hardship. The law covers applicants to and employees of most private employers, state and local governments, educational institutions, employment agencies and labor organizations.

If you believe that you have been discriminated against under any of the above laws, you immediately should contact:

The U.S. Equal Employment Opportunity Commission (EEOC)
1801 L Street, N.W.
Washington, D.C. 20507

or an EEOC field office by calling toll free 800-669-EEOC. For individuals with hearing impairments, EEOC's toll free TDD number is 800-800-3302.

Employers Holding Federal Contracts or Subcontracts

Race, Color, Religion, Sex, National Origin:
Executive Order 11246, as amended, prohibits job discrimination on the basis of race, color, religion, sex or national origin, and requires affirmative action to ensure equality of opportunity in all aspects of employment.

Individuals with Handicaps:
Section 503 of the Rehabilitation Act of 1973, as amended, prohibits job discrimination because of handicap and requires affirmative action to employ and advance in employment qualified individuals with handicaps who, with reasonable accommodation, can perform the essential functions of a job.

Vietnam Era and Special Disabled Veterans:
38 U.S.C. 4212 of the Vietnam Era Veterans Readjustment Assistance Act of 1974 prohibits job discrimination and requires affirmative action to employ and advance in employment qualified Vietnam era veterans and qualified special disabled veterans.

Applicants to and employees of companies with a Federal government contract or subcontract are protected under the authorities above. Any person who believes a contractor has violated its nondiscrimination or affirmative action obligations under Executive Order 11246, as amended, Section 503 of the Rehabilitation Act or 38 U.S.C. 4212 of the Vietnam Era Veterans Readjustment Assistance Act should contact immediately:

The Office of Federal Contract Compliance Programs (OFCCP)
Employment Standards Administration
U.S. Department of Labor
200 Constitution Avenue, N.W.
Washington, D.C. 20210
(202) 523-9368

or an OFCCP regional or district office, listed in most telephone directories under U.S. Government, Department of Labor.

Programs or Activities Receiving Federal Financial Assistance

Race, Color, National Origin, Sex:
In addition to the protection of Title VII of the Civil Rights Act of 1964, Title VI of the Civil Rights Act prohibits discrimination on the basis of race, color or national origin in programs or activities receiving Federal financial assistance. Employment discrimination is covered by Title VI if the primary objective of the financial assistance is provision of employment, or where employment discrimination causes or may cause discrimination in providing services under such programs. Title IX of the Education Amendments of 1972 prohibits employment discrimination on the basis of sex in educational programs or activities which receive Federal assistance.

If you believe you have been discriminated against in a program of any institution which receives Federal assistance, you should contact immediately the Federal agency providing such assistance.

Individuals with Handicaps:
Section 504 of the Rehabilitation Act of 1973, as amended, prohibits employment discrimination on the basis of handicap in any program or activity which receives Federal financial assistance. Discrimination is prohibited in all aspects of employment against handicapped persons who, with reasonable accommodation, can perform the essential functions of a job.

Exhibit 2

Example

Equal Employment Opportunity Policy

The *(name of your company)* Company has been and is fully committed to equal employment opportunity, both in principle and as a matter of corporated policy. Our commitment to a policy of non-discrimination in all aspects of employment has resulted in considerable progress being made to date. Much more needs to be done, however.

(Name of your company)'s policies on equal employment opportunity are consistent with objectives set forth by federal statutes and presidential executive orders. Our employment policies and practices require that we provide equal opportunity to all applicants and employees without regard to race, color, religion, sex or national origin and in full accordance with state and national policies pertaining to age. We shall take such affirmative action as is necessary to ensure implementation of these policies and practices as they apply to recruitment, hiring, placement, training, advancement, conditions and privileges of employment, compensation, transfer, termination and, in fact, all employment practices.

All levels of Company management are accountable for adherence to this policy and responsible for its dissemination to all employees under their supervision.

Corporate responsibility for coordinating policy implementation is assigned to _____, Director-Employment Opportunity Program. The Executive Committee will periodically review EEO progress measured against stated objectives.

_____   _____
Date   Chairman and
                                                     Chief Executive Officer

Exhibit 3

Government Code Section 12950(a) Requires All Employers to Post This Document

State of California

Department of Fair Employment and Housing

HARASSMENT OR DISCRIMINATION IN EMPLOYMENT

Because of

- Sex   - Race   - Color   - Ancestry   - Religious Creed
- National Origin   - Physical Disability (Including HIV and AIDS)
- Mental Disability   - Medical Condition (Cancer)   - Age
- Marital Status   - Denial of Family Care Leave

IS PROHIBITED BY LAW

The California Fair Employment and Housing Act
(Part 2.8 (commencing with Section 12900) of Div. 3 of Title 2 of the Government Code)

- prohibits harassment of employees or applicants and requires employers to take all reasonable steps to prevent harassment.
- requires that all employers provide information to each of their employees on the nature, illegality and legal remedies which apply to sexual harassment. Employers may either develop their own publication, which must meet standards as set forth in California Government Code Section 12950, or use a brochure which may be obtained from the Department of Fair Employment and Housing.
- requires employers to reasonably accommodate physically or mentally disabled employees or job applicants in order to enable them to perform the essential functions of a job.
- permits job applicants to file complaints with the Department of Fair Employment and Housing (DFEH) against an employer, employment agency, or labor union which fails to grant equal employment as required by law.
- requires employers not to discriminate against any job applicant or worker in hiring, promotions, assignments, or discharge. On-the-job segregation is also prohibited, and employers may file complaints against workers who refuse to cooperate in compliance.
- requires employers, employment agencies, and unions to preserve applications, personnel and employment referral records for a minimum of two years.
- requires employers to provide leaves of up to four months to employees disabled because of pregnancy, maternity, or childbirth.
- requires employers of 50 or more persons to allow employees to take up to four months leave in any two year period for the adoption or birth of a child or the care of an ill or injured spouse, parent or child.
- requires employment agencies to serve all applicants equally; to refuse discriminatory job orders; to refrain from prohibited pre-hiring inquiries or help-wanted advertising.
- requires unions not to discriminate in member admissions or dispatching to jobs.
- forbids any person to interfere with efforts to comply with the act. Authorizes the DFEH to work affirmatively with cooperating employers to review hiring and recruiting practices in order to expand equal opportunity.

REMEDIES TO INDIVIDUALS, OR PENALTIES FOR VIOLATION MAY INCLUDE:
hiring, back pay, promotion, reinstatement, damages for emotional distress, cease-and-desist order, or a fine of up to $50,000.

JOB APPLICANTS AND EMPLOYEES: If you believe you have
experienced discrimination, DFEH will investigate without cost to you.

For information contact the nearest office of the Department of Fair Employment and Housing:

BAKERSFIELD
1001 Tower Way, #250
Bakersfield, CA 93309-1586
(805) 395-2728

FRESNO
1900 Mariposa Mall, #130
Fresno, CA 93721-2504
(209) 445-5373

LOS ANGELES
322 West First Street, #2126
Los Angeles, CA 90012-3112
(213) 897-1997

OAKLAND
1330 Broadway, #1326
Oakland, CA 94612-2512
(510) 464-4095

SACRAMENTO
2000 "O" Street, #120
Sacramento, CA 95814-5212
(916) 445-9918

SAN BERNARDINO
1845 S. Business Ctr. Dr., #127
San Bernardino, CA 92408-3426
(714) 383-4711

SAN DIEGO
110 West "C" Street, #1702
San Diego, CA 92010-3901
(619) 237-7405

SAN FRANCISCO
30 Van Ness Avenue, #3000
San Francisco, CA 94102-6073
(415) 557-2005

SAN JOSE
111 North Market Street, #810
San Jose, CA 95113-1102
(408) 277-1264

SANTA ANA
28 Civic Center Plaza, #538
Santa Ana, CA 92701-4010
(714) 558-4159

VENTURA
5720 Ralston Street, #302
Ventura, CA 93303-6081
(805) 654-4512

TDD NUMBERS
Los Angeles (213) 897-2840
Sacramento (916) 324-1678

This notice must be conspicuously posted in hiring offices, on employee bulletin boards, in employment agency
waiting rooms, union halls, etc. For a copy contact the nearest DFEH office.

DFEH 162 (Rev. 12/92)

Exhibit 4

Example

Policy on Employment
of Persons with Physical and Mental Disabilities,
Disabled Veterans and Vietnam Era Veterans

The policy of the *(name of your company)* Company is to treat all applicants and employees fairly and without regard to (1) any disability they may have which is unrelated to job qualifications, or (2) the fact that they are veterans of the Vietnam Era. Accordingly, we have utilized and will continue to utilize positive practices in recruiting, employing and advancing qualified veterans and persons who are disabled.

All officers, managers and supervisors share in the responsibility for implementing this policy and for taking realistic affirmative action to seek, employ, advance and otherwise treat qualified persons without discrimination based on their disability or veteran status in all employment practices. These include, but are not limited to, recruitment, advertising, upgrading, demotion, transfer, termination, layoff, selection for training, rates of pay and other forms of compensation.

The Company will maintain at each facility an affirmative action program for employment of disabled persons and veterans. Each program will be audited periodically, updated annually, made available for applicant and employee inspection, and will assure compliance with regulations covering Section 402 of the Viet Nam Era Veterans Readjustment Assistance Act of 1974. In accordance with these actions and our Company policy, employees and applicants will be protected from any type of coercion, intimidation, interference or discrimination for filing a complaint or assisting in an investigation of such a complaint.

The Director-Employment Opportunity Programs is responsible for providing corporate guidance in affirmative action program development, coordination of implementation procedures and periodic auditing of employment practices and general program effectiveness.

_____   _____
Date   Chairman and
                                                                      Chief Executive Officer

Exhibit 5

Example

Family Care Leave

The following notice suggested for posting by the Fair Employment and Housing Commission contains only the minimum requirements of the law. Covered employers may develop their own notice or use this text, unless it does not accurately reflect their company policy.

Family Care Leave

Under the California Family Rights Act of 1991, if you have more than one year of continuous service with us and are eligible for at least one employee benefit, you have a right to an unpaid family care leave of up to four months in a 24-month period for the birth or adoption of your child or for the serious health condition of your child, parent or spouse. Granting this leave contains a guarantee of reinstatement to the same or to a comparable position at the end of the leave, subject to any defense allowed under the law. If possible, you must provide at least 30 calendar days written advance notice for foreseeable events (such as the expected birth of a child or planned medical treatment of a family member). For events which are unforeseeable 30 days in advance, we need you to notify us, preferably as soon as you learn of the need for the leave, but in any event no later than five working days form learning of the need for the leave.

Failure to comply with these notice rules is grounds for, and may result in, denial or deferral of the requested leave until you comply with this notice policy.

We may require certification from the health care provider of your child, parent or spouse who has a serious health condition before allowing you a leave to take care of that family member.

Any family care leave taken must be for at least two weeks, except that you may request a shorter leave (of anywhere from one day to two weeks) on any two occasions during a 24-month period or for planned medical treatments, such as chemotherapy, of a family member. If you are taking a leave for the birth or adoption of a child, you must initiate the leave within one year of the birth or adoption. If you are pregnant, you have certain rights to take a pregnancy disability leave; you should check regarding your individual situation. There are certain exceptions to eligibility for a family care leave and we are legally permitted to deny a request for leave under certain conditions. Also, taking a family care leave may impact certain of your benefits and your seniority date.

If you want more information regarding your eligibility for a leave and/or the impact of the leave on your seniority and benefits, please contact
_____.

Exhibit 6

EEOC Guidelines on Discrimination Because of Sex

Sex as a bona fide occupational qualification

A. The Commission believes that the bona fide occupational qualification exception as to sex should be interpreted narrowly. Labels — "men's jobs" and "women's jobs" — tend to deny employment opportunities unnecessarily to one sex or the other.

1. The Commission will find that the following situations do not warrant the application of a bona fide occupational qualification exception:

    a. The refusal to hire a woman because of her sex based on assumptions of the comparative employment characteristics of women in general. For example, the assumption that the turnover rate among women is higher than among men.

    b. The refusal to hire an individual based on stereotyped characterizations of the sexes. Such stereotypes include, for example, that men are less capable of assembling intricate equipment; that women are less capable of aggressive salesmanship. The principle of non-discrimination requires that individuals be considered on the basis of individual capacities and not on the basis of any characteristics generally attributed to the group.

    c. The refusal to hire an individual because of the preferences of co-workers, the employer, clients or customers except as covered specifically in subparagraph 2 of this paragraph.

2. Where it is necessary for the purpose of authenticity or genuineness, the Commission will consider sex to be a bona fide occupational qualification, e.g., an actor or actress.

Separate lines of progression and seniority systems

A. It is an unlawful employment practice to classify a job as "male" or "female" or to maintain separate lines of progression or separate seniority lists based on sex where this would adversely affect any employee, unless sex is a bona fide occupational qualification for that job. Accordingly, employment practices are unlawful which arbitrarily classify jobs so that:

1. A female is prohibited from applying for a job labeled "male," or for a job in a "male line of progression" and vice versa.

2. A male scheduled for layoff is prohibited from displacing a less senior female on a "female" seniority list, and vice versa.

B. A seniority system or line of progression which distinguishes between "light" and "heavy" jobs constitutes an unlawful employment practice if it operates as a disguised form of classification by sex, or creates unreasonable obstacles to the advancement by members of either sex into jobs which members of that sex would reasonably be expected to perform.

Discrimination against married women

A. The Commission has determined that an employer's rule which forbids or restricts the employment of married women and which is not applicable to married men is a discrimination based on sex prohibited by Title VII of the Civil Rights Act. It does not seem to us relevant that the rule is not directed against all females, but only against married females, for so long as sex is a factor in the application of the rule, such application involves a discrimination based on sex.

B. It may be that under certain circumstances, such a rule could be justified within the meaning of Section 703(e)(1) of Title VII. We express no opinion on this question at this time except to point out that sex as a bona fide occupational qualification must be justified in terms of the peculiar requirements of the particular job and not on the basis of a general principle such as the desirability of spreading work.

Job opportunities — advertising

It is a violation of Title VII for a help-wanted advertisement to indicate a preference, limitation, specification or discrimination based on sex unless sex is a bona fide occupational qualification for the particular job involved. The placement of an advertisement in columns classified by publishers on the basis of sex, such as columns headed "male" or "female," will be considered an expression of a preference, limitation, specification or discrimination based on sex.

Pre-employment inquiries as to sex

A pre-employment inquiry may ask "Male_____, Female_____"; or "Mr., Mrs., Ms. or Miss," provided that the inquiry is made in good faith for a non-discriminatory purpose. Any pre-employment inquiry in connection with prospective employment which expresses directly or indirectly any limitation, specification or discrimination as to sex shall be unlawful unless based upon a bona fide occupational qualification.

Relationship of Title VII to the Equal Pay Act

A. The employee coverage of the prohibitions against discrimination based on sex contained in Title VII is co-extensive with that of the other prohibitions contained in Title VII and is not limited by Section 703(h) to those employees covered by the Fair Labor Standards Act.

B. By virtue of Section 703(h), a defense based on the Equal Pay Act may be raised in a proceeding under Title VII.

C. Where such a defense is raised, the Commission will give appropriate consideration to the interpretations of the Administrator, Wage and Hour Division, Department of Labor, but will not be bound thereby.

Fringe benefits

A. "Fringe benefits" as used herein includes medical, hospital, accident, life insurance and retirement benefits; profit sharing and bonus plans; and other terms, conditions and privileges of employment.

B.   It shall be an unlawful employment practice for an employer to discriminate between men and women with regard to fringe benefits.

C.   Where an employer conditions benefits available to employees and their spouses and families on whether the employee is the "head of the household" or "principal wage earner" in the family unit, the benefits tend to be available only to male employees and their families. Due to the fact that such conditioning discriminatorily affects the rights of women employees, and that "head of household" or "principal wage earner" status bears no relationship to job performance, benefits which are so conditioned will be found a *prima facie* violation of the prohibitions against sex discrimination contained in the act.

D.   It shall be an unlawful employment practice for an employer to make available benefits for the wives and families of male employees where the same benefits are not made available for the husbands and families of female employees; or to make available benefits for the wives of male employees which are not made available for female employees; or to make available benefits to the husbands of female employees which are not made available for male employees. An example of such an unlawful employment practice is a situation in which wives of male employees receive maternity benefits while female employees receive no such benefits.

E.   It shall not be a defense under Title VII to a charge of sex discrimination in benefits that the cost of such benefits is greater with respect to one sex than the other.

F.   It shall be an unlawful employment practice for an employer to have a pension or retirement plan which establishes different optional or compulsory retirement ages based on sex, or which differentiates in benefits on the basis of sex.

Employment policies relating to pregnancy and childbirth

A.   A written or unwritten employment policy or practice which excludes from employment applicants or employees because of pregnancy is a *prima facie* violation of Title VII.

B.   Disabilities caused or contributed to by pregnancy, miscarriage, abortion, childbirth and recovery therefrom are, for all job-related purposes, temporary disabilities and should be treated as such under any health or temporary disability insurance or sick leave plan available in connection with employment. Written and unwritten employment policies and practices involving matters such as the commencement and duration of leave, the availability of extensions, the accrual of seniority and other benefits and privileges, reinstatement, and payment under any health or temporary disability insurance or sick leave plan, formal or informal, shall be applied to disability due to pregnancy or childbirth on the same terms and conditions as they are applied to other temporary disabilities.

C.   Where the termination of an employee who is temporarily disabled is caused by an employment policy under which insufficient or no leave is available, such a termination violates the act if it has a disparate impact on employees of one sex and is not justified by business necessity.

Chapter 16
Agencies and Contacts for Information

Equal Employment Opportunity Commission (EEOC)
901 Market Street, Suite 500
San Francisco, CA 94103
(415) 744-6500

Department of Fair Employment and Housing
2014 "T" Street, Suite 210
Sacramento, CA 95814-2919
(916) 739-4616

Fair Employment and Housing Commission
1390 Market Street, Suite 410
San Francisco, CA 94102
(415) 557-2325

California Chamber of Commerce
P.O. Box 1736
Sacramento, CA 95812-1736
(916) 444-6670

Index

California Chamber of Commerce
BUSINESS SURVIVAL GUIDES

Survival Guides to the Labor Law Jungle

■ **California Labor Law Digest**

Easy to use, describes complex state and federal labor laws in lay terms. Organized to help the reader find topics quickly. Describes the law and how to comply. Includes special sections on how to calculate overtime and vacation pay, exempt vs. non-exempt employees, alcohol and drug abuse, employee benefit plans and military return rights. Revised annually to reflect new laws, expanded advice on current problem areas of law.

■ **EEO Discrimination in Employment**

Clearly explains complex equal employment opportunity discrimination laws and how to avoid discrimination problems. Contains sample employment application and policies. Chapters on Americans with Disabilities Act, sexual harassment, AIDS, pregnancy, employees with disabilities, and statistics you must keep. Discrimination dos and don'ts.

Employee Handbook

■ **Employee Handbook: How to Write One for Your Company**

The California Chamber's recently developed guide explains why you should have a personnel policy. It then gives step-by-step instructions for writing a personnel policy for your business. The guide contains sample policies and a sample handbook, which will enable any company to develop its own written employee handbook with a minimum of time and confusion. Protect your business and avoid unnecessary costly litigation by having your personnel policy in writing.

■ **Employee Handbook Software**

Makes writing your employee handbook even easier. Select or modify the policies you need, push a button and print your customized, formatted employee handbook. Saves word processing time and makes future updates easy. *Bilingual* software lets you select pre-written policies in English, then print your handbook in both Spanish and English. Purchase of *Employee Handbook* is required so that you will have the legal reasoning and requirements behind the policies you select. (IBM PC-AT compatible — *not* XT; 3.5" or 5.25" diskette.)

■ **Employee Handbook Training Videos**

Two-tape set helps you introduce your employee handbook. One video shows managers how to introduce the employee handbook to workers to ensure the least resistance and best results. The second video explains the purpose and benefits of your employee handbook to employees. The English and Spanish version of the employee video are on the same tape.

ADA Compliance Kit

■ **ADA: 10 Steps to Compliance**

Easy-to-use, comprehensive guide shows you how to determine exactly what you need to do to comply with the Americans with Disabilities Act (ADA), the most complex, sweeping labor law in years. Includes examples, worksheets, checklists, sample forms. Explains key terms, such as "essential functions," "rea-sonable accommodation," "direct threat," "undue hardship."

■ **ADA Software**

Job descriptions identifying "essential job functions" are the best way to document your compliance with the ADA. This quality "graphical interface software" helps you write customized ADA-ready job descriptions quickly. Select from 1,300 sample complete job descriptions, then modify, combine, cut 'n' paste or add your own words.

■ **ADA Video Set**

Videos save you time and give you the assurance that everyone who oversees or interviews other people will have the knowledge to keep your company out of trouble. One video gives your managers an overview of the ADA. The other shows a manager in action trying to prepare for an interview.

The Recycling Kit for Business

■ **Recycling Handbook for Business**

Save time and confusion by starting your recycling and waste reduction program in an organized manner. The business person's guide to a cost-efficient waste reduction program. Follow the logical steps, fill out worksheets and refer to checklists. Model plans to follow for six industries — retail, wholesale, offices, manufacturers, construction and restaurants.

■ **Employee Training Video**

Help build employee enthusiasm, pride and support in every aspect of your business with "Reduce...Reuse...Recycle...The Bottom Line." This video demonstrates many techniques and concepts that small and large companies already are using and which can be adapted readily by smaller and medium-sized firms in nearly every industry. It's an ideal way to launch your recycling program.

■ **Recycling Organizer**

The *Recycling Organizer* will save you time, keep your program on track and document your waste reduction. It's a guide for the recycling novice and has easy-to-follow steps to document your recycling program. This well-planned system is a place to file your initial waste assessment, your waste reduction plan, vendor contracts and records of diverted waste. When the regulator calls, the *Organizer* is your proof that you're concerned and are already doing much to reduce solid waste.

Cal/OSHA Kit

■ **Cal/OSHA Handbook**

The *Cal/OSHA Handbook* is written for businesspeople who aren't safety experts. It tells how to find the regulations which apply to your firm. Then it gives step-by-step instructions to satisfy the regulations that apply to every firm, and also the most costly rules that apply to most industries. Know what to do when the inspector arrives, your rights, when to appeal a citation and how to do it.

■ **SB 198 Handbook**

SB 198 requires every employer to have a formal, written injury and illness prevention program. The *Handbook* was written with the premise that most employers can comply on a do-it-yourself basis. It contains legal requirements, sample plans to follow for various industries, fill-in-the-blank forms and step-by-step instructions.

■ **Hazard Communication Handbook**

Hazard communication standards apply to every firm where employees may be exposed to chemicals. If you receive an MSDS (Material Safety Data Sheet) from a supplier then you need a hazard communication program. The *Hazard Communication Handbook* gives clear guidelines on how to write your own program.

■ **Cal/OSHA Organizer**

The *Organizer* is a guide for the safety novice to comply with Cal/OSHA. Follow the steps in the *Organizer*. It refers to sections in the three companion handbooks where you'll get clear, detailed instructions on what you need to do, and cookbook-like steps on how to do it. Then file your safety programs and records right in the *Organizer.*

■ **SB 198 Software**

The California Chamber's *SB 198 Software* is made to be used with our *SB 198 Handbook.* It helps you write your SB 198 program and much more. The software is an ongoing recordkeeping system that will save you tremendous amounts of time. Organizes your records of training, accidents and injuries. Allows you to "batch" in updates instead of making single, time-consuming entries. Reminds you to do inspections and training. (IBM PC-AT compatible — *not* XT; 3.5" or 5.25" diskette.)

■ **SB 198 Video Safety Set**

Videos make it easy for you to train employees and managers about your injury/illness prevention program. One video lets your employees know safety is their responsibility and very important to your company. It offers commonsense instruction about safe work procedures. The second video tells your supervisors and managers how other companies are making their safety programs work and emphasizes the importance of training, hazard identification and inspections. Employee training video also available in Spanish.

Environmental Library

■ **California Environmental Compliance Handbook**

Overall guide to California's unique and far-reaching environmental programs. Gives an overview of more than 20 of the most significant environmental programs, along with the essential steps to take for compliance. Provides a thumbnail sketch of numerous additional, but less frequently encountered federal, state and local regulations that have an impact on business and local public facilities. The guide is your checklist and roadmap through California's maze of environmental regulations.

■ **Proposition 65 Compliance**

This complex and confusing initiative imposes many requirements on businesses that use or distribute chemicals and products which contain ingredients known to the state to cause cancer or reproductive toxicity. More than 300 substances are subject to the law. The proposition provides for government prosecutions, as well as "bounty hunter" rewards for informants and citizen plaintiffs. The handbook is your best explanation of the law and how to comply.

■ **Community Right-to-Know**

For firms that store, sell or use any of thousands of common materials or chemicals that are regulated by local governments under the concept of community right-to-know. Step-by-step instructions explain how to: determine if your firm handles hazardous materials, qualify for business plan exemptions, immediately report releases and how to develop a business plan in five easy steps.

■ **Hazardous Waste Management**

For any business that uses or handles chemicals. Tells how to determine if your business generates hazardous waste, what permits are needed, how to manage hazardous waste, how to ship and dispose of waste and how to determine where permits can be required for certain hazardous waste activities. This handbook explains how to comply with this complicated and stringently enforced area of environmental law.

■ **Environmental Organizer**

This compliance tool organizes your many environmental compliance programs and recordkeeping to demonstrate compliance. Divider sections in the *Organizer* provide thumbnail descriptions of each environmental program and how to comply, with references to the companion handbooks for details.

■ **California Regwatch**

A monthly newsletter to alert you to new environmental and Cal/OSHA regulations. It's your early warning system with concise news about proposed and enacted regulations. One-year subscription free with purchase of *Environmental Library.* Free to California Chamber members. Cannot be purchased.

Survival Guides to Avoid the Hidden Traps

■ **Guide to Hiring Independent Contractors**

Survive the IRS and state audit war against employers that misclassify workers as independent contractors. A single mistake can cost an employer $15,000 per worker per year. The guide details what factors the IRS looks for, explains special rules for over 300 industries and fatal flaws other companies have made. Contains a sample legal contract, pre-hire worksheet and required government forms.

■ **Employer's Survival Guide to Workers' Compensation**

Updated for 1993. Explains California's complex workers' compensation system, including how to avoid unnecessary costs and litigation. Explains anti-fraud provisions and limits on stress claims. Chapter on stress teaches you how to avoid and manage stress claims. New information on experience modification and workers' comp and the Americans with Disabilities Act. Includes free Workers' Comp Fraud Kit.

■ **Unemployment Insurance: A Cost You Can Cut**

Unemployment insurance benefit increases of 39 percent started in 1990, meaning wrongful claims and errors by the state and your firm will cost much more. The sweeping reform law that went into effect in 1990 provides protections to employers who know how the system works. Learn how to protest claims and how to audit every unemployment insurance form just like your firm audits any invoice.

For the New Small Business

■ **Business Start-Up Kits**

Provides every state, federal and most local government forms and permits necessary to start a business. Tells you what forms are necessary for your business and provides you with the forms, along with lay instructions on how to fill them out. Includes date reminder labels so you don't forget to file forms, and sample letters to government agencies. Three kits are available:

● **Sole Proprietorship/Partnership Kit** (18 forms)
● **Corporation Kit** (27 forms)
● **Employer Kit** (16 forms)

Free with each *Kit:* "Starting and Succeeding in Business," a 40-page booklet covering the 10 biggest pitfalls small business owners encounter.

■ **New American Business System**

Helps new small businesses succeed by helping you plan and stay organized. It's also your consultant with specific help on top problems new small businesses face: raising money, a business plan, a marketing plan, insurance, legal contracts, copyrights and trademarks, personnel, recordkeeping, accounting and budgeting, and 71 other essential topics. This 320-page loose-leaf kit also contains more than 80 forms, worksheets and checklists to help you plan and stay organized.

Other Employer Aids

■ **Employee Posters**

All 12 posters required by the government attractively printed on two 23 x 36-inch posters. Avoid the hassle of contacting seven different state agencies to get them. Available in English and Spanish. One set is free with your purchase of both *Survival Guides to the Labor Law Jungle.*

■ **Sexual Harassment Prevention Packet**

Starting January 1, 1993, all employers must distribute sexual harassment information to all employees. Packet includes: information sheet complying with the legal requirement to define sexual harassment and tell an employee what to do if it occurs, as well as conveying the company's willingness to correct the matter without outside intervention; policy and forms.

■ **Workers' Comp Fraud Kit**

Stop fraudulent workers' comp claims with the help of this kit designed to meet the requirements of the new workers' comp fraud prevention law. Contains: posters warning your employees that filing a phony workers' comp claim is a felony; stickers that you affix to workers' comp claim forms warning that fraud is a felony (meets your legal duty); checklist on how to spot fraud and what to do about it. In English and Spanish. One English kit is free with *Employer's Survival Guide to Workers' Compensation.*

■ **Workers' Comp Videos**

Each video begins with a strong statement that workers' comp fraud is a felony and that employees don't need a lawyer to get workers' comp benefits. These two videos target a major cause of skyrocketing workers' comp premiums: lawyers. The first video helps educate your employees about how the system works. A second and very similar video is to be shown to your injured workers. It reassures them their medical bills will be paid, they'll get cash benefits while out, and that you want them back on the job. Available in English and Spanish.

To Order Call
1-800-331-8877